DEPORTED

LATINA/O SOCIOLOGY SERIES

General Editors: Pierrette Hondagneu-Sotelo and Victor M. Rios

Family Secrets: Stories of Incest and Sexual Violence in Mexico
Gloria González-López

Deported: Immigrant Policing, Disposable Labor, and Global Capitalism
Tanya Maria Golash-Boza

Deported

Immigrant Policing, Disposable Labor,
and Global Capitalism

Tanya Maria Golash-Boza

NEW YORK UNIVERSITY PRESS

New York and London

NEW YORK UNIVERSITY PRESS
New York and London
www.nyupress.org

Library of Congress Cataloging-in-Publication Data
Golash-Boza, Tanya Maria.
Deported : immigrant policing, disposable labor, and global capitalism /
Tanya Maria Golash-Boza.
pages cm. — (Latina/o sociology series)
Includes bibliographical references and index.
ISBN 978-1-4798-9466-6 (cl : alk. paper) — ISBN 978-1-4798-4397-8 (pb   )
1. Illegal aliens—United States. 2. Deportation—United States. 3. Foreign workers—United
States. 4. United States—Emigration and immigration—Government policy. 5. United
States—Emigration and immigration—Economic aspects. I. Title.
JV6483.G637   2015
325.73—dc23   2015019580

Manufactured in the United States of America

10 9 8 7 6 5 4 3 2 1

Also available as an ebook

CONTENTS

On February 26, 1931, federal agents descended on La Placita, a public park in Los Angeles popular among Mexicans. Approximately 400 Mexicans were enjoying the afternoon when immigration agents arrived, wielded guns and batons, closed off the entrances, and ordered everyone present to line up and produce documentation of legal entry and residency or U.S. citizenship. About a week later, the first official repatriation train left Los Angeles for Mexico with more than 400 people on board (Balderrama and Rodríguez 2006; Olivo 2011).

In 1930, about 1.5 million Mexicans and Mexican Americans lived in the United States (as compared to nearly 30 million today). Estimates vary, but Balderrama and Rodríguez (2006: 151) calculate that immigration agents returned as many as one million Mexicans and their children to Mexico in the 1930s. This massive project of coercion involved local sheriffs, schools, social workers, and the Mexican consulates as well as U.S. federal agents (Hoffman 1974). These raids spread fear throughout the Mexican community and created decades of tension.

This mass repatriation of Mexicans occurred in the context of the Great Depression. In a time of fear and need, racial tensions were high. Many Americans perceived the mass deportation of Mexicans as a viable measure to ease economic pressures.

On July 30, 1952, about 100 Border Patrol agents descended on an area near Brownsville, Texas, at dawn and began to arrest recently arrived migrants—most of whom were coming to the United States for seasonal agricultural work. By the end of the day, they had made 5,000 arrests and had transported all of those people to the bridge that led back to Mexico. A rebounding economy in the 1940s may have prompted the easing of deportation rates, but Operation Wetback reinstated massive roundups of Mexicans. This initiative focused exclusively on border enforcement. Roundups like the one in Brownsville continued for years, and in October 1954, the Border Patrol announced it had deported more than one million Mexican immigrants in the preceding four years (Hernandez 2010).

Interest in keeping Mexicans and, more recently, Central Americans from immigrating to the United States resurged in the 1990s. The U.S. Immigration and Naturalization Service (INS) inaugurated Operation Hold-the-Line in 1993, Operation Gatekeeper in 1994, and Operation Safeguard in 1995 (Nevins 2002; Dunn 2009; Rosas 2012). As economic reforms and civil wars created turbulence in Latin American economies and societies, the United States attempted to keep potential migrants out. These initiatives failed remarkably to deter migrants, yet they succeeded in rendering migration journeys far more dangerous (Cornelius 2006).

Operations Wetback, Hold-the-Line, Gatekeeper, and Safeguard all focused on U.S.-Mexico border enforcement, while the U.S.-Canadian border did not experience this level of vigilance. During these operations, millions of would-be migrants were sent back at the southern border. In the first decade of the 21st century, immigration law enforcement shifted. In addition to returning large numbers of people at the border, immigration agents began to remove immigrants from the interior. While continuing to remove Mexicans, immigration law enforcement began to target other Latin American as well as Caribbean immigrants.

Just as the Great Depression had prompted massive roundups in the 1930s, the "Great Recession"—the worst economic crisis since the Great Depression—prompted arrests for violations of immigration law in the interior. In 2012, the Department of Homeland Security broke another record: It removed nearly 420,000 noncitizens. By the spring of 2014, there had been two million removals under the Obama administration—more in just over five years than any previous administration and more than the sum total of all documented removals prior to 1997. (The 1930s mass repatriations were not recorded as removals.)

This most recent mass deportation also occurred during a period of high unemployment, especially for men. Three quarters of the eight million jobs lost in the United States during the Great Recession were lost by men, particularly in the occupational sectors of construction and manufacturing where Latino immigrant men have been concentrated. In 2008, annual removals broke 300,000 for the first time in history, and they rose in subsequent years. These removals have primarily targeted Latino men.

Some critics have suggested that President Obama pushed immigration law enforcement in an effort to make a compromise with Republicans to get immigration reform passed. Others called Obama a hypocrite—insofar as he rallied for immigration reform while deporting more than 1,000 immigrants a day. I argue that a focus on Obama's executive decisions and partisan interests provides too narrow an answer to this big question. Understanding mass deportation requires a broader lens.

Mass deportation has global implications and is intimately tied to the worldwide movement of people and goods. In short, it is not simply a domestic policy issue. The larger economic picture—especially in the countries to which the United States sends deportees—has shaped the development of mass deportation. Many scholars have found that globalization and economic restructuring have produced global migration. In this book, I argue that the current phase of mass deportations is produced by neoliberal reforms and the intensification of economic inequality. I further contend that deportation maintains a system of global apartheid.

To make this argument, I draw from the narratives of deportees, and I place their stories and experiences in the wider context of global capitalism, neoliberalism, and racialized social control. Through their life histories, I identify the elements of the current era of global capitalism that have rendered mass deportation possible:

- Global inequality, which leads migrants to travel across borders in search of better opportunities than that which their country of birth provides
- Systems of border control and immigration policing, which make international migration difficult and render working-class and poor international migrants vulnerable
- Economic and social changes in the United States in the 1980s that led to changes in the labor market, which have greatly reduced the availability of low-skill jobs that pay a living wage and a concomitant increase in temporary and low-paying jobs in the United States that immigrants are qualified to do
- The rise in unemployment in the context of the Great Recession

- A system of racialized social control that focuses on black and Latino men and ensures that those migrants who eschew low-wage jobs are arrested and deported if they are noncitizens

The above list includes factors that have made mass deportation possible from the U.S. side. Additionally, I will explain the role that deportees play in global capitalism once they are deported. Countries that receive deportees have found rhetorical and practical uses for their returning citizens: They serve as scapegoats or bilingual low-wage workers in their countries of origin.

I interviewed 147 deportees in Guatemala, the Dominican Republic, Jamaica, and Brazil. Placing their stories in a larger context reveals that mass deportation is critical to the sustainability of global capitalism—both in the United States and elsewhere.

ACKNOWLEDGMENTS

As I sit down to write these acknowledgments, I am overwhelmed with gratitude for the countless people who have helped make writing this book possible. I have a truly amazing intellectual community and am grateful for the inspiration I draw from these wonderful people.

This book was certainly not written in isolation. From Tepoztlán, Mexico, to Yosemite, California, and back to Merced, California, this book was written and conceptualized in the midst of amazing and generous scholars. Thanks to all of the people who participated in workshops, conferences, and writing retreats and who shared their brilliance with me.

Many thanks to the audience members at talks I have given while writing and thinking about this book at California State University, Channel Islands; California State University, Long Beach; the University of California at Los Angeles; the University of California at Davis Law School; the University of Oregon; Washington State University; Northern Illinois University; the Unitarian Universalist Church of Santa Monica; the University of Oxford; California State University, Sacramento; the University of California at Santa Cruz; the University of California at Santa Barbara; Vanderbilt University; Providence College; Central Oregon Community College; University of South Carolina at Columbia; Duke University; the University of Hawaii at Manoa; the Universidade Federal de Goiás; the University of Kansas; the University of California at Merced; and the Universidade Federal de Brasilia. Your comments and insights helped to push my thinking on this project forward.

Numerous scholars have selflessly donated their time and energy to read and provide feedback on portions of this manuscript. For that, I am grateful to Zulema Valdez, Helen Marrow, Jody Agius Vallejo, Christina Lux, Gilberto Rosas, Jemima Pierre, Vilna Treitler, Daisy Reyes, Megan Thiele, Irenee Beattie, David Torres-Rouff, Joane Nagel, Shannon

Gleeson, Laura Enriquez, Sandy Darity, Leah Schmalzbauer, Mael Vizcarra, Ximena García Bustamante, Elliot Young, Kimberly Hoang, and Laura Hamilton.

A few very special and generous colleagues also were kind enough to read the manuscript in its entirety. For that, I am grateful to Joanna Dreby, Christina Sue, Pierrette Hondagneu-Sotelo, Kate Epstein, and the two anonymous reviewers. Thanks also to my research assistant, Joshua Mason, and my brother, Justin Golash, who read the entire manuscript and helped prepare it for publication.

An awesome virtual community has also kept me on task in the last stages of writing this book. That community includes Amani Nuru-Jeter, Ana Aparicio, Nitasha Sharma, Vilna Treitler, Crystal Fleming, and Zulema Valdez. Thanks and I look forward to seeing you online soon!

I am also grateful for collaborations with esteemed colleagues Pierrette Hondagneu-Sotelo, Cecilia Menjívar, and Zulema Valdez, which helped to sharpen my thinking on race, gender, deportations, and human rights.

The research for this book would not have been possible without the generous support of Bernard Headley in Jamaica, Miguel Ugalde in Guatemala, Rene Vicioso and María del Carmen Vicente in the Dominican Republic, and Izabel Missagia in Brazil. Thanks so much to these colleagues as well as many others who helped me to complete the ambitious task of conducting interviews with deportees in four countries.

I am grateful to the New York University press acquisitions editor, Ilene Kalish, who expressed interest in this project in its early stages, as well as the series editors, Pierrette Hondagneu-Sotelo and Victor Rios, who gave me crucial support toward the end.

I am eternally grateful for the love and support provided by my husband, Fernando Boza, and the patience and encouragement provided by my children, Tatiana, Soraya, and Raymi Boza. Writing this book and being a scholar have been made much easier by my family as well as my dear academic friends who are always there for me: Christina Lux, Zulema Valdez, Jemima Pierre, Vilna Treitler, Angela Black, Ana Aparicio, France Winddance Twine, Amani Nuru-Jeter, and Ayu Saraswati. I have not enough words to thank you all.

Finally, I am very grateful for the funding that made this project possible. The bulk of the funding for the research came from the

Fulbright-Hays Faculty Research Abroad Award. I also am grateful for funding from the University of Kansas General Research Fund and the Institute for Policy and Social Research at the University of Kansas as well as the School of Social Sciences, the Humanities and the Arts and the Faculty Senate Research Award at the University of California at Merced.

Introduction

Mass Deportation and the Neoliberal Cycle

I could tell immediately, as with so many others, that he had lived in the United States since he was a child: His smooth skin, the swing in his step, and his calm but guarded demeanor gave him away as a U.S. Latino. I was standing on the tarmac watching as he descended from the plane.

He told me his name was Eric. I asked him about himself and we chatted for a few minutes as he waited for Guatemalan immigration agents to process him as an arriving deportee. He wrote down his number and I told him I would call him in about a month to see how he was doing. He said he wasn't sure he'd still be in Guatemala by then.

When I was in Guatemala in 2009, I witnessed thousands of deportees like Eric returning to their countries of birth. When I returned in 2013, I found that deportations had accelerated even further. Four to six planeloads of deportees arrive at the Guatemalan Air Force base each week—more than 45,000 people each year.[1]

Just over a month after Eric arrived, we met up in Metro Norte, a modern shopping center in one of the rougher neighborhoods of Guatemala City—Zone 18—close to where Eric was staying. Eric told me he had traveled to the United States when he was 11 to join his mother, who had left three years prior. He went on an airplane alone, with a tourist visa, as his undocumented mother could not come for her son or apply for an immigrant visa for him. Eric enrolled in middle school in Inglewood, Los Angeles, where his mother worked at a garment factory. In his last year of high school, Eric's mother injured her back and was unable to continue working. Eric had to drop out of school and get a job to keep the family afloat. He had no trouble finding low-wage work, and he worked two jobs. He met a Salvadoran woman who is a legal permanent resident of the United States, and they got married.

Once Eric had a job, he purchased a car to drive to work each morning. On weekends, Eric spent time with his wife and friends. One Saturday afternoon, Eric's friend asked him for a ride, and Eric took him to the other side of town. Shortly after he dropped his friend off, a police officer pulled Eric over and arrested him as an accomplice in the car theft that his friend had allegedly committed. Once they arrived at the Los Angeles County Jail, a police officer ran Eric's fingerprints through an immigration database, because the police district participated in the Secure Communities program. This program—designed to find and deport dangerous noncitizens—enables police officers to determine if an arrestee is in the country legally. The police discovered he had overstayed his visa and held him until immigration agents came to take him into custody, even though the car theft charges had been dropped. Immigration agents took Eric to a privately owned Corrections Corporation of America (CCA) detention center, and they held him until he was deported from the United States. Neither Eric's innocence nor his pending application for legalization on the basis of his marriage prevented his deportation, and he had to leave his mother and pregnant wife behind.

In Guatemala City, Eric moved into his aunt's house, where he had lived before leaving the country when he was 11. Soon after arriving, Eric secured a job at a call center, where he answers calls from customers in the United States. As a bilingual deportee familiar with the social and cultural norms of the United States, he is an ideal worker for this transnational corporation. His labor is also significantly cheaper than it would be in the United States: His job pays $400 a month—enough to support himself in Guatemala but not sufficient for raising a family.

Eric's story lays bare what I call a "neoliberal cycle" because of the interrelated nature of each of the events in Eric's life, and their connection to neoliberal reforms—economic changes focused on opening up the economy to global markets and reducing state spending on social welfare. The neoliberal cycle refers to the interconnected aspects of neoliberal reforms implemented in the United States and abroad. These elements include outsourcing; economic restructuring; cutbacks in social services; the enhancement of the police, the military, and immigration enforcement; and the privatization of public services. Neoliberal reforms generally involve cuts to government funding—with the notable

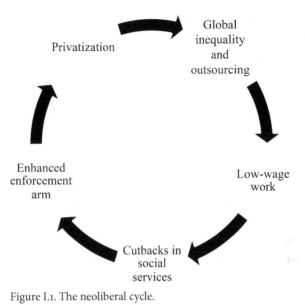

Figure I.1. The neoliberal cycle.

exception of the military and law enforcement—and are designed to integrate countries into the global economy. These reforms constitute a cycle insofar as they lead to and reproduce one another. This cycle of restricted labor mobility and deportation is crucial to the maintenance of global apartheid—a system where mostly white and affluent citizens of the world are free to travel to where they like whereas the poor are forced to make do in places where there are less resources (Nevins and Aizeki 2008). Global apartheid would not be feasible without deportation, as deportation is the physical manifestation of policies that determine who is permitted to live where.

Eric's story fits neatly into this cycle. His family felt compelled to leave Guatemala because of the economic havoc that neoliberalism wreaked on their home country (Robinson 2000, 2008). Once in the United States, Eric's mother found a low-wage job in the garment industry. Manufacturers have moved most garment industry jobs abroad, and those jobs that remain are low-paid and offer few to no benefits (Louie 2001). As an undocumented worker, Eric's mother was less likely to challenge her low pay and lack of benefits. When she became ill, there was no safety net—another factor related to cutbacks in social services under neoliberalism (Harvey 2005; Wacquant 2009). Eric was then obliged to leave school and work two jobs.

Although the state did not provide resources to help this family in troubled times, the coercive arm of the state is robust. California built 23 major prisons, at a cost of about $300 million each between 1984 and 2005, amid growing poverty and inequality (Gilmore 2007). The escalation in law enforcement spending facilitated Eric's arrest and deportation. The heavy policing of poor neighborhoods predominated by people of color made it much more likely that Eric would be arrested, even though he had not in fact committed a crime. Once arrested, Eric was placed in a private prison—privatization of public services is another key element of neoliberalism, as is the profitability of prisons.

Globalization, enhanced by neoliberal reforms, facilitates the movement of capital across borders while restricting the mobility of workers. This makes it possible for Eric, a deportee, to work for a U.S. corporation in his homeland. The arrival of 45,000 deportees a year into Guatemala ensures a steady supply of bilingual workers for this transnational corporation—about half of the workers in the call center where Eric works are deportees. As this book will show, by elaborating on each aspect of the neoliberal cycle, mass deportation from the United States is critical to the sustainability of neoliberal economies. And, although mass deportation is carried out in the name of national security, these stories will reveal that it creates insecurity.

Eric was detained and deported because of a program called Secure Communities. However, it should be clear from his story that this program does not make communities more secure. Instead, it creates instability and insecurity. Angela García and David Keyes (2012) authored a report that documents the everyday lives of undocumented immigrants in North County, San Diego, the first community in California to sign on to Secure Communities. They completed 30 in-depth interviews with migrants, in addition to 851 surveys. Their study revealed that undocumented migrants were reluctant to report crimes, out of fear they could be arrested and deported. In addition, many undocumented migrants reported that they avoided public places and even walking down the street. Some parents stopped picking their children up from school once they perceived there was a crackdown in immigration law enforcement. In sum, undocumented migrants often live in fear and experience substantial insecurity in their daily lives. This fear comes from the threat of deportation and is a consequence of record-high deportations.

The United States is deporting more people than ever before. Obama hit an all-time record high of more than 400,000 deportees in 2012. These numbers are unprecedented: In the first five and a half years of his presidency, President Obama deported more than two million people—more than the sum total of all people deported before 1997. Why are deportations at a record high? Why at this historical moment? Many deportees are people like Eric who have close ties to the United States. The vast majority of deportees are men of color. Why are they the primary targets?

When I share my work on deportees and mass deportation, people often ask me why Obama, a liberal Democrat, has deported record numbers of people. As a student of political economy, however, I know that the answer to why mass deportation is happening now has to move beyond questioning Obama's political motivations. To be sure, Obama—as the head of the executive branch—has been facilitating mass deportation. However, an explanation for why it is happening must be much broader. The answer I offer in this book comes primarily from talking to deportees. There are other ways to answer these questions: One could analyze congressional debates, interview public officials, or try to make sense of the patchwork of available statistical data. However, I contend that deportees' stories are the best way in which to capture the nuance and complexity of mass deportation and the impacts of neoliberal reforms on their overall migration trajectories. When we listen to deportees, it becomes evident that deportees are immigrants, low-wage workers, people of color, and parents. When we listen to their stories, and place them in the broader political, social, and economic context, it becomes clear why they have become the latest version of disposable workers.

I argue that mass deportation of men of color is part of the neoliberal cycle of global capitalism. I further argue that mass deportation is a U.S. policy response designed to relocate surplus labor to the periphery and to keep labor in the United States compliant. The U.S. public accepts this policy response because it targets mainly immigrant men of color, who are perceived to be expendable in the current economy and unwanted in the broader society. To make this argument, I explain how neoliberal economic changes created migration flows, attracted migrants to the United States, required a disposable labor force, and, of late, have made migrant labor disposable.

We must look at mass deportation as part of the neoliberal cycle of global capitalism because mass deportation is only the latest permutation of this cycle that began in the 1980s. Understanding this requires stepping back and taking a critical look at the social and economic processes that produced global migration from the South to the North, the current state of the neoliberal economy, the rise of the coercive arm of the state, and the uneven integration of developing countries into the global economy. A consideration of mass deportation from this standpoint provides a comprehensive explanation for why it is happening now.

Mass Deportation

Deportation is the forced removal of a noncitizen from a host country. I refer to the current wave of immigration law enforcement as "mass deportation" because the raw numbers of deportees are significantly higher than they have been in any previous period in history. Moreover, deportations have accelerated even as the number of new immigrants has declined—and the population of undocumented immigrants has shrunk.

In 2011, the U.S. Department of Homeland Security (DHS) deported a record high of 396,906 people—10 times as many as in 1991, more than during the entire decade of the 1980s, yet just short of its quota of 400,000 removals per year. In an internal memo made public in March 2010, the Immigration and Customs Enforcement (ICE) director, James M. Chaparro, informed ICE field office directors that the department has an annual goal of 400,000 deportations. In fiscal year (FY) 2012, this goal was finally surpassed, with more than 419,000 deportations. As seen in figure I.2, the numbers of deportations are at a historic high. During the George W. Bush administration, there were a recordbreaking number of deportations—more than two million—and, yet, by 2014 the Obama administration had already surpassed this massive number.

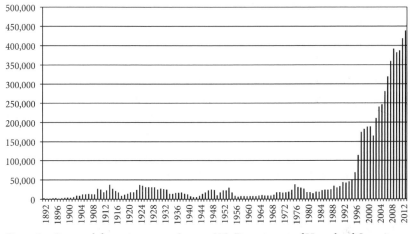

Figure I.2. Removal data, 1892–2012. Source: U.S. Department of Homeland Security removal data (2013), online at http://www.dhs.gov/yearbook-immigration-statistics -2013-enforcement-actions.

Legislation passed in 1996, combined with a massive infusion of money into immigration law enforcement in the aftermath of the September 11, 2001, terrorist attacks, rendered this escalation in deportations possible. The 1996 laws were passed in a moment of racialized fears related to crime. These laws, however, have not changed substantially since then. Instead, Congress has continued to appropriate increasing amounts of money for immigration law enforcement. The FY 2011 budget for DHS was $56 billion, 30 percent of which was directed at immigration law enforcement through ICE and Customs and Border Patrol (CBP). Another 18 percent of the total goes to the U.S. Coast Guard and 5 percent to U.S. Citizenship and Immigration Services—meaning over half of the DHS budget is directed toward border security and immigration law enforcement.[2] To put this $56 billion in perspective, the Department of Education FY 2011 budget was $77.8 billion, and the Department of Justice budget was $29.2 billion.[3] The rise in deportations over the past decade primarily stems from executive branch decisions to expand immigration law enforcement, as part of the broader project of the War on Terror. When you have more than a thousand people deported every day, that's a policy of mass deportation.

These unprecedented numbers of deportees mask the reality that most people who could be deported are not. There are approximately 11 million undocumented people in the United States. According to statistics that the ICE provided to the journalist Alan Gomez, in FY 2013, there were 133,551 interior removals and 180,970 border removals—representing a substantial decrease in interior removals from the year before. At this pace, it will take more than 80 years to deport all of the 11 million undocumented migrants currently living in the United States, and more time is required to deport others eligible for deportation: those who have committed crimes among the 13 million legal permanent residents, and unknown millions of legal visitors who have committed visa violations. DHS will never remove all undocumented migrants or all deportable people. A mass deportation policy does not aim to remove all deportable people—there are simply too many. It does aim, as Nicholas de Genova (2005) argues, to keep large sectors of the U.S. population deportable and thus vulnerable.

Faced with the gargantuan task of enforcing unenforceable laws, DHS claims it targets the "worst of the worst." The reality, however, is that immigration policy enforcement targets Afro-Caribbean small-time drug peddlers and Latino undocumented workers—not hardcore criminals or terrorists. Nearly all deportees—97 percent—are from Latin America and the Caribbean. DHS rarely deports any of the approximately 25 percent of undocumented migrants in the United States that are from Asia and Europe. Nearly 90 percent of deportees are men, although about half of all noncitizens are women (Golash-Boza and Hondagneu-Sotelo 2013). Additionally, dangerous noncitizens account for a small percentage of deportees.

On April 6, 2014, the New York Times reported that nearly two-thirds of the two million deportations since Obama took office have involved either people with no criminal records or those convicted of minor crimes.[4] Just two days later, the Transactional Records Access Clearinghouse (TRAC) Immigration issued an even more detailed, and more damning, report.[5] The report, which looks at deportations carried out by ICE, found that 57 percent of ICE deportations in 2013 were of people who had criminal convictions. However, this statistic hides the fact that most of these convictions are minor. The authors write,

ICE currently uses an exceedingly broad definition of criminal behavior: even very minor infractions are included. For example, anyone with a traffic ticket for exceeding the speed limit on the Baltimore-Washington Parkway who sends in their check to pay their fine has just entered ICE's "convicted criminal" category. If the same definitions were applied to every citizen . . . evidence suggests that the majority of U.S. citizens would be considered convicted criminals.

In other words, not only have nearly half of all deportations involved people with no criminal record whatsoever, large numbers of "criminal" deportations involve people with traffic offenses.

The TRAC report is notable because it provides a close look at the criminal convictions of deportees—data that had not previously been available. The report further reveals that, although the percentage of deportations that involved a criminal conviction increased for each year of the Obama administration, most of these convictions were minor. Some of these convictions would only be considered criminal in a very broad definition of the term. For example, about a quarter of the criminal convictions involved the immigration crime of "illegal entry." The difference between a person deported on noncriminal grounds for being undocumented and one deported on criminal grounds for "illegal entry" is almost entirely a question of prosecutorial discretion. In other words, these 47,000 people deported for illegal entry were converted into criminals for reporting purposes.

The next largest category is traffic offenses—the majority driving under the influence or speeding—which account for nearly another quarter of all criminal deportations. In common parlance in the United States, people with traffic convictions are not usually called "criminals." The third largest category is drug offenses. Notably, the most common offense in this category was marijuana possession, which has recently been decriminalized in Washington State, Colorado, and other locations.

The TRAC analysis renders it clear that the increase in the number of noncitizens who have been deported on criminal grounds under the Obama administration is mostly a consequence of an increase in the deportation of noncitizens with immigration and traffic violations—convictions that are only considered criminal in a very broad definition of the term. In fact, based on ICE's own definition of a serious or "Level 1" offense, only 12 percent of all deportations in 2013 were of people convicted of such offenses. According to ICE, Level 1 criminals are people who have been convicted of two or more felonies. Level 2 criminals are those convicted of one felony or three misdemeanors. Level 3 criminals are those convicted of misdemeanors, or crimes punishable by less than one year of jail time.

These details put the DHS's 2012 data into perspective. In 2012, DHS deported nearly 200,000 "criminal aliens." Almost a quarter of these deportations were for immigration offenses, another 23 percent for traffic violations, and 21 percent for drug violations. Relatively few people deported on criminal grounds had been convicted of violent crimes: 2 percent for sexual assault; 2 percent for robbery; and 6 percent for assault. And more than half of the 419,384 people deported in 2012 had no criminal conviction (Simanski and Sapp 2012). Despite official rhetoric, deportations do not focus on the "worst of the worst."

Deporting undocumented workers, traffic violators, and drug users and sellers does not make America any less susceptible to terrorist attacks. DHS almost never deports people to countries that the U.S. Department of State identifies as sponsoring terrorism: Iran, Iraq, Syria, Libya, Cuba, North Korea, and Sudan. In 2010, for example, 387,242 people were deported. Among these were 55 Iranians, 54 Iraqis, 48 Syrians, 95 Cubans, and 21 Sudanese. (Data were not available for Libya, yet "all other countries" accounted for a total of 106 removals, and there were a total of 326 removals to North and South Korea combined.)[6] Instead, deportees are citizens of countries that are the United States' allies in the Western Hemisphere. The most recent escalation in deportations has occurred in the context of the War on Terror, and yet it doesn't seem to further that war. Instead, with large numbers of black and Latino men being deported, mass deportation shares many similarities with mass incarceration.

Instead of making us safer, mass deportation tears families apart and prevents immigrants from applying for legalization or citizenship even when they qualify. Enhanced deportation tactics increasingly deport people with strong ties to the United States. A recent report revealed that DHS deported more than 45,000 parents of U.S. citizen children in

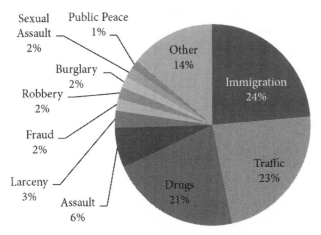

Figure I.3. Leading crime categories of convicted criminal aliens removed: Fiscal year 2012. Source: Simanski and Sapp 2012.

the first six months of 2011—meaning that likely almost 100,000 parents of U.S. citizens were deported in 2011 alone (Wessler 2011). This marks a ten-fold increase—it previously took a decade (between 1997 and 2006) for DHS to deport 100,000 parents of U.S. citizens (Golash-Boza 2012). Prior to 1996, the deportation of parents of U.S. citizens was fairly uncommon, as those immigrants were eligible for appeals and potential cancellation of removal, based on family ties to the United States. Deportation of parents of U.S. citizens does vast damage to U.S. citizens deprived of parents and spouses. A consideration of neoliberalism and its relationship to global capitalism will shed light on why we have seen this escalation in immigration law enforcement directed at black and Latino men.

The Neoliberal Cycle

Neoliberalism has three manifestations: It is (1) an ideology that the state's primary role is to protect property rights, free markets, and free trade; (2) a mode of governance based on a logic of competitiveness, individuality, and entrepreneurship; and (3) a policy package designed to slim down social welfare and integrate countries into the global economy (Harvey 2005; Steger 2010; Steger and Roy 2010).

According to neoliberal ideology, the free market will best address the needs of the poor: The state should not intervene and provide social assistance. The United States has implemented neoliberal policies in order to make the country more competitive in the global economy and to protect the interests of the corporate class. In developing countries, neoliberal reforms have been at the core of their insertion into the global economy. Countries around the world, often at the behest of the International Monetary Fund (IMF), have implemented economic reforms based on neoliberal ideologies. These reforms include (1) deregulation; (2) privatization of public enterprise; (3) trade liberalization; (4) promotion of foreign direct investment; (5) tax cuts; and (6) reduction in public expenditures (Harvey 2005; Steger 2010).

Each of these neoliberal reforms is designed to bring foreign currency into the national economy and to prepare the country to enter the global economy (Robinson 2004, 2008). Deregulation creates favorable conditions for investment by both allowing the currency to fluctuate and removing protections for workers and the environment. When public enterprises are privatized, the purchasers are often foreign investors and this process creates an infusion of dollars into the economy. Trade liberalization involves the reduction of tariffs, which promotes international trade. Tax cuts favor foreign investors. Finally, the elimination of a safety net ensures a compliant labor force and frees up government money to pay off foreign debts. The spread of neoliberalism around the globe has pulled countries into the global economy, transformed peasants into international migrants, and lured immigrants to toil in low-wage jobs in countries like the United States.

Neoliberalism and Emigration

Developing countries around the world implemented neoliberal economic reforms during and after the 1980s. In many cases, leaders of countries did this in response to demands by the IMF that they impose structural adjustments onto their economies. To explain a complicated process briefly, during the 1960s and 1970s, many poor countries around the world borrowed money from the World Bank for development projects. These development projects included building dams for electricity, constructing ports, and modernizing agriculture toward the production of cash crops. The intent of these projects was to bring these developing countries into the global economy—these development projects would enable them to import items from abroad and export their cash crops and natural resources. In the 1980s, however, interest rates and oil prices skyrocketed and many countries were unable to pay back their loans. They thus turned to the IMF to request assistance in stabilizing their economies and paying their debts. The IMF agreed to lend money, but under the condition that the countries implement structural adjustment.

Structural adjustment is a package of neoliberal reforms. The standard package recommended by the IMF includes privatization, trade liberalization, tax reductions, deregulation, and cutbacks in social services (Steger 2010). One of the most important aspects of each of these reforms is that they are designed to generate the foreign currency necessary for these countries to repay their debts.

In general, neoliberal reforms exacerbated inequality, led to internal migration, and created severe disruptions in countries' economies. These disruptions have, in turn, led to emigration—a process I explain in more detail in chapter 1.

Emigration does two things for the local economy: (1) It shrinks the ranks of the unemployed, and (2) emigrants often send money home, filling a crucial need for families unable to subsist on their meager wages. In some countries these remittances become vital for the overall economy: In 2009, remittances accounted for substantial portions of the gross domestic product (GDP) in Tajikistan (35 percent), Honduras (19 percent), and El Salvador (16 percent).[7] For people to migrate and send remittances, however, there must be a need for their labor in receiving countries. In the next section, I detail how neoliberalism has created a labor market primed for immigrant labor in the United States. Just as globalization, modernization, and neoliberal reforms created a mass exodus of workers from Jamaica, the Dominican Republic, Brazil, Guatemala, and other countries, neoliberal reforms in the United States led to economic restructuring and created an abundance of low-wage jobs in the service sector that immigrants were able to fill (Massey et al. 2002; Varsanyi 2008). In chapter 1, I elaborate further on the connections between neoliberal reforms and emigration.

Neoliberalism and Immigration

Changes in foreign economies made neoliberal economic reforms in the United States possible. The U.S. economy changed in two important ways during the era of globalization that took off in the 1980s: (1) Manufacturing jobs have gone abroad, and (2) the service sector has expanded. These trends have continued up to the present day. There were about 27 million jobs created in the United States between 1990 and 2008; 98 percent of these jobs were in the nontradable sector, which produces goods and services for domestic consumption.[8]

Instead of expanding the manufacturing sector in the United States, U.S. corporations have moved production overseas. In order for manufacturing jobs to go abroad, there must be international agreements between U.S. employers and foreign governments. Trade agreements such as the North American Free Trade Agreement (NAFTA) have been a major part of neoliberal reforms. Neoliberal economic reforms in the United States have facilitated the restructuring of the U.S. economy— from an economy based on manufacturing to one based on services. After World War II, the U.S. economy grew rapidly with the production of automobiles and steel. These manufacturing jobs often paid well and came with benefits. Mostly men worked in these jobs, and many earned a "family wage"—enough to support their wives and children. Between 1950 and 1960 the average incomes in the United States increased steadily. However, these increases began to level off, and by the 1970s incomes for the working poor stopped increasing. The average income for someone with less than a high school diploma decreased from $30,015 in 1967 to $23,419 in 2010 (in constant 2010 dollars).

In the 1980s, these well-paying manufacturing jobs began to disappear due to global competition and increased outsourcing. As it became easier for U.S.-based manufacturers to move production abroad, many did. While manufacturing jobs disappeared, there was an increase in jobs in the service sector. Service jobs include high-paid workers such as lawyers and investment bankers and low-paid workers such as gardeners and nannies (Louie 2001). High-level service professions such as lawyers and bankers are often concentrated in large urban areas, yet they require a different skill set than those men that worked in factories had—leaving many of these latter men jobless.

The men who had worked in factories often were not in a position to retool themselves and take on the new service jobs. Instead, immigrants have filled many of these low-paying service jobs (Louie 2001; Massey et al. 2002; Boehme 2011). Immigrants are concentrated in low-paying and dangerous industries. In 2010, immigrants made up 16 percent of the workforce and were overrepresented in specific industries: construction, food services, agriculture, household employment, and hotels (Singer 2012). Many of these employment sectors are also highly gendered—male immigrants work outside in construction and gardening and women are inside houses in childcare and housekeeping. Immigrants made up 49 percent of all private household employees in 2010 (Singer 2012).

Inequality has grown with economic restructuring: In 1980, when manufacturing dominated the economy in the United States, CEOs earned, on average, 42 times more than the average worker. Today, that figure is 380.[9] This increase in inequality is a consequence of the bifurcation of the U.S. labor force into two kinds of employment: high skill and low skill. Economic restructuring, designed to keep the United States competitive in the global arena, has led to the impoverishment of large swaths of society and to the enrichment of a few (Harvey 2005; Louie 2001).

David Harvey (2005) contends that the neoliberal turn in the United States began in the late 1970s in New York City, marking a change from the more socially conscious government of the 1960s and early 1970s, where the federal government had expanded its urban funding to create jobs and raise the standard of living of city dwellers. Once President Nixon declared the urban crisis over, he withdrew federal funding, and the New York City government decided to implement wage freezes and cut back funding for education, transportation, and public health. This marked the beginning of the neoliberal turn in the United States, where it became increasingly acceptable for city, state, and federal governments to cut social spending, invest in public safety, and implement policies that favored the wealthy. This version of trickle-down economics took off across the country—and around the world—in the 1980s, creating vast inequality.

Neoliberalism in developing countries has created economic conditions that lead to emigration by attracting migrants from the countryside into the cities and then creating economic instability and inequality, which makes leaving the country an attractive option. Without these disruptive economic changes in countries such as Mexico, Guatemala, and the Philippines, the United States would not have had the compliant workforce it needed to make its own economic transition. The trade liberalization and incentives for foreign direct investment that are central to neoliberal economic reforms created the conditions abroad for U.S.-based manufacturing factories to relocate. Absent these favorable conditions, it would not make sense for U.S.-based manufacturers to outsource production. For example, U.S. manufacturers would not move to Mexico if they had to pay high tariffs on exports or if Mexican laws required adequate wages and permitted unions to demand workers' rights.

Although neoliberalism at home and abroad has created powerful push and pull factors for labor migration, open borders for capital have not led to open borders for labor. The U.S. economy depends on immigrant labor, yet it offers potential migrants few options for legal immigration. Monica Varsanyi calls this the "neoliberal paradox" and asks, "How can nation-states manage the tensions that emerge between the seemingly contradictory forces of economic openness and political closure?" (2008: 879). Similarly, Philip Kretsedemas (2012) points to a contradiction where neoliberal economic practices welcome new migrant flows yet fund an enforcement apparatus designed to keep migrants out. And Stephen Castles (2011: 312) contends that restrictions on labor flows in the context of free flows of capital constitute a "global class hierarchy, in which people with high human capital from rich countries have almost unlimited rights of mobility, while others are differentiated, controlled, and excluded in a variety of ways." Building on this work, I argue that, in the context of the Great Recession, the enforcement apparatus keeps migrant labor compliant. Whereas Castles (2011) focuses primarily on nation and class in his construction of the concept of a "global class hierarchy," I find Joseph Nevins and Mizue Aizeki's (2008) concept of "global apartheid" more compelling insofar as race maps neatly onto this global hierarchy of labor mobility. Accordingly, in the context of global apartheid, mass deportation reinforces the limited mobility and enhanced vulnerability of black and brown labor.

Neoliberalism and Deportation

At the same time that global economic developments that encourage international migration have unfolded, the United States has witnessed an augmentation of the coercive arm of the state. Remarkably, those scholars who focus on the connections between global capitalism and immigration rarely engage with those who focus on neoliberal reforms in the United States and their relationship to the rise of mass incarceration. A study of deportation helps us to see the connections between mass incarceration, global capitalism, and economic restructuring in the United States.

Scholars who consider why deportation happens generally provide two related explanations: (1) Deportation functions as social or migration control (Welch 2002; Bloch and Schuster 2005; Gibney 2008; Bosworth 2011; Brotherton and Barrios 2011; Collyer 2012), and (2) deportation creates a vulnerable workforce (de Genova 2005). I place these arguments in a broader context. I agree that deportation functions as both social and migration control. It is also clear that deportation incites fear in migrants who have not been deported. The question I set out to answer is why deportation is being used in the current historical moment for these purposes.

Loïc Wacquant (2009) argues that there is a "close link between the ascendancy of neoliberalism . . . and the deployment of punitive and proactive law-enforcement policies" (1). Wacquant notes that the primary victims of enhanced law enforcement are men of color. He contrasts the 2.1 million people in the incarcerated population (nearly all men) to the 2.1 million on welfare (nearly all women). He further notes that the United States designed both welfare policies and the War on Drugs not to protect the poor but to transform them into "compliant workers fit or forced to fill the peripheral slots of the deregulated labor market" (101). This argument has great resonance with the experiences of deportees.

Although neoliberalism demands that the state cut back on social services, at the same time, it requires that the state strengthen enforcement. Insofar as neoliberalism diminishes opportunities and services for the poor, the state must ensure that working-class and poor people do not pose a threat to the rich. The state's cutbacks in social services often lead to dissent and increases in crime on the part of frustrated workers. The state responds by enhancing the police force and the military. Under neoliberalism, "forms of surveillance and policing multiply: in the United States incarceration became a key state strategy to deal with problems arising among discarded workers and marginalized populations. The coercive arm of the state is augmented to protect corporate interests and, if necessary, to repress dissent" (Harvey 2005: 77).

The current economic crisis has created high rates of unemployment, meaning there are large numbers of expendable workers. Many of the diminished markets for workers had employed immigrant men. For example, the construction industry lost more than a quarter of its jobs in five years: Whereas in April 2006, there were 7,726,000 jobs, in May 2011, there were only 5,516,000 jobs.[10] In the same time period that 2,210,000 jobs were lost in the construction industry, over 1.5 million people—mostly men—were deported. Both incarceration and deportation remove people from society and work to keep people compliant. Additionally, both regulatory policies cost taxpayers billions and harm communities.

Incarceration and deportation both require substantial financial outlays, which supposedly should not be part of neoliberal governments. However, insofar as neoliberalism creates economic insecurity, it requires the state to strengthen its coercive arm. In a neoliberal state, economic crises occur frequently, and the people at the lowest rungs of society suffer the most (Harvey 2005). As the economic crisis deepens, it threatens the economic security of the middle class: 40 percent of Americans say they are struggling "a lot" in the current economy, and 37 percent of these people identified themselves as being in the middle- or upper-middle class.[11] Economic worries translate into a general sense of insecurity (Hacker, Rehm, and Schlesinger 2013). Politicians—anxious to distract us from real economic issues—attempt to assuage people concerned about their economic situation with promises to deport all undocumented immigrants and strengthen crime enforcement (Davis 1998; Simon 2007).

In the United States, the War on Drugs and the War on Terror involve massive outlays of cash—expenditures that could be used to provide financial security for people teetering on the edge of foreclosure, bankruptcy, and unemployment. However, in a neoliberal climate that demands government cutbacks in social services, the state cannot extend unemployment insurance, subsidize homeowners, or invest in public housing. Instead, politicians assure people that the Wars on Drugs and Terror enhance public and national security. Security from terrorism and crime replace financial and social security.

As Wacquant and Harvey suggest, neoliberalism requires docile workers willing to work for less than a living wage. Noncitizens in the United States provide this necessary labor force in a neoliberal economy. However, as inequality has increased, real wages have dropped, and unemployment has risen, the state has become increasingly repressive to ensure workers are compliant. I met many Dominicans who arrived in New York City and worked in low-wage jobs for years before getting tired of the low pay, long hours, and lack of benefits. They turned to the illegal economy to supplement their income. However, they were caught, arrested, and deported. These men told me they wished they could go back to the United States so they could have another chance to do things the right way. The right way, it seems, is to accept jobs that pay $8 an hour or less. Even though these men will not have the chance to do things the "right way," their deportation sends a message to their communities that subservience to the global economy is the best way to survive. Workers who might entertain the thought of eschewing low-wage labor fear deportation and keep their heads down. The threat of deportability—similar to the threat of incarceration—encourages workers to self-govern, which is another key element of a neoliberal era.

Criminal aliens, similar to felons, have become expendable and serve as an example to others who may consider transgressing the law. With no powerful lobbies to defend them, working-class, immigrant men of color who break the law experience harsh castigation. Their punishment serves two purposes: (1) Law makers and enforcers have statistics to show how effectively they are using public funds, and (2) the draconian consequences keep potential transgressors in check and willing to work in dead-end, low-wage jobs that barely ensure their subsistence. Stories of deportation that circulate in immigrant communities and in the media encourage immigrants to keep their heads down, stay away from drugs, and accept work in low-wage jobs.

Neoliberalism, Global Capitalism, and Mass Deportation

My arguments with regard to why we are in an era of mass deportation are based in large part on interviews I conducted with 147 deportees. Read together, the stories of deportees reveal the elements of neoliberalism and global capitalism that make mass deportation possible. Three elements create this neoliberal cycle of migration and deportation: stark inequality, social and border control, and economic shifts.

Global inequality is one of the prime reasons for international migration: There is tremendous inequality between countries, so people seek out their fortune in wealthier countries when they have the opportunity to do so. For many people, simply moving to a new country can significantly increase their income. For example, 80 percent of the people in Côte d'Ivoire earn less than the poverty threshold in Italy. Were these Ivoirians to move to Italy, they would be better off, even if they joined the working poor in Italy.[12] Similarly, when working-class Guatemalans move to the United States and join the U.S. working poor, they still can earn several times more than they could have in Guatemala.

Deportees I interviewed consistently told me they or their parents came to the United States in search of a better life. People who migrate to the United States also encounter significant inequality here: In 2012, the richest 20 percent of people in the United States earned 16 times more than the poorest 20 percent. In 2007, the share of the income in the United States held by the top 1 percent of earners was higher than it had been since 1917 (Morris and Western 1999; McCall and Percheski 2010). Wealth inequality in the United States is staggering: 1 percent of Americans own nearly half of the wealth in the country (Norton and Ariely 2011). As I explain above, this high level of inequality is due in part to the shifting nature of the labor market.

High levels of inequality at the global level lead to international migration. At the national level, they often lead to discontent. Both of these responses—migration and discontent—have engendered a state response of control. The United States has erected an elaborate system of border control, ostensibly to keep unwanted immigrants out and to create a complex system of immigration policing to render those immigrants that are there more vulnerable. The border control system does not actually keep migrants out—it simply makes their passage more difficult (Cornelius 2006). And immigration policing does not remove all migrants who are in the country illegally, yet it does create fear in migrant communities and renders migrant labor more vulnerable.

Immigrants have been able to fill jobs in the new economy in the United States. However, often these jobs are undesirable and various systems of social control have emerged to ensure that immigrants stay in these jobs and don't disrupt the economy. These systems of control include border enforcement, immigration law enforcement, zealous criminal law enforcement, and migrant self-policing.

Methods and Case Selection

The arguments I present in this book are based primarily on 147 interviews I conducted over 14 months between May 2009 and August 2010 in Jamaica, Guatemala, the Dominican Republic, and Brazil, as well as follow-up observations in Guatemala in 2013. I spent a minimum of three months in each country, and I was able to interview at least 30 deportees in each country. I employed local research assistants to help me find interview candidates. In Jamaica, I found two assistants—both of them deportees—who assisted me in locating interview candidates. In Guatemala, students with connections to the migrant community as well as a deportee were able to find interview candidates. In Brazil, university students helped me to locate interview candidates. And in the Dominican Republic, a deportee and a student helped me find people to interview.

Using a variety of entry points, I obtained a sample that closely resembles the overall deportee population in each country. I selected interviewees who had spent varying lengths of time in the United States, who were deported on criminal and noncriminal grounds, who had served varying prison sentences, and who had gone to the United States at various ages. Although the deportee population in each of the countries is nearly all male, I interviewed women to gain their perspective as well. The interviews ranged in length from 20 minutes to more than two hours and were all audio-recorded, transcribed, and coded.

I interviewed deportees in the two countries to which the United States sends the highest proportion of criminal deportees (Jamaica and the Dominican Republic) and the two with the lowest proportion

TABLE I.1. Top 10 Countries of Origin of Deportees, Fiscal Years 2005 and 2006 Combined

Country	# of Deportees	% Criminal
All	527,405	36%
Guatemala	35,049	**17%**
Brazil	11,314	**18%**
Honduras	42,632	20%
Nicaragua	3,738	25%
Ecuador	3,240	27%
El Salvador	19,355	34%
Mexico	355,757	40%
Colombia	5,382	50%
Dominican Republic	6,317	**71%**
Jamaica	3,685	**74%**

Source: Department of Homeland Security, "Yearbook of Immigration Statistics, 2005 and 2006."

of criminal deportees (Guatemala and Brazil). The concentration of deportees in a handful of countries made it relatively easy to choose sites for this project. Overall, 92 percent of the 527,405 people deported in FY 2005 and 2006 were from just nine countries: Mexico, Honduras, Guatemala, El Salvador, Brazil, the Dominican Republic, Colombia, Nicaragua, and Jamaica—in descending numerical order (2005 and 2006 Immigration Enforcement Data Tables—DHS). Fewer than 20 percent of the Guatemalans and Brazilians deported in 2005 and 2006 had been convicted of crimes in the United States, compared to 74 percent of Jamaicans and 71 percent of Dominicans.[13] (See table I.1 for details.)

In addition to the interviews, I draw from DHS statistics on immigration law enforcement, DHS published statements and reports, as well as data from the TRAC, which publishes data on immigration law enforcement and court proceedings.

Overview of Rest of This Book

This book explains the neoliberal cycle of emigration, immigration, and deportation. For this reason, I have organized the book around the journeys of immigrants who eventually became deportees. My analyses of their narratives make clear the mechanisms through which stark inequality, social and border control, and economic shifts—the undercurrents of neoliberalism—underlay their experiences. I develop arguments in each chapter that describe the mechanisms by which global capitalism drives mass deportation, and I use deportees' stories to illustrate their positions within the cycle.

In chapter 1, "Growing Up," I tell the stories of several deportees to describe the conditions these deportees left behind in their home countries. These stories show how global inequality compelled people to leave their countries of birth. The deportees we will meet in this book traveled to the United States because they knew someone else who had done so before them and because they had good reasons to do so. When these deportees and their families migrated, they were playing a crucial role in global capitalism—that of providing their labor where it was needed. However, these deportees likely would never have left their home countries if global capitalism had not already made them economically vulnerable. They became necessary cogs in the migration machine primarily because it was the best option available to them.

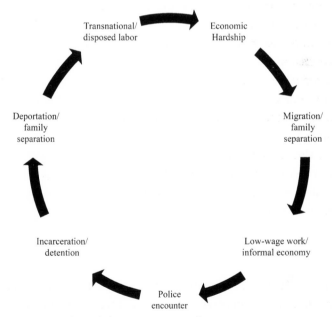

Figure I.4. The path from migration to deportation.

In chapter 2, "Crossing Over," I detail the experience of crossing over into the United States and document the consequences of enhanced border enforcement. We see that migrants who traveled earlier tended to find it fairly easy to get into the United States, whereas those that came in the recent era of enhanced enforcement have had more harrowing experiences. I asked each of the deportees I met to describe to me his or her experience of trying to make it to the United States. The stories were often traumatic adventures across sea and land. They are also a testament to the risks migrants must endure in order to make it to the United States.

In chapter 3, "Becoming (Black and Latino) American," I consider the lives of young immigrants coming of age in the United States and how their parents' marginal positions in the economy combined with heavy policing in their neighborhoods affected their lives. Many of the deportees I met spent their formative years in the United States. Their stories make it clear that immigrant children who grow up in the United States have distinct experiences based largely on the situation into which they arrive and the ability of their family to adapt to the new situation. Whether the journey culminated in a reunion with parents after years of separation or immigration had been with their families intact, whether they settled in New York City or other places, all affected the experiences of deportees growing up in the United States.

In chapter 4, "The War on Drugs," I tell the stories of Jamaican and Dominican immigrants who were deported on drug charges. Dominicans and Jamaicans are the two immigrant groups most likely to be deported on criminal grounds and most often deported on drug charges. Their stories lay bare the intersections between the War on Drugs and the War on Terror through a consideration of how the War on Drugs has affected their neighborhoods and how small-time drug dealers have been targeted in the War on Terror. This chapter renders it evident how mass incarceration and heavy policing affect immigrants in a neoliberal era.

Chapter 5, "Getting Caught," tells the story of how deportees got caught up in the deportation dragnet. This chapter draws from the narratives of deportees to explain how criminal law enforcement contributes to the skewed nature of immigration law enforcement and to illuminate how the stories of immigration law enforcement that circulate in immigrant communities contribute to a climate of social control.

Chapter 6, "Behind Bars," describes deportees' experiences behind bars—in jails, prisons, and immigration detention centers. Many of the deportees spent time both in prison and in immigration detention centers, experiencing varying levels of mistreatment. A look inside detention centers and prisons reveals the underbelly of global capitalism. Both prisons and detention centers are a literal manifestation of the coercive arm of the state under neoliberalism.

Chapter 7, "Back Home," details the struggles deportees face in their countries of birth. Many face stigma, exclusion, and even legal sanction. We see how the context of reception matters in these homecomings. The Dominican Republic treats arriving deportees as unwelcome criminals; Guatemala ushers the English-speaking workers into jobs at transnational telemarketing centers, while eschewing those who have tattoos; Jamaica blames its crime wave on the influx of criminal deportees; and Brazil, with a growing economy, barely notices its returning citizens.

The conclusion recaps key policy lessons and discusses the most recent policies and proposals in light of my findings.

Each of these chapters provides insights into a critical aspect of the neoliberal cycle. In the first chapter, we will consider how global inequality and economic restructuring in Jamaica, the Dominican Republic, Guatemala, and Brazil accelerated emigration flows from these countries.

1

Growing Up

Yearning for a New Life

What would it take for you to leave your country? Living in the country where you were born comes with tangible and intangible privileges: citizenship, belonging, family ties, and rights, for example. Leaving these rights and privileges behind is no small matter. Yet people leave their countries of birth every day. Today, there are nearly a quarter of a billion international migrants around the world. About half of these migrants are women; about a fifth live in the United States.[1]

Why do people migrate? People migrate not solely because they are poor, but because they have a better opportunity elsewhere and they have the networks and resources to leave. There are many poor people around the world who will never emigrate because their position in the global economy does not facilitate the possibility for international migration. This fact can be seen by looking at who migrates to the United States: Of the more than one million immigrants who became legal permanent residents in 2009, only 6,718 of them hailed from the five poorest countries in the world.[2] Immigrants in the United States do not come from the poorest countries in the world; they come from the countries where the United States has close ties that facilitate and encourage their migration.

Scholars who offer structural theories of migration argue that histories of colonization; economic, political, and historical ties; and contemporary international relations and foreign policy can help us understand migratory patterns around the world (Sassen 1989). Beginning in the 1960s, Asian, Latin American, and Caribbean countries began to be pulled into the global economy and politics through U.S. investors and the involvement of the U.S. military. These linkages eventually translated into mass migration. In 2006, 43 percent of all legal permanent residents and 64 percent of all undocumented migrants came from

Mexico, China, India, the Philippines, and Vietnam—all countries that have long-standing and close military, political, and economic ties to the United States (Golash-Boza 2012).[3]

One poignant example of these ties is that Mexican migrants often come to the United States to work in the same sector that they worked in prior to migration. This trend began with the bracero program and continues today. To meet labor needs during World War II, the U.S. government created the bracero program in 1942, an arrangement to bring in temporary workers from Mexico. Between 1942 and 1964, 4.6 million Mexicans, called *braceros* (after the Spanish term roughly translated as "farmhands"), came to work in agriculture in the United States. In large part due to criticism over widespread labor violations, the program ended in 1965. However, the linkages created during the bracero program meant that Mexican migration continued. Growers had become dependent on Mexican farm labor, and Mexican households had become dependent on the additional income. Today, several decades after the end of the bracero program, Mexicans continue to make up the bulk of farmworkers in the United States (Massey et al. 2002).

The relationship between transnational ties and international migration is evident in a variety of sectors of the labor market. Sanderson (2014) found that the majority of Mexicans who work in food processing, agriculture, and construction in Mexico also worked in those same sectors after migrating to the United States. This process is called "occupational channeling" and can be explained by the development of a transnational food system spanning all of North America. U.S. companies such as General Mills and Smithfield Foods invested substantial amounts of money into food production in Mexico. This has been ongoing since the early 1980s, and it accelerated with the North American Free Trade Agreement (NAFTA). As a consequence, U.S.-based firms own over half of the total foreign direct investment (FDI) in Mexico's food industry (Sanderson 2014). These linkages have, in turn, translated into transnational migration.

Scholars of international migration generally agree that people migrate due to a combination of structural and individual factors. The structural factors include employment opportunities, family reunification, and the flight from persecution. Most people in the world, however, who might wish to migrate, do not. This is where the individual factors come into play—people migrate when they know someone who has migrated, when they know a job is available in a specific place, and when they have the resources to leave their homes. Finally, people migrate to very specific places; people leave one village in Thailand or Mexico to rejoin relatives and friends in a particular neighborhood in San Francisco or Los Angeles (Rumbaut 1994; Massey et al. 2002). In the stories we will read, we will see that most Jamaicans and Dominicans rejoined family members in New York City; Guatemalans often went where other Guatemalans were, as did Brazilians. We also will see the costs and benefits of international migration and how children are often pulled along in their parents' quests for better lives.

This chapter explores the lives of deportees before they left their countries of origin to shed light on why they left. We will see that, although their migration journeys ended in deportation, they began just as other migrants' journeys began—with a decision to seek out a better life. We also will learn that the four countries under study here— Jamaica, the Dominican Republic, Brazil, and Guatemala—all have very close ties with the United States, and each underwent economic and social shifts due to neoliberal policies in the late 20th century. These ties and neoliberal changes work as both push and pull factors that lead migrants to leave their countries. The details of each country are distinct but they all share the commonality that neoliberal reforms accelerated the flows of international migrants.

All four countries implemented neoliberal reforms into their economies at the behest of the International Monetary Fund (IMF). These reforms were designed to further integrate these countries into the global economy. These reforms also accelerated emigration, thereby filling a need for labor in the United States (and in Europe, although the European case is not discussed here). Emigration from these countries did not begin with neoliberal reforms. However, these reforms created the conditions that led to larger numbers of emigrants. These emigrants often chose the United States as their destination because of long-standing ties between these countries and the United States—ties created through military intervention, labor recruitment, and foreign direct investment (Golash-Boza 2012).

The migration flows of Jamaicans, Dominicans, Guatemalans, and Brazilians differ in the details of their histories although they share many commonalities. Jamaicans have a long history of emigration to other countries in the Caribbean, the United Kingdom, and, since the 1960s, the United States. Dominicans also began to come to the United States in large numbers in the 1960s. The Jamaicans largely came on employment-based visas in the 1960s, as housecleaners and nurses. The Dominicans came because they were fleeing political turmoil in the 1960s, then overwhelmingly for economic reasons. The migration histories of Guatemala and Brazil are more recent. Guatemalans began to leave their country en masse in the 1980s, due to an ongoing civil war and economic turmoil. Brazilians trickled into the United States in the 1980s and 1990s, when Brazil began to have economic problems. Now that Brazil is experiencing an economic boom, fewer Brazilians are coming to the United States. As I explain further below, the timing of the migration flow is important because of a spate of changes in U.S. immigration law that affected the legal status of immigrants.

Specialists in international migration have long argued that there are connections between the global flow of capital and the movement of people across borders. However, few researchers make this link explicit through the examination of large-scale economic changes alongside individual migration stories. Additionally, insofar as many migration researchers focus on one country such as Mexico or Brazil, it is often difficult to see commonalities across countries. In this chapter, I make linkages between migration and global capitalism explicit through a discussion of several deportees' migration trajectories. This discussion also renders it clear that U.S. involvement in the internal politics of these countries often served as a catalyst for emigration. This book focuses on the stories of deportees, and insofar as their stories begin with emigration, it is critical for us to explore why they left their homelands in the first place.

Growing Up in Jamaica

Jamaicans who leave their home country for the United States join millions of fellow countrymen who have also left the island: Half of the Jamaican population lives abroad (Thomas 2009). These migration flows are not new. In the 19th century, thousands of Jamaicans emigrated to Central America and other Caribbean islands in search of employment. Jamaicans continued to leave the island throughout the 20th century, although emigration slowed substantially during the Great Depression (Vickerman 1999). At the end of World War II, Jamaicans left for Great Britain by the thousands. This flow subsided in the 1960s when Great Britain passed a series of restrictive immigration laws. Just as emigration to Great Britain subsided, the United States passed amendments to the Immigration and Nationality Act in 1965 that facilitated Jamaican immigration.

This act, also called the 1965 Hart-Cellar Act, was one of the most significant changes to U.S. immigration law in the 20th century. It put an end to the racially biased quotas set forth in the 1924 Oriental Exclusion Act and the Immigration Act of 1924. In the spirit of the civil rights movement, the 1965 act set a universal quota for every country in the world. Each country could send up to 20,000 qualified immigrants a year, with no racial restrictions. Potential immigrants could qualify for entry based on either family ties to the United States (relatives could petition for their entry) or their skills (employers could request immigrants based on their skills and education). The 1965 act had two main consequences: (1) It increased immigration from Asia, Latin America, and the Caribbean, and (2) it increased undocumented immigration from Mexico.

By 2009, there were about 637,000 Jamaican migrants in the United States (Glennie and Chappell 2010), most of them concentrated on the East Coast. Nearly half the Jamaicans in the United States live in New York City; another 28 percent live in south Florida. There are also significant populations in Connecticut, New Jersey, Washington, D.C., and Atlanta (Vickerman 1999). Notably, over half of Jamaican migrants to the United States have been women. The preponderance of women among Jamaican immigrants is a reflection of economic restructuring in the United States and the concomitant growth in traditionally female labor sectors such as service, health care, microelectronics, and garment industries (Kasinitz et al. 2008; Model 2008; Foner 2009; Glennie and Chappell 2010).

Emigration from Jamaica is closely related to the transformation of the economy and its demographic composition over the past 50 years. In 1950, 80 percent of the Jamaican population was rural. By 2010, the majority of Jamaicans (60 percent) lived in urban areas. In the 1950s and 1960s, Jamaica diversified its economy through investments in bauxite, tourism, and manufacturing. The bauxite industry, for example, was established in 1952. By 1976, with the help of foreign investors, Jamaica became the leading exporter of bauxite—a key raw material in the production of aluminum. These investments helped the gross national product (GNP) to grow, and things were going fairly well until soaring oil costs hit in the 1970s. The Jamaican government responded by negotiating new agreements with the bauxite and sugar industries and by facilitating loans to small farmers. These reforms, however, did not help Jamaica pay its growing debt. In 1977, Prime Minister Manley turned to the IMF, which lent money to Jamaica but demanded that Manley implement structural adjustments in return for the loan (Hahamovitch 2011).

Jamaica's economy continued to worsen, unemployment soared, and the next prime minister, Edward Seaga, borrowed more money from both the IMF and the World Bank. The 1980s brought substantial growth to the Jamaican economy, with development in tourism and exports—both of which generated foreign currency. During the 1980s, most of the state funding in agriculture went to large-scale sugar and banana farmers, not to small-scale farmers who produced goods for local consumption. By the end of the 1980s, only a quarter of Jamaica's workforce was engaged in agricultural labor, and Jamaica had become dependent on cheap, subsidized foreign imports for most of its food. To take milk as an example, the combination of the elimination of tariffs and the importation of milk from subsidized dairy farms in the United States meant that domestic milk production fell by one-third between 1992 and 2000 in Jamaica, due to consumers opting for cheaper, imported, powdered milk. Many of these out-of-work farmers moved to Kingston, looking for work (Weis 2004; Clarke and Howard 2006).

Structural adjustment had also hit Jamaica's capital city and largest urban area—Kingston. Employment in manufacturing in Free Trade Zones near Kingston grew a little in the 1980s, but most of these factories closed in the 1990s, as the foreign owners left for other countries that could pay even lower wages for workers. Under global capitalism, companies are free to seek out the lowest wages around the world, whereas workers are often restricted to seeking out opportunities in their countries of birth. In Jamaica, structural adjustment also brought cuts in government employment: More than a quarter of employed workers in Kingston worked for the government in 1977, and government jobs shrank by more than a third by 1989, leaving large numbers of Kingston residents unemployed (Clarke and Howard 2006). Overall unemployment increased from 24 percent in 1974 to 31 percent in 1980. At the same time, inflation caused by devaluation of the currency made it difficult for wage earners to survive (Clarke and Howard 2006).

Emigration provided some relief from these social pressures. The Jamaican government was well aware of this and Prime Minister Manley asked the U.S. government to expand the guestworker program such that more Jamaicans might be able to travel abroad and earn much-needed cash to support their families (Hahamovitch 2011). Although the guestworker program allowed Jamaicans to seek out higher wages in the United States, the program placed severe restrictions on their mobility once in the United States—they were obliged to remain with the employer who had hired them. If the guestworker found a way to escape from the sugarcane fields in the United States, he would become an undocumented immigrant: another vulnerable category of workers.

Economic and social changes in Jamaica have led to massive displacement. Moving to Kingston brought opportunities for some Jamaicans, but many other Jamaicans opted to emigrate to the United States, the United Kingdom, and Canada. Some Jamaicans emigrated directly from the countryside, but many others first moved to Kingston, where they gained the cultural, social, and economic capital necessary to leave the country. This process of two-stage migration is common across the globe; peasants first move to cities where they work in transnational or national industries, and then they emigrate abroad (Sassen 1989; Louie 2001). One reason for this is that peasants often lack the resources to emigrate: In urban areas it is often easier to accumulate the cash and social networks you need to leave your country.

A few of the Jamaican deportees I interviewed traveled to the United States when they were very young. When I asked them about their lives in Jamaica prior to migration, they struggled to remember details. Their lack of knowledge of Jamaica, of course, made their subsequent deportation back there much more difficult.

Those Jamaicans who could tell me why they traveled to the United States spoke of a desire for a better future for themselves and their families. Women who struggled as single mothers in Kingston traveled to the United States to create more opportunity for their children. Men who earned little money working in Jamaica spoke of a desire to earn more money and to provide for their families. Those deportees who traveled to the United States as minors followed their parents who had traveled abroad to provide a better future for them. Hakim is one example. He told me:

> My mama tried hard; that's why she ended up in America. The aspiration of working people is always to try to rise, trying to look for better. Everybody wants to migrate to where they think it is a better life, you know. She had left the island early. She left about 1962 or 1963, then she came back and she left again. I remember when she came back; she took my younger brother.

Hakim's mother's migration was part of one of the early waves of Jamaicans leaving the island for New York City. These early migrants made subsequent migrant flows possible, due to family reunification laws in the United States. Hakim's family decided he should stay in Jamaica when his mother left so that he could complete his schooling at Kingston College—a competitive public high school in Kingston. As they knew well, the education he would receive at Kingston College would be much better than at a public high school in a low-income neighborhood in the United States. When his mother traveled, he stayed behind with his aunt. It was (and still is) typical for Jamaican women to leave their children behind with female relatives until they are settled in the United States (Waters 1999; Pottinger 2005). A moniker, barrel children, has emerged to describe these children because they received barrels full of provisions from their mothers from time to time.

A few years after his mother left, Hakim joined the Rastafarian movement. When Hakim was 12, Haile Selassie, an Ethiopian leader whom Rastafarians believe to be their Messiah, came to Jamaica. After this visit, Hakim became interested in the Rastafarian movement and became a Rastafarian at age 14. By that time, his mother had left Jamaica, and Hakim was living with his aunt in downtown Kingston. I met many Jamaican deportees like Hakim whose mothers had left them behind with relatives while they got settled in the United States. Likely because this practice is fairly common (Waters 1999), the men I met did not express bitterness that their mothers left them with relatives. They viewed it as a necessary step toward their eventual reunification. Hakim, however, would have been happy to remain in Jamaica, where he found a place in the Rastafarian community.

In Kingston, Hakim did well in school until the principal found out Hakim had become a Rastafarian. The principal confiscated his Rastafarian literature and his red, gold, and green hat. Because of this harassment, Hakim left school and went to live in a Rastafarian community outside of Kingston. In the community, Hakim and other Rastafarians were able to survive by making herbal tonics and juices and selling them. They also did some small-scale farming but mostly lived cheaply. When Hakim's mother found out he was living in a Rastafarian community, she decided it was time for him to move to the United States. Hakim moved with her to Cleveland, Ohio, when he was 19, but he soon left for New York City to join a Rastafarian community there. On his own in New York, Hakim was able to practice his religious beliefs without interference from his family. Hakim's family was among the earliest wave of Jamaicans who traveled to the United States once the 1965 Immigration and Nationality Act was passed, which enabled many Jamaicans to enter the United States legally and to bring their families. Hakim's mother, like many Jamaicans before her, sought opportunities abroad when the prospects looked better than they did in her home country.

Elias traveled to the United States in 1979, the last year of Michael Manley's first stint as prime minister of Jamaica. Elias's family was much poorer than Hakim's. The first wave of Jamaican immigrants to the United States in the 1960s arrived with visas to work—many as nurses or household employees. By the 1970s, Jamaicans were more likely to emigrate on family-based visas (Foner 2009). When this happened, the class composition of Jamaican emigrants shifted, and more poor Jamaicans, like Elias's mother, were able to emigrate on these family-based visas. Elias's mother was able to travel to the United States as a legal permanent resident because her sister was already in the United States. Elias told me his family was poor in Jamaica, and his mother, like Hakim's, left him behind with family members when she traveled. When I asked him about growing up in St. Thomas, Jamaica, he told me:

Well, you know, it was rough. My mom got a break and she left to work in America. Then she sent for me and my little sister and my stepdad. I left here when I was 13 years old, in 1979. . . . We were poor; I mean, I have memory of wearing no shoes and the pants ripped up. But, I'm saying, that was back in the days. But life was rough. I mean, my grandmother, she used to make these belts that they plait for a living and my grandfather, he was a farmer. And, basically, that's how we survived until [we migrated] . . . 'cause I was living with my grandmother, you know, as a baby.

Elias lived with his grandmother, as was typical of Jamaican youth whose parents migrated (Waters 1999). Elias's mother left him in Jamaica with his grandmother when he was about six years old when she went to work as a housecleaner for a lawyer in New York City. Elias's mother joined many Jamaican women who took household jobs in New York to meet the growing demand. Elias joined her a few years later in New York. Elias's grandparents were barely able to eke out a living through their traditional handicrafts. This trend is also typical; as countries transition into the global economy, local industries and handicrafts lose out due to global competition. For Elias's family, the best solution was to send a family member abroad to earn much-needed income. While abroad, Elias's mother, like many Jamaican emigrants, sent home toys, clothes, and money, thereby ensuring the material wellbeing of her family left behind.

The Jamaicans who migrated in the 1960s and 1970s often traveled legally on family- and employment-based visas. In the 1960s, more than one-third of emigrants from Jamaica to the United States were skilled workers. Some scholars imply that this out-migration constituted a brain drain insofar as these workers were educated and trained at a cost to the Jamaican government whereas the United States reaped the benefits (Cooper 1985).

Over time, this pattern shifted and emigration from Jamaica became more of an escape valve than a brain drain. In the 1990s, it was difficult even for skilled Jamaicans to enter the United States legally. The situation in Jamaica, meanwhile, had gotten worse, largely due to structural adjustment policies implemented in the 1990s and the consequent escalation of political violence (Gray 2004). Philip's story is typical of migrants who left in this period, in that he traveled on a temporary visa and eventually fell into an undocumented status.

Philip grew up in downtown Kingston, where he ran for the track team at the local high school. He excelled in running and was selected to participate in an international track meet held in Orlando, Florida, when he was 21. He obtained an athletics visa to participate in the meet. He saw this as an opportunity to escape the poverty he and his mother experienced in Kingston. As a single mother, working as a house-cleaner in Kingston, his mother barely earned enough to get by. Thus, after Philip ran in the track meet in 1994, he decided he did not want to return to Jamaica. Philip told me he had moved to the United States to "escape from the hard life" because "Jamaica's very hard." After the track meet, Philip went to stay with the only person he knew in the United States: an American woman he met in his neighborhood in Kingston. She had come to visit friends there, and they developed a romantic relationship. Once he was in the States, they decided to make their lives together and get married.

Many of the deportees I met described similar lives of deprivation in Jamaica prior to leaving. Ken, a deportee who grew up in Trenchtown, recounted that before he migrated, relatives sent him clothes and food because they lived in poverty, "a real hard situation." Philip's mother also supplemented her meager income with remittances from her daughter who lived in England.

Their stories show how emigration has both been a brain drain and an escape valve. Large-scale emigration has relieved some of the economic pressure felt in Jamaica since the 1960s; by emigrating, these Jamaicans don't join the ranks of the unemployed, and the remittances they send home help their family members left behind survive. Employers in the United States recruited Jamaicans to fill service and technical jobs in the United States in the 1960s. Provisions in U.S. immigration law at the time made that feasible. Connections between the United States and Jamaica were strengthened through foreign direct investment, particularly in the bauxite and sugar industries. Jamaicans who emigrated in the 1960s laid the foundation for their fellow countrymen to follow their paths and migrate to the United States—nearly every Jamaican I spoke with traveled to the United States to join a family member already there.

The twists and turns of the Jamaican economy under structural adjustment provided motivation for ambitious Jamaicans to leave. The openings in the U.S. labor market and their ties to Jamaicans in the United States gave them somewhere to go. Massive emigration has helped Jamaica avoid political and social upheaval as discontented people leave as opposed to staying and engaging in political protest. Migration as a strategy to avoid political dissent is particularly obvious in the Dominican Republic, where the U.S. consulate granted visas to dissenters in the 1960s (Wiarda 1980; Brands 1987).

Growing Up in the Dominican Republic

Emigration is also very common in the Dominican Republic: By 1997, nearly 10 percent of people of Dominican origin were living in the United States. Large-scale Dominican migration to the United States began in the 1960s, after the assassination of President Rafael Leonidas Trujillo, who had restricted emigration during his three decades of despotism. Trujillo's economic strategy involved developing the industrial and agricultural sectors, which required large numbers of laborers. For this reason, Trujillo restricted emigration. The growth in the industrial sector was primarily in urban areas, which led to large-scale internal migration from rural areas to Santo Domingo in the 1940s and 1950s (Torres-Saillant and Fernandez 1998).

After the 1961 assassination of Trujillo, who had close ties to Washington, D.C., Dominicans elected left-leaning Juan Bosch to the presidency, with more than 60 percent of the popular vote. After just a few months in office, opposition forces, led by Dominican General Elias Wessin, deposed Bosch. This overthrow was possible in large part because the United States provided material support to the right-wing opposition (Brotherton and Barrios 2011). The coup led to political instability, and the United States, worried about the threat of communism and the possibility of allying with Fidel Castro, intervened militarily in the Dominican Republic (Brands 1987). U.S. military troops arrived in the Dominican Republic on April 28, 1965, with the intention of ensuring that Bosch would not return to the presidency (Wiarda 1980). During this time of intense involvement of the United States in Dominican affairs between 1961 and 1968, more Dominicans entered the United States than from any other country in the Western Hemisphere, except Mexico (Golash-Boza 2012). Remarkably, these Dominicans entered on skills- and family-based visas—not as refugees—even though many were fleeing political violence from the former supporters of Trujillo and later from those who had supported Bosch.

The U.S.-organized elections in the Dominican Republic enabled Joaquín Balaguer to win the presidential elections. Balaguer's government from 1966 to 1978 was characterized by a reign of terror against dissidents. Meanwhile, the U.S. consulate granted visas to potential dissidents (Wiarda 1980; Brands 1987). There was no formal written agreement between the United States and the Dominican Republic with regard to emigration and the control of dissidents. However, the Balaguer government readily issued passports and the United States built a new consulate office in Santo Domingo to facilitate the granting of visas. This strategy benefited Balaguer as it rid him of both excess workers and potential political dissidents. It benefited the United States insofar as Balaguer—who was friendly to U.S. investors—remained in office (Torres-Saillant and Fernandez 1998).

Balaguer also opened up the Dominican economy to more foreign investment, particularly from the United States. As neoliberal reforms often do, the economic changes led to growth in the industrial sector but also created unprecedented rates of unemployment in the Dominican Republic. Dominicans protested in response to the massive economic changes, but, with the help of the Pentagon, the CIA, and the U.S. State Department, the Dominican government was able to squash the dissidence.

In 1978, the Dominican Revolutionary Party (PRD) came to power, and it implemented a series of social democratic reforms; the government raised wages, imposed price controls, and created jobs in the public sector. However, in 1982, with a new president, the PRD changed course, and the new Dominican president, Jorge Blanco, as Michael Manley had done in 1979, began to negotiate with the IMF. These negotiations led to an agreement whereby the Dominican government implemented a series of structural adjustments, including a reduction of public expenditures, trade liberalization, and the free-floating of the Dominican peso. These changes helped the Dominican economy pay off some of its debts, but they also created high levels of unemployment and inflation. In 1986, Balaguer won the election again, this time on a platform critical of the IMF and its neoliberal policies. However, his statist policies increased the deficit and Balaguer soon found himself obliged to negotiate with the IMF and implement more neoliberal reforms (Espinal 1995). Over the course of the 1980s, Dominicans witnessed the gradual withering away of the state. These neoliberal cutbacks led to protests, economic strife, and more emigration to the United States. The 1980s was marked by increased legal as well as illegal Dominican immigration.

More than 250,000 Dominicans came to the United States legally during the 1980s; in the 1990s it was 335,221. Tens of thousands of other Dominicans entered illegally or on temporary visas. More than half of Dominican migrants have settled in New York City (Levitt 2001; Duany 2004; Sagás and Molina 2004). The Dominican deportees whom I met, like the Jamaicans, generally migrated to the United States with hopes for a better life and with the purpose of reuniting with family members.

Those Dominicans who had been very young when they migrated often weren't sure exactly why their parents left for the United States, but they presumed it was either due to the political turmoil or the lack of economic opportunities. All of these men who migrated as children went as legal permanent residents on family-based visas to the United States.

Dominicans who left in the 1960s often did so for political reasons—to get away from the turbulent times that followed the assassination of Trujillo in 1961. Mike, for example, was born in 1956 in a middle-class neighborhood. His father had a government job in the Trujillo administration. When Trujillo was assassinated, Mike's parents fled to the United States. His parents left hastily, and they left Mike and his six brothers and sisters with their grandmother. Once his parents were able to get legal permanent residency in the United States, Mike's mother came back for the children. That was in 1965.

Renaldo also left for political reasons. Unlike many of the deportees who hail from poor neighborhoods, Renaldo was raised in a middle-class neighborhood. Renaldo's father was a military officer under the Trujillo regime. Renaldo described an idyllic childhood, eating mangos from neighborhood trees and running around the streets until night-fall. When he reached adolescence, however, things began to change. He told me:

> The decade when Trujillo died was a bloody one. We saw the death of the Mirabal sisters, the government of Balaguer, the exodus of Trujillo's children, the coup by Juan Bosch, the Revolution of 1965, and the first government of President Balaguer, which was a criminal regime. In that time, to be young and to think was dangerous. Now, looking back, I can understand what was going on during that time. It was the infamous Cold War, and the United States and Russia; well, I won't place blame with either. It was a question of political and military control. I entered into the Universidad Autónoma de Santo Domingo in 1968 as a product of the Revolution. . . . I entered into the university to study law. My mother didn't want me to study law because she thought, erroneously, that those who studied law were future communists. Just imagine the mentality of people during the Revolution. . . . I did get involved in a Dominican communist party, and one of my great friends, Otto Morales, a great revolutionary, was shot by the Intelligence Services. . . . In 1970, I became involved with a famous lawyer, Dr. Plinio Matos Moquete. He was an urban guerrillero. . . . During that time, my friends and I began to commit military actions, burn cars, and buses, those sorts of things.

Renaldo befriended revolutionary leaders in the Dominican Republic and became involved in the opposition movement. His father, a military officer, disapproved of his involvement. When tensions heightened, Renaldo's father intervened and sent him to the United States, ostensibly to study but really to avoid Renaldo getting arrested or killed. Renaldo was one of many dissidents sent to the United States in the 1960s and early 1970s. The United States, hoping to avoid instability in the Dominican Republic, and especially to avoid a socialist government, readily accepted Dominican dissidents.

The Dominicans I met who left for the United States in the 1980s and 1990s did not cite political reasons for their departure. Instead, they left for economic motives and to join family members. In the various decrepit neighborhoods that border the Ozama River, emigration is exceedingly common and seen as one route out of poverty. Homero, for example, was born in 1958 in Santo Domingo, in Los Guandules, a poor neighborhood that borders the Ozama. His single mother cleaned houses for a living to support Homero and his four siblings. Homero's father was electrocuted and died in a work-related accident when Homero was just eight months old. With no social safety net to help out this family in the aftermath of the loss of the primary breadwinner, Homero decided to drop out of school and get a job in a garment factory that made clothes for export to the United States. Once Homero started his own family, it became evident that his income was not enough to make ends meet. Thus, in 1991, when Homero was 32 years old, he decided to go to the United States on a yola (a fishing boat). A childhood friend of his sent him money to pay for the trip to Puerto Rico by boat and to New York City by plane. Homero's story shows how low wages, the lack of a social safety net, and linkages to the United States can easily translate into emigration for Dominicans.

Those Dominicans who migrated on their own as adults often had considered emigration from a young age: Many of them grew up watching boats full of cargo leave the port of Santo Domingo for the United States. Juan Pablo, for example, spent his childhood at the seashore. Born in 1973 in Santo Domingo, in the working-class neighborhood of Villa Juana, Juan Pablo preferred swimming at the beach in downtown Santo Domingo to going to school. When his father, a construction worker, found out he was skipping school, he beat Juan Pablo soundly and insisted he get an education. Juan Pablo chuckled as he remembered that his father would ask his cousin to lick his arm to see if it was salty to find out if Juan Pablo had been to the beach. Juan Pablo got around this by hosing himself off with fresh water in a gas station on the way home so that his skin would not be salty. By the time he was 14, Juan Pablo's parents gave up, took him out of secondary school, and put him to work with his brother who was a mechanic. Not too long afterward, he got on a yola to travel to the United States, where he hoped to earn more money.

Many of the Dominican deportees I met had worked at the port in Santo Domingo, loading ships with cargo destined for the United States, until the day came that they decided to stow away on one of those cargo ships. Jose, for example, was born in 1952, in a Santo Domingo neighborhood called María Auxiliadora, which is right on the Ozama River, which leads to the Caribbean Sea. Jose was raised by his single mother, who could not afford to send him to school. Jose only finished the first grade. When he was eight, his mother did not have enough money for books and Jose had to work as a shoeshine boy to bring in extra income. When he was 18 and old enough to get an identity card, Jose got his first formal job in the port. He worked there for several years, loading and unloading cargo to and from large ships. When he was 25 in 1977, Jose summoned the courage and stowed away on one of the ships, headed to Puerto Rico, where he made his way to his brother's house. It was not unusual for Dominican migrants to have relatives in the United States: Nearly every Dominican I met who traveled to the United States had relatives there.

Like Homero and Jose, Pedro is also from a neighborhood near the port of Santo Domingo, Villa Francisca. Pedro's father was a soldier and was killed when he was a baby. He was raised by his single mother. Pedro, who was born in 1964, told me:

> When I was younger, we used to get so excited when we saw our older friends coming back from New York and Puerto Rico. Because, at that time, you could just get on any of those boats that left from the pier. It was easy for us, because the pier was right there. We lived right there, right next to the pier. We used to take food to the dockworkers. I left when I was 12 years old. I didn't go straight to the United States. I got on a boat that was going to Saint Thomas, and from Saint Thomas to Puerto Rico.

Pedro, like many Dominicans who lived near the ports, boarded a cargo boat that would take him to the same places that the goods on the ships were being transported. Whereas it was legal to transport cargo, Pedro had no legal avenue to travel to the United States.

I did my fieldwork and interviews in the Dominican Republic's capital city of Santo Domingo. Thus, most of the Dominican deportees I met were born in Santo Domingo. Maximo, however, was born in 1979 in Samaná, in a small fishing village on the northern coast. Maximo finished the 11th grade of school but dropped out to work when he was 15. His first job was as an auto mechanic. When he was growing up, Maximo's aunt lived in the United States. She called frequently and came to visit each Christmas. She always brought clothes and other gifts for Maximo. Like many Dominicans, Maximo saw people coming from the United States returning with dollars, nice clothes, and fancy cars. Seeing people come back with riches led him to decide that he, too, wanted to go to the United States. In 1999, Maximo got on a yola that took him to Puerto Rico.

Homero, Pedro, Jose, and Maximo went to the United States for economic reasons—they saw themselves resigned to a life of poverty in the Dominican Republic and wanted more out of life. Their emigration, in turn, fueled the Dominican economy through the remittances they sent home. As we can see in these stories, Dominicans often migrated to the United States for a better life. Depending on the laws in place at the time, some were able to migrate legally, whereas others had only illegal options available to them. The circumstances in the Dominican Republic pushed them out, but the United States was their chosen destination because of strong ties between the two countries and, specifically, between people in their networks in the Dominican Republic and their fellow compatriots in the United States. Those Dominicans who emigrated in the 1960s left for explicit political reasons. However, we can also see how massive emigration in the 1970s, 1980s, and 1990s relieved social, political, and economic pressures by giving potential dissidents an alternative.

Growing Up in Guatemala

Guatemalans have had many reasons to leave their country: economic turmoil, violence, and political disorder. Guatemalans began to immigrate to the United States during their long and bloody civil war, in which the United States was heavily involved. In 1954, a CIA-sponsored military coup overthrew the democratically elected government of Jacobo Arbenz Guzman. This led to a civil war, which did not officially end until the peace accords were signed in 1996. During this 42-year war, a series of military officers ruled the country. Guerrilla armies frequently challenged their rule, and this conflict caused intense violence, particularly in the countryside. Rural inhabitants suspected of involvement in guerrilla activity were killed en masse. The U.S. government provided military aid to the government of Guatemala and trained

Guatemalan military officers to fight in the civil war. The brutal practices of the Guatemalan military created an exodus of refugees, particularly in the 1980s—although few of these refugees have been officially
recognized as such (García 2006). Today, although the civil war is officially over, poverty, high unemployment, and social disorder are left in
its aftermath. And the country is still on a long, rough road toward integration into the global economy.

In the 1980s, the Guatemalan government implemented a series of
neoliberal reforms— trade liberalization, the promotion of foreign
direct investment and exports, and tax cuts for investors—intended to
integrate the country into the global economy. These reforms generated
some jobs in Guatemala but mostly in temporary, low-skill, low-wage
occupations such as maquiladoras (factories) and tourism. Similar to
changes in Jamaica and the Dominican Republic, these reforms did not
create long-term stability in the country and eventually led to increased
urbanization and emigration (Robinson 2000).

Today in Guatemala most working-class jobs do not pay enough
to support a family, leading many parents to immigrate to the United
States to feed their families. In addition, there has been a surge in violence, and increasing numbers of people are fleeing the country in fear
of violence and extortion. In a suburb of Guatemala City called Mixco,
apparel workers assemble garments for export to the United States.
Workers there who have tried to form unions have been terrorized. A
new unfortunate twist to this story is that workers are being forced to
pay a "tax" of 20 quetzales (US$2.50) every two weeks to local extor-
tionists or face being beaten or even killed.[4] The rise of extortionists in
recent years has enhanced the insecurity that the Guatemalan working
class and peasantry face.

The poor economic and social situation, combined with strong ties
to the United States, continues to push many Guatemalans to emigrate.
Given the difficulties involved in acquiring permission to enter the
United States, around half of the estimated one million Guatemalans
in the United States lack the legal paperwork to remain in the country
on a permanent basis (Menjívar 2007). Although Guatemalans ranked
15th in terms of the legal permanent resident population in 2007, they
ranked third in the number of undocumented migrants in 2008, behind
El Salvador and Mexico (Hoefer, Rytina, and Baker 2009; Rytina 2009).

Guatemalans in the United States are less likely to have legal status than immigrants from other nationalities such as Dominicans because of the nature of U.S. immigration policy. Dominicans and Jamaicans benefited from the fact that many of their countrymen came in the 1960s when the United States had more visas available relative to the number of applicants. Dominicans and Jamaicans often can qualify for family-based visas because of this. In contrast, few Guatemalans came to the United States in the 1960s or even the 1970s. By the time Guatemalans were pushed out of their country, there were few to no visas available. And the U.S. government often does not recognize the horrendous violence in Guatemala as sufficient grounds for granting asylum to Guatemalans. Thus, many Guatemalans remain undocumented.

Many of the deportees I met were taken to the United States as children by their parents and have no or very few memories of their childhood in Guatemala. Larry, for example, left in 1988 when he was six. His parents left him for a brief time in Guatemala with his grandmother, but he doesn't remember much about that period. He just knows that his parents felt that emigration was their best choice, even if it meant they would be temporarily separated from him and live as undocumented immigrants in the United States.

Another group of deportees was left behind in Guatemala by their parents who never came to retrieve them. Overton is one example. He was born in 1979 in the outskirts of Guatemala City. When his father abandoned his mother and her six children, his mother left her children with Overton's grandmother and traveled to the United States, where she hoped to earn enough money to send for her children. With six children, Overton's mother had been trying to make ends meet by selling food on a street corner. This strategy left her with barely enough for herself and her family to eat. Many Central American and Mexican single mothers see emigration to the United States as their best option for providing for their children (Schmalzbauer 2008; Dreby 2010). Without a safety net, uneducated women in Guatemala rarely can earn enough to support their families.

When Overton's mother first left, they did not hear from her for more than a year. During that time, his grandmother earned enough to feed Overton and his five siblings by washing clothes and selling cooked meals. When his mother began to send remittances, things got a bit easier, although there was never enough money. When Overton was 15, he began to work. His first job was as a mechanic's assistant, which did not pay very much. He finally got a decent job working for a water company when he was 18. Overton was fortunate to find a job in a company that paid a living wage and provided benefits. However, his employer, like many other similar companies, folded when a foreign company came in and undercut the business. The neoliberal economic policies passed in Guatemala opened up the economy to foreign investors. The arrival of these investors who often had much more capital was often detrimental to smaller Guatemalan companies. When local companies closed, many Guatemalans, like Overton, lost their jobs. When Overton was laid off, the company gave him severance pay. He used that money to pay a coyote (a human smuggler) to take him to the United States, where he hoped to have more economic opportunities and to reunite with his mother. Overton waited until he was a young adult to venture out to look for his mother. Many Central American children, like 16-year-old Enrique in the book Enrique's Journey (Nazario 2007), leave at a much younger age and face grave risks in their quest to find their mothers.

Mateo also left Guatemala at a young age, yet he remembered his childhood in Guatemala vividly. He was born in 1975 in Zone 3 of Guatemala City. This central city neighborhood was dangerous when he was growing up and drugs were commonplace. Mateo recalled that one day he found a large bag of marijuana outside. He didn't know what it was and took it home to show to his parents. His parents were scared and asked him where he found it, but they didn't want to tell him what it was. His father immediately took it from him. When his father came home, he had bags of food. Mateo imagines he must have sold the marijuana, because they never had much food. Mateo recalls growing up in poverty and living in fear of his father's heavy hand. When Mateo was eight, his father told him he had to leave school and work. Mateo got a job in construction. He recalled the day he got his first paycheck. The guys he worked with asked him to go out drinking with them, as it was payday. Once they started drinking, they invited Mateo to join them. Mateo got drunk and woke up the next morning with his first hangover.

The next day I got up and my worst mistake was that I asked my mom to make me a soup, the one that she used to make my dad, you know, when he was hungover. [Laughs] My dad was like, "Come here . . . I smelled you yesterday. I didn't say nothing. And now you come and ask your mom for soup? My soup!" You know what? He took everybody out. I had little brothers. He took everybody out. He talked to me. He was like, "You know what? You drink one more time in this house and I'm not only just going to beat you, I'm going to get you out there naked and I'm going to beat you out there." I was like, "All right, no problem." I never did it again.

When Mateo was 10, he left his job in construction and began to work in a paper factory. While working there, he met people who were planning to travel to the United States. He began to save his earnings so that he could pay a coyote to take him as well. He was anxious to escape his bad family situation in Guatemala, and he figured he could make a better living elsewhere. Like many Guatemalan migrants, Mateo had family in the United States—he hoped to make it to his aunt's house near Washington, D.C. At the young age of 10, Mateo set out with a group of Guatemalans for the United States. He left a note with his parents and didn't call them until several years later to let them know he was alive and in the United States.

Although most of the deportees I met experienced deprivation in Guatemala, a few of the Guatemalans I met grew up in relative privilege. Mariluna and Rafael, for example, are a married couple from elite families in Guatemala City. Their story bears some resemblance to that of middle-class Dominicans who were forced to flee the Dominican Republic during turbulent times. Mariluna was born in 1946 into a wealthy family that lived in the center of Guatemala City, when rich people still lived in the city center. Mariluna enjoyed remembering the good old days:

It was very clean. Before, people were very elegant. When I was small, I went out in the afternoons with a hat and gloves to visit friends and take tea with them. I am the niece of the Vice President of Guatemala. . . . My mother is from an upper-class family and I was raised well. In those days, rich people lived in the historic center. That is why the houses are very large. . . . Doctors and other honorable families used to live here in the center. But things have changed.

Mariluna went to a private French school, another indicator of her class status. Her mother was a pediatrician and her father a psychiatrist. Mariluna met Rafael at the university, where she studied medicine. She left her studies after marrying Rafael and becoming pregnant with their first child. Rafael is four years younger than Mariluna; he was born in 1950, in another central city neighborhood. Rafael spent much of his childhood in Antigua, a historic city about an hour away from the capital. For high school, Rafael studied in the English American School. After finishing high school, he went to the University of San Carlos, where he met Mariluna. After graduation, Rafael traveled back and forth to the United States for business. Rafael never intended to stay permanently in the United States.

In 1989, however, everything changed. Rafael had to flee Guatemala because he was a witness to a political assassination while visiting the house of one of his left-leaning university professors, who was a candidate in the upcoming elections. When Rafael and the professor were walking back toward the professor's house after dropping the professor's sons at the bus stop, armed gunmen came out of a parked vehicle and began to shoot. The men ran in separate directions. Rafael managed to escape, but not without seeing the men who shot and killed the professor. The assassins found out who Rafael was and began to look for him. It was under these circumstances that Rafael fled the country. His wife and two daughters accompanied him shortly afterward and they made their home in the United States until they were deported, many years later.

Although Rafael seems to have had a good case for political asylum, he never was able to attain it. In 1984, only 3 percent of Guatemalan petitioners were granted asylum, as President Reagan's official policy was that they were economic migrants, not refugees. This remarkably low approval rate for asylum cases raised the ire of religious and other communities in the United States because of the tremendous violence in Central America, as well as the involvement of the United States in this conflict. In 1991, there was a settlement with American Baptist Church in a court case that eventually led to a Temporary Protected Status (TPS) for some Guatemalans. Rafael should have been included in this settlement. However, it appears that his lawyer was not sufficiently savvy and Rafael was not included.

The deportees I met in Guatemala who left when they were old enough to remember attributed their leaving to either economic or political troubles in their home country. Many did not intend to remain permanently in the United States, but the fact that conditions have not improved greatly in Guatemala, combined with the passing of many years, created a situation where many Guatemalans had no concrete plans to return home. This, in turn, made their eventual deportation more difficult.

Growing Up in Brazil

With a gross domestic product (GDP) of over 2.2 trillion in 2013, Brazil had the seventh largest economy in the world, the largest in Latin America. With strong ties to the United States, Brazil is a major trading partner. Brazil was a net migrant-receiving country until the early 20th century, when it began to experience economic decline. By the late 20th century, Brazil began to become a country of emigration, and many Brazilians left for the United States. One reason Brazilians travel to the United States is because of the ties created between the two countries through mining partnerships: U.S. companies began mining mica (a mineral used in the production of electronic devices) in the Brazilian state of Minas Gerais in the mid-20th century. At the same time, U.S. corporations were involved in building the railroad in Minas Gerais (Golash-Boza 2012). These ties later translated into substantial numbers of economic migrants.

The flow of emigrants from Brazil to the United States began in the 1960s and accelerated in the 1980s, when Brazil experienced political and economic changes. On January 15, 1985, Brazil had its first democratic elections in 21 years, and the country began its full-scale integration into the global economy. Between 1987 and 1995, trade as a percentage of gross domestic product (GDP) rose from 17 to 27 percent. Foreign direct investment in Brazil increased from $1 billion in 1991 to $30 billion in 1999. This was due to trade liberalization, currency stabilization, and regional market integration—all neoliberal reforms. Due to these and other reforms, privatization initiatives generated approximately $60 billion for federal and state governments between 1995 and 1998 (Wolford 2005). By 2000, the total income from privatization had reached $83 billion (Amann and Baer 2002). The 1990s were a "neoliberal decade" (Wolford 2005: 246) for Brazil, and, by the 21st century, the Brazilian economy had become much more integrated into the global economy.

The massive privatizations in Brazil led to a drop in industry and manufacturing jobs as new corporations took over and installed more advanced technology to replace workers. Many of the workers who had previously been employed in stable public utility jobs found less secure and less well-compensated jobs in the service and in informal industrial sectors. Privatization also led to increases in prices of public utilities: In Rio de Janeiro, for example, the price of public services tripled between 1994 and 2000 (Amann and Baer 2002).

Economists consider the 1980s in Brazil a lost decade because of high inflation and low economic growth. The neoliberal policies of the 1990s were meant to increase growth, but, like neoliberal reforms everywhere, they created structural changes in the economy that increased inequality and led to more emigration. In the 1980s and 1990s, it was relatively easy for Brazilians to get tourist visas to the United States, and many did. In 1981, Brazilians were tenth among recipients of nonimmigrant (tourist or student) visas, and, by 1991, they climbed to fourth (Goza 1994). In the 1980s, many Brazilians would travel to the United States on tourist visas, work for a year or two, then return (Margolis 1993). This became more difficult as the United States changed its policies on tourist visas, and those Brazilians who wished to immigrate to the United States often had to do so illegally by crossing the southern border from Mexico. By the 1990s, nearly two million Brazilians were living abroad, about 800,000 of whom were living in the United States.

Brazilians who migrate to the United States usually do not leave Brazil out of a need to survive; instead, they see migration as a way to accumulate enough capital to invest in a small business and attain a better standard of living in Brazil. Unlike Guatemalans, many Brazilians are able to go back to their countries of origin, and many do, once they have saved up enough investment funds. Not all have had financial success, however, and some have found it difficult to return to their homes in

Brazil after they and their families became accustomed to living in the United States (Siqueira 2007a, 2007b).

Zelda and Octavio, for example, were able to get tourist visas because of their stable jobs as schoolteachers. I met this married couple at their house in a small city in Goiás. Zelda and Octavio's house is very nicely decorated. We sat at their large cherry-colored wood dining table in their kitchen, which was fully equipped with new, modern appliances. From where we were sitting, I could catch a glimpse of the fine furniture in their living room as well as a large flat-screen television. They also had a new car parked in the garage. Zelda and Octavio come from very humble origins and have come quite far in life through years of hard work—both in Brazil and in the United States.

The majority of Brazilian immigrants in the United States come from Minas Gerais. The neighboring state of Goiás has emerged as a major sending area, in part because of its proximity to Minas Gerais and in part because many Goianos are themselves internal migrants from Minas Gerais. Zelda was born in Minas Gerais yet came with her family to Goiás in the late 1960s when she was a small child. Her father came to Goiás as a sharecropper. He rented land from a landowner and gave the landowner a portion of his harvest as payment. Zelda described her childhood as arduous. Octavio's story is similar, except his parents came to Goiás from Minas Gerais before he was born. Octavio, as the only male child, had to help his father on their land from a very young age. When Octavio finished primary school, he went to the city to study secondary school. Before finishing his studies, Octavio returned to his hometown and to Zelda.

Once reunited, Octavio and Zelda decided they would drop out of school and get married. Zelda was 17 and Octavio was 19. Getting married young was common in their town, so their parents didn't think anything was wrong with their decision. Soon, however, they found themselves with three small children, and Octavio's salary as a farmworker was barely enough to get by. Eventually, they were able to save up enough money to move to the city. With primary school finished, Octavio was able to get a job as a schoolteacher. Two years later, Zelda began to teach at the same school. At that time, in the early 1980s, you could teach primary school with only a primary education yourself. However, as teachers, they were encouraged to finish their schooling.

Octavio and Zelda both finished high school through an accelerated program. Once their children were old enough, Zelda decided she
wanted to study at the university. She earned her degree in four years,
studying and working the whole time. Then it was Octavio's turn, and
he went through the same process. Octavio and Zelda, children of poor
farmworkers, were able to establish a decent life for themselves and their
children. They instilled the values of hard work and wanting more out
of life into their children. Their children, however, decided to pursue
this dream in the United States.

In 2001, when Zelda graduated from the university, she and her
19-year-old son went to the U.S. embassy in Brasilia to request tourist
visas. They were granted the visas. Zelda, however, did not travel. Her
son did, and he made his way to Massachusetts to a town where others
from their town in Goiás had settled. Their son began to work in construction and sent word home that life was good in Massachusetts and
that there was money to be made. In 2003, their eldest son tried to get
a visa. He was unsuccessful and decided to travel with a coyote through
Mexico. He made it across the border and made his way to Massachusetts. In 2005, Octavio and their youngest son were able to obtain tourist
visas to go to the United States. Octavio did not travel, but their son did.

Octavio and Zelda used their professional positions to help their children attain visas to travel to the United States. In 2007, they decided to
join them. Their motives were twofold: They wanted to see their sons,
who had settled in the United States, and they hoped to earn money to
finish their house and buy a car. Their salaries as teachers were enough
to survive, but they wanted more economic stability and middle-class
comforts in life. They asked for an extended leave of absence from work
and went to the United States. With their tourist visas, they were able
to board a plane and go straight to Massachusetts. They planned to stay
there for a couple of years, save money, and return home—with enough
capital to finish their home and perhaps start a business. They achieved
some of their goals, but their deportation was also a setback.

For Brazilians, traveling to the United States on a tourist visa is an
option only available to people who have enough resources to obtain
the visa and pay the airfare. Because of the high cost of traveling to the
United States legally and the exorbitant cost of traveling illegally, Brazilians who migrate are not usually the poorest of the poor. Instead, they

are often people like Octavio and Zelda who are getting by yet want more financial stability, or people who had been doing well yet fall prey to hard economic times.

William, for example, was doing well in Brazil until a recession in Brazil affected his business and he saw migration as a viable economic alternative. William was born in 1960 in a small town in Goiás called Jaraguá, which has become famous for its clothing manufacturing. When he was growing up, Jaraguá was still a small town. William's parents owned a small farm, and they earned enough so that William could finish high school. After graduation, he began to work in clothing manufacturing. He accumulated enough money to buy his own machines and set up a small business making clothes, with some help from his parents. In the 1980s, Jaraguá was rising as a small-scale clothing manufacturer, with many companies producing counterfeit designer jeans for a good profit. William explained that he began to have financial issues with his business in the late 1990s, although he did not make it clear whether or not that was related to the crackdown on counterfeit manufacturers during that time. In 2002, William decided to join the exodus for the United States, as many other people from Jaraguá had set out for Danbury, Connecticut. He saw a friend of his go to the United States for four years and come back with enough money to buy six houses. His plan was to do the same. In Brazil, William may have been able to get back on his feet. Traveling to the United States seemed to be a way to accumulate wealth faster.

Tom's story is similar to William's. Tom was born in 1980 in Inhumas, Goiás—a small town in the center of Brazil. When he was four, his family moved to the countryside. When he was six, they moved back to the small town of Matrinchã so he could go to school. His parents separated when he was a child, and his single mother did not earn enough to support him. For this reason, Tom went to school in the mornings and worked on a farm in the afternoons. He was able to finish high school but did not have the money to go on to the university. Tom was able to get a job in the mayor's office. He supplemented his income by buying and selling perfumes. Tom heard of people going to the United States and earning money and resolved to go as well so that he could have a more comfortable life. He grew up watching his single mother work hard, yet never having much to show for it. As he got older, he saw many people leave his small town to work in the United States. They returned with their houses completed, new consumer goods, and money to start a business. Like many Brazilians, Tom intended to return to Brazil after working and saving money for a few years. In 2005, he set out for the United States and managed to cross the border from Mexico. At that time, Brazilians could obtain a visa to travel to Mexico and then travel illegally from there to the United States. Many Brazilians I met took this path. Tom, like many others, went to the United States to work as many hours as he could and return to Brazil with enough capital to start a business.

Many of the Brazilians I interviewed told me a similar story: They grew up in poverty, worked hard to get ahead, yet encountered difficulties along the road to financial stability. Some of them lost their jobs due to privatization; others lost their farms or small businesses due to trade agreements; all of them saw the United States as the solution to paying off their debts and accumulating savings and consumer items. Antonio, for example, was born in 1980 in the capital of Goiás. His father decided to bring his family back to farm life when Antonio was 11. After finishing high school, Antonio got into the dairy business with his father. They did quite well, and Antonio had a new car and was leasing a large piece of land. In 2007, however, the federal government of Brazil decided to import large amounts of powdered milk from Argentina so that poor people could have cheaper milk. This was devastating to small farmers like Antonio. The price of milk plummeted from 75 cents a liter to 25 cents and it was no longer worth it for Antonio to sell milk.

After the dairy farm was no longer a viable business, Antonio decided to try his luck in the United States. He had always dreamed of living there, primarily because of films he had seen and stories people had told him. In 2007 Antonio sold his cattle and paid a coyote about $6,000 to guide him to the United States. Antonio, like most Brazilians I interviewed, did not intend to stay in the United States. Most told me they were Brazilians to the core and wouldn't dream of permanently relocating abroad. But they wanted to live in Brazil debt-free, with the comforts of modern life, and to be able to provide an education for their children. Thus, they chose to take the risk and immigrate to the United States—legally or illegally, depending on the available options.

Marly is an exception—unlike most Brazilian deportees I met, she not only grew up poor but she was also able to emigrate even though she was also poor as an adult. Marly was born in 1963 in Pirenópolis, a small town with a small economy based in part on tourism. Her father died when she was young and she began to work as a maid when she was eight. Because of this, she hardly went to school and only finished the second grade. Marly knows how to read—just barely—and can only do math with a calculator. Marly was sitting in the door of her small store in Jaraguá when we first met. She invited me to sit with her on the stoop and asked me about the purpose of my study. I explained it to her, and she told me she had been deported in 2007. She wanted to know what I thought about her chances of returning to the United States.

I demurred, having little expertise on the subject, but this opening led to an interesting interview. Marly is a fair-skinned woman with brown hair who looks younger than her 47 years, despite the fact that she has had a hard life. She married when she was 14 years old to a man who was 19. Ten years later, he died—at the age of 29—of heart problems. At the time, he and Marly were living on a farm. Widowed at 24, Marly had four children and few options for gainful employment due to her low level of education. Marly moved in with her mother and struggled to make ends meet.

Marly told me of how she'd come to try her luck in the United States. It began in 1998, when Marly was 35 years old. An ex-boyfriend asked her to go with him to a travel agent in Anápolis to find out about his chances of visiting the United States. The travel agent told Marly's ex-boyfriend that his best option was to get married and apply for a visa to go on his honeymoon in the United States. Marly agreed to marry him so that he could get his visa. Because it was a honeymoon, he also had to get her a passport and visa—which he did.

Although Marly had a passport and visa, she did not have the money to travel. Her chance didn't come for a year. A friend of Marly's paid for her ticket because she wanted companionship for her own trip. Marly did not even have clothes to put in a suitcase. But a neighbor gave her a suitcase full of clothes and Marly and her friend got on a plane to the United States. That was in 1999, when Marly was 36 years old. Her oldest son was 22, and her youngest was 18. Marly went straight to

Danbury, Connecticut, a common destination for people from Jaraguá. She immediately found work in housekeeping.

Marly's story shows how difficult it can be for poor Brazilians to get to the United States, yet also how crucial connections can be. It took her several instances of good luck to make it all the way from Jaraguá to Danbury, and more than a few people were willing to help along the way.

These Brazilians chose to try their luck in the United States because they saw it as an opportunity to work and accumulate capital. The long-standing linkages between Brazil and the United States made emigration a viable option. These linkages, however, are highly localized. In some towns in Goiás, such as Jaraguá, Matrinchã, Itapuranga, and Itaberaí, most people know someone who has traveled abroad. In contrast, this is not the case in nearby Ciudade Goiás—where few people move away.

Sometimes all it takes is one or two people from a town to set off a trend. In the early 1990s, two Jaraguenses traveled to Danbury. There, they found a community of Brazilians—mostly from Minas Gerais. These two pioneers established themselves. One became the regional manager of Dunkin Donuts. Other Jaraguenses soon followed. Many found work in Dunkin Donuts, where the manager from Jaraguá gave preference to people from his hometown. Others worked in landscaping or laying foundation. Most of the women worked in housecleaning.

These early migrants returned to Jaraguá with their houses finished and with new cars, and they bought farms and livestock around Jaraguá. With the Brazilian Real at R$4 for US$1, their savings went far in Jaraguá. They were able to save thousands of dollars by working 60, 70, 80 hours a week—or more. People in Jaraguá watched those migrants return and began to build their own dreams and their own plans. Instead of working for 10 or 20 years to save up for a house in Jaraguá, they could go to the United States and have the money in two to four years.

This is how migration happens. The local conditions do not provide ambitious young people with opportunities to thrive. They seek out opportunities abroad. Others follow. This combination of structural and individual factors has created a culture of emigration in several towns in the state of Goiás, Brazil.

Wanting More from Life

A peek into the lives of immigrants before they left their country of origin reveals that many migrants travel to the United States to seek a better life. They hear tales of the American Dream and set out to see if they, too, can make that dream a reality. They know that U.S. streets are not actually paved with gold, but they believe it is a place where, if you work hard, you can save money and build a better future for yourself. It is this dream of a better life that leads parents to leave children behind and husbands to leave their wives. If and when the family reunites, children are taken from their caregivers and brought to a new life in the United States.

Everyone I interviewed came to the United States with the resolve of doing better. Most of the migrants had worked exceedingly hard for most of their lives, even from young ages. Many were unable to complete their schooling because they had to work as children to help support their families. When they found an opportunity to travel to the United States, they seized it.

The Dominicans and Jamaicans primarily intended to settle permanently, taking their families with them. The Brazilians usually had specific goals to meet: to earn a certain amount of money and return. The Guatemalans emigrated with various intentions, but many Guatemalans who had intended to return end up building lives in the United States that make leaving difficult. As we will see later, deportation was most devastating for those migrants who had settled permanently in the United States. For many Brazilians, although deportation was humiliating, the most serious consequence was a personal financial crisis. In contrast, for those Dominicans, Jamaicans, and Guatemalans who knew no country other than the United States, deportation, for them, amounted to banishment and felt like an extraordinarily cruel punishment.

Many of the stories also show how temporary migration becomes permanent when the crisis fails to end. In the story of Overton from Guatemala, for example, we can see how neoliberal reforms pushed his mother to emigrate, and then, Overton, decades later. Neoliberal reforms in Guatemala meant that there were no social services to help Overton's mother when the father of her children abandoned her. For her, the best option seemed to be to travel to the United States so she could send money back to her children. When Overton was old enough to work, he did. However, when the water company he worked for was sold off to a transnational corporation, migration seemed like a good option for Overton as well. The possibility of emigration for Overton and his mother ensured their survival.

One can also see how emigration may have helped to quell social unrest in Guatemala and the other countries profiled here, as emigration provided an escape valve for ambitious people. If these people had no other options, perhaps they would have stayed at home and fought against the neoliberal reforms that were wreaking havoc on their home countries. In Brazil, the economic situation is not as dire. Nevertheless, we can see how emigration allowed the people of some of these small towns to purchase houses and start businesses, thereby injecting new flows of capital into their communities. Had emigration not been a possibility, these towns may have confronted different economic possibilities. And the townspeople may have been more discontented with their economic options. In each of the countries profiled here, emigration provided relief from economic turmoil and likely served as an escape valve for dissent, allowing the countries discussed here to make their economic transitions.

Listening to the stories of migrants, we learn how and why they emigrated. Their tales are often stories of personal resolve. The migrants themselves are unlikely to point out either the globalizing forces that pushed them from their homes or even that U.S. military involvement in their home countries was one of the causes of political turmoil. However, they do point to individual cases of political violence and economic insecurity. Their stories render these connections easy to discern, once we look at their accounts alongside the political and economic conditions. Across these four countries, we hear stories of farmers forced to leave the countryside because it is no longer profitable to farm, of unemployment and poverty in urban areas, of political violence, and of instability and crime.

We also see that emigration is not just about leaving—it is also about going to a particular place, a place where emigrants have family members and they know jobs await them. Even the adventurous Dominicans who stow away on cargo ships have a particular destination in mind: the ports that send these huge ships to their city. They don't take cargo ships to Spain because there are none. Instead, the cargo ships take them straight to Puerto Rico, Miami, and New Orleans. With these cargo ships, we are witnessing a direct manifestation of the relationship between international trade and international migration—between global capitalism and global migration. In the next chapter, we will look at what was entailed in the journeys for these opportunities and the great challenges some migrants endure to make it to the United States.

Chapter 1 Timeline

- *1950s–60s*—Jamaica expands development into global industry
- *1952*—Bauxite industry established in Jamaica
- *1954*—CIA stages a coup in Guatemala to overthrow the democratically elected government of Jacobo Arbenz Guzman
- *1961*—Dominican Republic's Trujillo is assassinated, thereby ending his policies that restricted immigration
- *1961–1968*—Massive wave of immigration from the Dominican Republic (DR) to the United States (due to political turmoil and the convenient passing of the Immigration and Nationality Act)
- *1962*—Hakim's mother leaves Jamaica for New York
- *April 28, 1965*—American boots hit the ground in the DR to prevent leftist Juan Bosch from becoming president
- *1965*—The Immigration and Nationality Act passes (ending discriminatory racial quotas and establishing the universal 20,000 migrant quota for all countries, and family- and skill-based preferences)
- *1965*—Mike (from the DR) leaves his country because of political conflict after Trujillo's assassination
- *1969*—Hakim and his mother leave for Cleveland, Ohio
- *1970s*—Oil prices soar, leaving Jamaica financially strapped
- *1974–1980*—Unemployment increases from 24 percent to 31 percent in Jamaica
- *1976*—Jamaica becomes the lead exporter of bauxite
- *1977*—Prime Minister Manley turns to the IMF to service Jamaica's debt at the expense of structural adjustment commitments
- *1978*—The Dominican Revolutionary Party comes to power and begins to raise wages, control prices, and invest in social welfare
- *1979*—Elias travels to the United States from Jamaica

- *1980s—*
  - The DR begins to economically degrade in the wake of structural adjustment policies
  - The Guatemalan government also attempts to restructure its economy to integrate with the international community by implementing neo-liberal reforms
  - Jamaica borrows more money; tourism and exports begin generating serious foreign currency and economic development (a small period of growth)
- *1982*—President Jorge Blanco of the DR begins negotiating with the IMF, just as Manley did in Jamaica
- *1985*—Brazil has its first democratic elections in 21 years and begins its full-scale integration into the global economy
- *1986*—Balaguer wins the DR presidency, employing a platform that views IMF agreements critically
- *Late 1980s*—Jamaica invests too much money in the production of selected exports; begins to kill its own domestic market
- *1988*—Larry leaves Guatemala with his family in search of opportunity
- *1989*—Mariluna and Rafael flee Guatemala after witnessing a political assassination
- *1990s*—Further structural adjustment ramps up political violence in Jamaica
- *1991*—Homero leaves in a fishing boat in search of economic opportunity
- *1994*—Philip runs in an international track meet in Orlando, Florida, and decides to stay in America
- *1996*— Peace accords are signed in Guatemala, which finally ends their civil war
- *1997*—10 percent of the Dominican population lives in the United States
- *1999*—Domingo boards a yola and heads for the United States amid economic hardship
- *2005*—Tom sets out for the United States through Mexico from Brazil
- *2007*—Octavio and Zelda join their family in the United States by traveling on a tourist visa from Brazil
- *2007*—Price of milk plummets in Brazil due to importation of powdered milk from Argentina
- *2007*—Antonio tries to enter the United States from Brazil by traveling illegally through Mexico

2

Crossing Over

Risking Life and Facing Increased Border Security

In August 2010, Mexican authorities discovered the bodies of 58 men and 14 women stacked in a small room on a ranch near the Mexican border city ominously named Matamoros, which means "killing Moors." The bodies belonged to migrants from Brazil, Ecuador, Guatemala, and other countries. As of 2014, there are still no criminal convictions for this case. However, many people believe that the Zetas, a paramilitary criminal organization in Mexico, are responsible and that these migrants had either refused to become hit men or drug couriers or were unable to pay enormous ransom fees to the Zetas.[1] In the first six months of 2011, human rights organizations estimated there were 10,000 kidnappings of migrants attempting to cross Mexico.[2] Getting across Mexico was the most dangerous part of the journey for many of the Brazilian and Guatemalan deportees I interviewed. Stories of kidnappings abound and Guatemalan deportees often told me their greatest fear with regard to returning to the United States was being kidnapped in Mexico.

The people I met who traveled illegally to the United States did so either because they had no option to do so legally or because their legal options entailed waiting several years for their paperwork to process. Deciding to migrate to a new country is a momentous decision, even for those who are able to do so legally. Deciding to do so illegally requires no small amount of courage, even recklessness. Dominican migrants often travel to the United States on rickety fishing boats known as yolas. Other Dominicans stow away on cargo ships. Brazilians and Guatemalans must trek through Mexico and then across the dangerous terrain of the U.S.-Mexico border. On average, at least one person dies every day attempting to cross this border. Between 1994 and 2009, between 3,861 and 5,607 people have died attempting to cross the southern border, leading the American Civil Liberties Union to call this a "humanitarian crisis."[3] An unknown number of people die at sea or are drowned or eaten by sharks as they attempt to cross from the Dominican Republic to Puerto Rico or from Cuba to Miami by sea. Their border-crossing journeys involve much more than jumping a fence separating the United States and Mexico—for these migrants, the border extends through all of Mexico or across the expanse of the Caribbean Sea.

People who decide to migrate without permission are actively resisting a system of borders and migration control that traps poor people born in poor countries into a lifetime of deprivation. Within the system of global apartheid, citizens of wealthy countries and highly skilled professionals often have the option of emigrating if they so choose. This, however, is not the case for the vast majority of people in the world, due to visa restrictions, which provide citizens of wealthier and more democratic countries with more freedom of movement across international borders. For example, citizens of Belgium, Germany, Sweden, and the United States enjoy the right to travel to 155 countries without a visa; Sudanese, in contrast, can only enter 26 countries without a visa, Pakistanis can go to 25 destinations, and Afghans, 22 (Mau 2010). Individuals are positioned differentially with regard to their options for international migration, according to their countries of birth. The people discussed in this chapter chose to seek out the best options for themselves and their families by leaving their countries of birth.

In a vastly unequal world, it is not surprising that people born into poorer countries would want to move to richer ones. Of course, the wealthier countries feel obliged to protect their borders and prevent the poor people of the world from voting with their feet and moving into wealthier areas. To prevent this mass exodus, affluent countries have enhanced visa restrictions and fortified their borders. However, these efforts have not kept determined migrants out. Instead, as these stories show, enhanced border security makes the journey more difficult and renders international migrants even more vulnerable.

I asked each deportee I met to describe the experience of trying to make it to the United States. Some of their stories were harrowing adventures across sea and land. They are also a testament to the risks some migrants are willing to endure in order to make it to the United States. As noted in table 2.1, there was quite a bit of variation in the

TABLE 2.1. Method of Entry into the United States—First Attempt (n = 147)

	Airplane	U.S.-Mexico border	Cargo ship	Passenger boat	
Jamaicans	100%	—	—	—	n = 37
Brazilians	57%	40%	—	3%	n = 30
Guatemalans	38%	62%	—	—	n = 34
Dominicans	46%	7%	11%	37%	n = 46

method of entry but there are clear patterns by nationality. Whereas all of the Jamaicans entered via airplane on temporary or permanent visas, the Guatemalans were the most likely to cross the U.S.-Mexico border illegally. The Dominicans were the most likely to enter the United States via the Caribbean Sea, although I met one Brazilian who also had come on a passenger boat. The various methods of entry mean that people from these nationalities tend to have distinct border-crossing experiences. These experiences are determined by geography, opportunity, and the history of U.S. immigration laws as they pertain to entry, residency, and citizenship.

Jamaicans: From Kingston to JFK

All of the Jamaicans I interviewed traveled to the United States on airplanes, making their border-crossing experiences relatively uneventful. Usually, they were able to travel by plane because they qualified for legal permanent residency visas. Others went on tourist visas, and a few used fabricated passports and visas to enter. Some of the Jamaicans went via roundabout ways to the United States via other islands, but they always went by airplane. Jamaica sits in the Caribbean Sea just south of Cuba and west of Haiti. It would be difficult for a Jamaican to enter the United States by sea, but not impossible, as he could travel either to Cuba or to Haiti, cross by land, and then take a fishing boat. Jamaicans could also stow away on cargo ships—and they do occasionally.[4] However, none of the Jamaican deportees I interviewed seemed willing to risk their lives by venturing out to sea on rickety boats. Nevertheless, the experience of crossing over to a new land was significant in and of itself.

Alberto traveled to the United States as a child, and became a legal permanent resident (LPR), but he recalled the day he migrated quite vividly. Alberto grew up in a middle-class family in Uptown, Kingston. He earned a full merit-based scholarship to attend Kingston College, the same prestigious high school attended by Hakim. He had to give up his full scholarship, however, when he was 15, as his parents decided to migrate to the United States in 1969. His mother went first, as a legal permanent resident, and he, his father, and his brother followed soon afterward.

Like most Jamaicans I spoke with, Alberto went to New York City. Alberto's plane descended at night in October 1969. Alberto told me:

> I didn't really have any great expectations. I was just excited to see what America was about. I didn't expect anything. It was something else; I was going someplace new, and I was just open to seeing what it was all about. I didn't expect to become a movie star overnight or anything like that, you know, I was just . . . I couldn't wait. All I remember is that the night we got there, there was so much light. It looked very nice landing. And when I got to Brooklyn I couldn't wait to see what the place looked like in the morning 'cause I couldn't really see what it was at night. I remember I got up in the morning and I looked outside. When I got up in the morning and looked out across the street, the streets were so dirty and a bunch of guys—they were winos—they were drinking. As my mother took me out it was broad daylight; I saw the men drinking. They weren't bad people, they were just beer drinkers, you know.

Alberto's neighborhood in Kingston had looked a lot better. Like many Jamaicans who arrived in New York City in the 1960s and 1970s, Alberto was surprised to learn that the land of milk and honey had such filthy streets.

Alberto's migration was emotional and momentous, but it wasn't dangerous. Traveling on an airplane with a visa in hand eliminated the potential violence of the border crossing. Some Jamaican migrants I spoke with experienced peril, not from terrain or elements, but because they were smuggling drugs to the United States. Naimah, for example, grew up in a poor neighborhood in South St. Andrew called Rema with her great-grandparents. Her grandmother lived nearby and her mother lived with them on and off. She never knew her father.

Naimah's great-grandmother sold fish and her great-grandfather swept the streets. Naimah dropped out of school when she was 16 and pregnant. She had three more years before she would have finished high school. The first time Naimah went to the United States was in 2002, when she was in her late 20s. She had a friend who had been there several times as a drug smuggler. Naimah's friend knew that Naimah was struggling to get by as a single mother and suggested she try carrying drugs to the United States. She told Naimah she would earn US$2,000. Naimah took the offer but never earned the money: She was apprehended at the border and spent one year in prison after customs agents found a kilo of cocaine in her luggage.

Naimah explained what happened.

> When I got to the airport, I went through okay. When I went to JFK they were checking and checking and they did not say anything. They say I must go in a room and after I went in the room I was there for a while before somebody come and talk to me. The stuff was in the luggage at the time. I see the police come in and they say they have to lock me up. They showed me what they found. I did not put it in the luggage. They just met me at the airport and gave me a suitcase. They booked the flight. They had the ticket and everything. . . . I was just paid to carry the package. Because my friend just told me she just carried a package. She was back and forth, back and forth, and she said the money was all right because it has been helping her and she has four kids. Sometime when she is gone they would stay with me and I would watch them for her.

Naimah preferred not to know what was in the package she was asked to carry. She agreed to carry it so that she could earn much-needed cash. The stories of the four female Jamaican deportees I met were all fairly similar: Three were drug couriers and one was caught with drugs inside the United States. All of the Jamaican deportees I met who were drug couriers were women. These women chose to transport drugs for the same reason: They are single mothers and needed money to support their families. As Julia Sudbury (2002: 70) argues, "The failure of the legal economy to provide adequate means for women's survival is the key incentive for those who chose to enter the drug trade." The female Jamaican drug couriers I interviewed fit the profile of the typical Jamaican drug courier: poor single mothers from the inner city (Sudbury 2002). These women engaged in illegal activity not for their personal gain, but to provide for their families that which the state denied them: adequate schooling, health care, and food. Neoliberal reforms in Jamaica privilege the market over people's needs, pushing many people to turn to underground markets for survival.

I have not seen data on the percentage of Jamaicans who travel to the United States illegally, but it appears that the most common mode of entry for Jamaicans is with a visa. The Jamaican deportees I interviewed were all able to travel to the United States with visas.[5] Thus, their stories of crossing over to the United States did not involve journeys through rugged terrain. Dominican, Guatemalan, and Brazilian deportees were often not as fortunate.

Dominicans: Across Sea, Land, and Air

Some of the Dominicans were able to travel to the United States legally on tourist or immigrant visas. Their stories are similar to the Jamaicans who arrived on airplanes in New York City. Many others, however, traveled illegally. There are four ways they did this: (1) on yolas; (2) as stowaways on large cargo ships; (3) with fabricated passports; and (4) through Mexico. The majority went by sea on yolas or cargo ships. In contrast, only two entered the United States with fabricated passports.

Cristobal, for example, began to work in construction when he dropped out of school at age 16, and he remained in that profession until he made up his mind to try his fate in the United States, to see if he could better his life there. I asked him why he took the risk of going on a yola. He responded, "You have to go on a yola, because there is no way they will give you a visa. To get a visa, you have to own a bank and have a million documents to prove it. If you are poor, you will never get a visa." Cristobal's claims are hyperbolic but reflect the fact that it is difficult to acquire a visa: In 2013, 40 percent of Dominicans who paid the $100 fee and provided all of the requested documents were still denied a temporary entry visa at the U.S. embassy.[6] With no chance of getting an entry visa, in 1998, Cristobal boarded a yola headed to Puerto Rico. He spent one month in Puerto Rico before taking a plane to New York City.

Stowing away on cargo ships was also common. Carlos, for example, was born in 1949 in a rural area near the capital city. When he was 19, he moved to Santo Domingo and got a job on the docks. His job was to help load cargo ships destined for the United States. Carlos didn't know much about the United States yet had heard that there was money to be made there. In 1970, when Carlos was 21, he loaded himself onto the cargo ship to travel for 30 hours with other Dominicans to Puerto Rico. They managed to sneak off of the cargo ship and enter Puerto Rico. He stayed in Puerto Rico for one year, working in a restaurant and getting the money together to make the trip to New York. Finally, Carlos arrived at 107th Street, near Harlem, at the house of a friend who had worked with him on the docks in Santo Domingo.

Other Dominicans told me they traveled with fabricated or borrowed passports, but they preferred not to provide too many details about how they did that. Many of those who went with fake passports were reentering the United States after having already been deported. One Dominican explained that he arrived in Santo Domingo, turned around, and took the next plane out. That was in the 1980s, when the technologies of control at the border were much less developed than they are today. David Brotherton and Luis Barrios (2011), however, found that there continue to be ways for Dominicans to enter the United States with fabricated documents.

A few Dominicans went to the United States via Mexico. Darius, for example, took a plane to Guatemala in 1980, when he was 36 years old. He crossed Mexico by land and made it to New York City shortly thereafter, where he moved in with his sister in Washington Heights. Many Dominicans who originally went to the United States illegally were eventually able to legalize their status, either through the 1986 amnesty or through marriage to a U.S. citizen—options that are generally no longer available in U.S. immigration law. The vast majority of Dominicans who traveled to the United States illegally went by sea.

Although Juan Pablo—whom we met in the previous chapter—liked to play in the sea as a child, he was scared to take a fishing boat across the sea to Puerto Rico. Juan Pablo told me he never intended to get on a yola. He had planned to go to the United States as a stowaway on a cargo ship, which he thought would be much more secure. He actually tried getting on a cargo ship once and was unsuccessful. He told me, "Even though I wanted to go to the United States, and didn't have any way to go legally, I still didn't want to go on a yola. I was scared of yolas because I like water, but only to a certain point." Juan Pablo's fears were not unfounded: In 2004, the engine of a yola died en route between the Dominican Republic and Puerto Rico and half of the 80 passengers died of drowning, starvation, or dehydration before Dominican authorities rescued them after two weeks at sea (Nevins and Aizeki 2008).

One day, Juan Pablo's brother asked him if he would accompany him to Miches, a small seaside fishing village in the province of El Seibo, where his brother was going to take a yola to Puerto Rico. His brother assured him that he just wanted him to go with him to Miches and that he did not have to get on the yola. Juan Pablo and his brother were in Miches for two nights until the yola was ready to leave.

Juan Pablo explained that there is a river that goes out to the sea, and you have to push the yola out onto the river toward the sea. His brother asked him to help push. Through means I never entirely understood, pushing the boat turned into riding the boat. The yola left the coast at 5 am one morning and did not reach Puerto Rico until nearly 5 am the next morning. They spent almost 24 hours on the boat without food or water. The trip should only take 12 hours, but it takes longer when one has to outmaneuver the Coast Guard. Juan Pablo recounted that there were more than 120 people in the yola, which had a capacity of 80 people. He was standing up straight for 24 hours, but he couldn't see outside the yola except for once when he pulled himself up and saw sharks in the water bigger than the yola itself. He told me that they made it across the Mona Passage only by the grace of God.

When the yola arrived in Puerto Rico, Juan Pablo jumped off the boat into the darkness and swam to shore. Everyone on the boat had to run in different directions, as the Coast Guard knew the yola had arrived. Juan Pablo didn't know what happened to his brother, as everyone had to swim on their own to shore. Once on shore, they began to walk toward the street. Juan Pablo and a few other people were ushered into a car and they sped off. However, when it became clear that the Coast Guard was pursuing them, the driver stopped the car and told everyone to run and not to get caught. Juan Pablo had no idea where he was or where he was supposed to go. He did know that he did not want to be caught. Even though he hadn't planned to come, now that he'd been through so much, Juan Pablo wanted to be able to stay in Puerto Rico.

After getting out of the car Juan Pablo ended up with one other person—Renato, a kid from his neighborhood—who had also just got off the boat. Neither of them had any idea where they were or where they were going. They just kept walking. While walking, they spotted a car parking and saw four officers get out of the car. They ran, and the officers started running after them. Juan Pablo cut into an alley and hid underneath a house. It turned out there was a dog inside the house, and, because the floor of the house was made of wood, the dog noticed they were there and began to bark. Scared the barking would call attention to him, Juan Pablo left that house and began to run again.

Juan Pablo and Renato ran and ran, with no idea where they were headed. Eventually, they saw a hill that seemed it would provide some protection. There was an older man sitting by the hill. Desperate, Juan Pablo said to the man, "I am Dominican and I just got here on a yola and the police are after me. I need your help, please." The man, a Puerto Rican, said he didn't want to get into trouble but that they could hide in the hillside and should be safe. They went into the hills and found large plants with thorns but carefully made their way through the brush to a clearing, where they sat and waited for what seemed like hours.

When they left the brush the Puerto Rican man was gone. They saw two young guys walking down the street. They asked them what time it was and the boys told them it was 7:30 am. Juan Pablo could not believe only three hours had passed since they arrived in Puerto Rico, because it seemed as if they had been running for an eternity.

Juan Pablo and Renato knew they should seek a safe house—a house where someone would hide them from the police until things cooled down. They asked people on the streets and found out about a safe house within walking distance. The people in the house gave them food and let them clean up. They were also able to call Renato's family members in Puerto Rico. When Renato's brother came to pick them up, the people at the safe house told him he had to pay to get both Renato and Juan Pablo out. Renato's brother refused to pay for Juan Pablo.

The owner of the safe house told Renato's brother that he didn't have to pay for Juan Pablo; he just had to take him. Renato's brother refused at first, but Renato told his brother that Juan Pablo had helped him escape from the police, so he finally agreed to take Juan Pablo with him to San Juan. It would be several days before Juan Pablo found his brother, who had his own arduous adventure running from the police and the Coast Guard.

Juan Pablo and his brother, like many Dominican migrants (Brotherton and Barrios 2011), spent a few months in Puerto Rico working and saving up money until they had the funds to pay for airline tickets to New York. Although they were able to find work in Puerto Rico, they had heard there were more lucrative opportunities on the mainland. At that time—in the late 1990s—you did not need a U.S.-issued ID to get on a plane. With the security measures put into place in the aftermath of the terrorist attacks of September 11, 2001, it has gotten more difficult for undocumented Dominicans to travel from Puerto Rico to New York City.

Scholars have commented that the U.S.-Mexico border has become militarized (Dunn 1996). For this reason, it is important to point out that the U.S. Coast Guard is one of the five armed forces of the United States. Thus, Dominicans who attempt to enter the United States via the Caribbean Sea have to evade these military personnel.

Despite myriad dangers involved in this sea voyage, as well as increased border security, many Dominicans continue to make the dangerous trek from their island nation to Puerto Rico and then on to New York. Efforts by the Coast Guard to deter people who ride on yolas have made the journey more difficult, yet people who are determined to seek out a better life continue to risk their lives for their piece of the American Dream. The same is true for Guatemalans, whose primary peril is crossing the dangerous terrain of Mexico.

Guatemalans: When All of Mexico Is a Border

In August 2012, Juan David Gonzalez, a six-year-old Central American migrant, appeared in court by himself—with no lawyers and no parents to help him navigate the complex U.S. immigration court system. He was one of thousands of children who face deportation on their own each year in the United States. Many of these children are fleeing the violence in their home countries and hoping to reunite with their parents who live illegally in the United States. Parents pay thousands of dollars to coyotes to transport their children to the United States.[7] Juan is one of the children whom the Border Patrol caught, arrested, and detained. The United States greatly enhanced the Border Patrol presence in the 1980s, again in the 1990s, and even more drastically in the first decade of the 21st century. In 1983, for the first time since 1954, Border Patrol apprehensions surpassed one million in one year. Border apprehensions reached a peak of 1.7 million in 2000.[8]

Although the numbers of apprehensions have fluctuated in recent years and generally decreased, the number of Border Patrol agents has increased steadily. In 2000, when apprehensions reached their peak, there were a record high of 9,621 Border Patrol agents. Since then, the number of agents has increased to 21,391 in fiscal year (FY) 2013—despite the decline in apprehensions to less than half a million.[9] These enhancements to border security—what many refer to as a "militarization of the border" (Dunn 1996) or "low-intensity warfare" (Rosas 2012)—did not deter Juan's parents from hiring a coyote to transport him to the United States. When people have good-enough reasons to leave their countries or to travel to the United States, it is very difficult to deter them, no matter the risks or the costs. Enhancements to border security simply make the journey more dangerous.

The crossing through Mexico that Guatemalans who enter the United States illegally often must endure has gotten increasingly dangerous since the 1980s. In fact, many deportees cited the violence in Mexico, particularly the risk of being kidnapped by criminal gangs, as the primary reason they were scared to return illegally to the United States. Despite this violence and their fears, many deportees told me they planned to reunite with their families in the United States and would take the risk. Guatemala shares a border with Mexico, so Guatemalans intending to reach the United States by land must first cross this border and then make it all the way across Mexico before attempting to cross the U.S.-Mexico border.

Roberto was born in 1964 in Zone 5 of Guatemala City, where he finished primary school. Roberto dropped out of school in his first year of secondary school. He was 14 and got a job helping a mechanic so that he could earn more money. He grew up in a poor neighborhood, and he had always dreamed of going elsewhere and of having more things in

life. His desire to know other places and to have more material possessions eventually led him to emigrate. When he was 16, he left Guatemala
for Mexico. He spent three years in the border town of Nuevo Laredo,
where he worked as a mechanic.

In 1983, when Roberto was 19, he crossed the border to the United
States. There were one million people apprehended at the border that
year, but Roberto was able to evade the Border Patrol. He told me that
it was fairly easy, and he had no trouble getting to Houston, Texas,
where he had some friends. He stayed in Houston for three years, working as a mechanic. But he grew tired of the Texas heat. He got together
with a group of friends and they decided to hitch a ride on a train.
Roberto hoped to go to Miami, but his friends grabbed a train headed
for Chicago.

As the train headed north, however, Roberto noticed it was getting
colder and colder. When they reached Cincinnati, he told his friends he
was getting off at the next stop. They agreed to get off the train in Toledo,
Ohio. His friends planned to continue to Chicago but disembarked in
Toledo to make sure Roberto found a place to stay. Walking around
town, they were able to get a short-term job cleaning a vacant lot next
to a mechanic shop owned by a Mexican. Roberto's friends got back on
the train to Chicago, but Roberto got a job as a mechanic and ended up
spending the next 18 years in Toledo.

Mateo, whose story I told in the previous chapter, set out on this voyage across Mexico alone at age 10 in 1985. Mateo is slim and brown-
skinned, has strong indigenous features, and is missing one of his two
front teeth. I asked him to tell me his life story, and he proceeded to do
so with very little questioning on my part. Speaking in English with a
strong New York accent, Mateo told me that he left school when he was
eight to work, then left his country when he was 10.

Mateo found his opportunity to migrate to the United States while
he was at work. He overheard some of his work colleagues talking about
traveling to the United States. He told them that he wanted to go with
them as he knew he had an uncle in Washington, D.C. They said that if
he got the money together, he could. Mateo had 300 quetzales saved up
and used that money to pay for his trip to Mexico.

Once in Mexico, Mateo lost his guide. Mateo was disoriented but
determined to make it to the United States. He described walking down

the highway and seeing two signs. One said "Mexico City" and the other read "Monterey." He headed toward Mexico City, as he had no idea where Monterey was. It took him about two months to get to Mexico City, because he had to work to get bus money for each leg of the trip. Once in Mexico City, Mateo got a job loading lettuce onto trucks and ended up spending five years there. He spoke about those five years and his decision to leave Mexico in vivid detail:

> At that time, there were a lot of kids working there, unloading the lettuce trucks. They used to pay you good money. I paid for my apartment. I actually got me an apartment, not just a room. I started making friends until I got to a point that I was getting comfortable. Then, I thought to myself, "You know what? I came here because I'm supposed to go to the United States, not just stay in Mexico. So what the hell am I doing here?" And, just from one day to another, I packed my stuff up and I told the guys, "I'll see you. You're not going to see me anymore." I just grabbed my stuff and the next night, I grabbed the bus, and I went to Matamoros. I had money to pay the guy that was going to pass me through to the United States, but he actually robbed me. I called here to Guatemala.
>
> When my uncle heard my voice, he was like, "Oh my God, Mateo. You, oh my God! You're alive. We thought you were dead. We couldn't find you here in Guatemala. You left a note. You were going to go to the United States. Are you there yet?" "Well, I'm halfway there. I just got my money robbed, and I need to get there." They were like, "Don't worry. I'm going to get your aunt's phone number." I called her. She was like, "Oh my God, Mateo, you're still there. Oh my God, what are you doing?" And she told me the place where I could go and pay the coyote so he can take me to Houston, Texas, and then from Texas to Washington. And I went. And I told the guy, "Listen, you know. My aunt is going to pay you the money. Here's her phone number. You can call her up." The guy spoke with my aunt and he said that it was going to be $1,000 at the time. She sent him $500.
>
> Once I was in Texas and he put me on the bus, then she would send the other $500. Now, when I got there it was fine. Everything was fine. We walked for three days and two nights, but there was no immigration the whole way. Nothing. It was calm. Everything was smooth. No food, no drinks. We just had a gallon of water, and we had to split that for the

three days and the two nights. So, it was hard, but we made it with the little food that we had. When we finally made it to the house, they let everyone out except for me, because my aunt hadn't paid the other $500. We went to his house and he actually took out a gun out of his waist. And he called his cousin, I remember. They were like, "Yo, listen. Keep a good look on this guy because I think he wants to run away. This guy told me that that's his plan, to leave and not to pay the money. He thinks he's already in the States, you know, so just keep an eye on him. If he tries to run away, just shoot him."

But something happened that my aunt couldn't send the money out on that day. So it took a week before she could send them the money and the guy was actually worried. They were like, "Yo, dude, I think I'm just going to disappear this guy." He was talking in the backyard with his cousin, I think. "I think we should just take him over there to the woods and just disappear him, huh? They're not going to send the money out." And, exactly that day, my aunt called. What a relief! Then the guy went and the next day in the morning, he woke me up around five o'clock. Six o'clock I was taking a shower. I was eating breakfast. In addition, I remember that he took me up to a thrift store and he went and bought me some clothes. He didn't even buy me new clothes. I remember. And he was like, "You gotta blend in. So, since you gotta blend in, I bought you this sombrero, these boots, and I bought you these tight jeans and this shirt. You gotta wear these so they can't tell you're Mexican." I was like, "Well, I got a sombrero. I got boots. I got tight pants. I'm a target, dude. Hello. All I need is a sign." "Hello, I'm Mexican!" Well, I'm not Mexican, but you know. Anyway, I had to wear those clothes, and he gave me a duffel bag, $50, and a bus ticket.

The bus took Mateo to Washington, D.C., where he stayed at his aunt's house. It took him five years to cross through Mexico, but he made it to the United States.

Roberto and Mateo traveled to the United States in the 1980s when the passage was not as difficult, expensive, or dangerous as it is now. Roberto was able to enter with the help of a few friends, yet Mateo sought out the services of a coyote, which made Mateo more vulnerable and the trip more costly. As border enforcement has tightened, increasing numbers of migrants must rely on coyotes to cross.[10]

Similar to other Guatemalans who crossed Mexico in the 1980s, Roberto and Mateo were able to work their way (literally) across Mexico by picking up odd jobs along the way and moving from town to town. The relative ease with which Roberto crossed all of Mexico and then the U.S.-Mexico border contrasts with border-crossing stories in the late 1990s and in the 21st century.

Noe also traveled to the United States illegally as a child, although, unlike Juan and Mateo, he traveled with his parents. Noe's parents went to the United States when he was very young, and they left him with his grandmother. Noe recalled the precise moment in 1996 when his mother returned for him.

N: One day I was watching a show called A-Team and I saw a lady to my right, and I turned around and there was like this weird . . . I thought it was a weird lady, right? So, then when I turned to my right, she was holding her hands out and I was like, "What? What's wrong with her?" And then I looked closer and closer and I walked closer and closer; I realized it was my mom. So I was like, "Damn, you're here. That's cool." Then she told me, "You're not gonna suffer no more." She stayed for, I would say, about three months maybe and then we took off with her. She told us that we were gonna go get clothes, so she packed us all nice and everything. So we went, and I guess we ended up traveling through all Mexico. I don't remember much of it until one day my brother got lost.

When we got there, we didn't find my brother, but he actually arrived in the D.F. [Mexico City]. But he was young. I don't remember much of it. . . . It took us a long time to get to the States, man. I think it did 'cause from what I remember, we became like a different family. Like I had to be called somebody else's kid. But we traveled all through Mexico.

Once we got to the States, not to the States but to the border of Mexico, I remember we had to, like, my mom had to get naked and stuff and walk through the river. And then we got into Laredo. In Laredo, I guess we had to meet my uncle there. My uncle is a resident 'cause he went to the States when he was young. When he went there, I guess for me being young and stupid, I was excited to see him. I hadn't seen him forever. I didn't even know who my uncle was. I kept looking back at him and I guess we got in trouble for me doing that.

T: For looking back at him?

N: Yeah, 'cause we were in the States and he was a resident and I wasn't. So, we got caught. And we said we were Mexican and we remembered all the things. My mom remembered all the things, I guess. So, then we got deported to Mexico just across the border, right. I mean, no biggie. And we went back. And in that time we finally made it. And we made it to Texas. . . . We ended up in Texas. Not for long, like two months maybe. Then we went to California. In Cali, we stayed in this rough neighborhood. From what I think, it was Compton because we lived in a bad area where there was black people everywhere, and my mom didn't like it 'cause my cousin got shot.

Noe was only seven years old when he, his mother, and his brother crossed all of Mexico and then the U.S.-Mexico border, with the help of several coyotes. As he explained, they walked across the Rio Grande near Laredo, Texas. In Laredo, the river is about 200 feet across in some places. Although it is only about three feet deep, the current can be strong, and about 70 migrants drown each year in their attempts to cross this river.[11]

Noe and his family crossed over in 1996, after border enforcement had been intensified in the early 1990s but before the militarization of the late 1990s and early 2000s. Today, getting to the United States from Guatemala often requires hiding from Mexican police and criminal gangs across the long routes from Guatemala to the United States. In addition, Guatemalans must worry about whether or not their Guatemalan coyotes will pass them off to unscrupulous coyotes in Mexico who may steal their money and threaten their lives. Several deportees explained to me that there is a division of labor with coyotes and that some of the Guatemalan coyotes only take you to the northern border of Mexico, where they then must find someone else who can help others make it across the U.S.-Mexico border. Usually, people have to have very good reasons to take these enormous risks.

When Noe crossed over—in the mid-1990s—it was no picnic. However, passage has become increasingly difficult as the United States engages in new levels of "low-intensity warfare" (Rosas 2012: 7) at the

U.S.-Mexico border. During the 1990s, the United States implemented successive operations in attempts to keep swelling numbers of Mexicans and Central Americans from crossing over. Operation Hold-the-Line took off in 1993, followed by Gatekeeper in 1994 and Safeguard in 1995 (Nevins 2002; Dunn 2009; Rosas 2012). As neoliberal reforms created turbulence in Mexico's economy, the United States attempted to keep potential migrants out. These attempts were remarkably unsuccessful in deterring migration, but there is no doubt they made the journeys more dangerous (Cornelius 2006).

Raquel Rubio-Goldsmith and her colleagues explain:[12]

> In the mid-1990s, the U.S. government implemented a "prevention through deterrence" approach to immigration control that has resulted in the militarization of the border and a quintupling of border-enforcement expenditures. However, the new border barriers, fortified checkpoints, high-tech forms of surveillance, and thousands of additional Border Patrol agents stationed along the southwest border have not decreased the number of unauthorized migrants crossing into the United States. Rather, the new strategy has closed off major urban points of unauthorized migration in Texas and California and funneled hundreds of thousands of unauthorized migrants through southern Arizona's remote and notoriously inhospitable deserts and mountains. (1–2)

Rubio-Goldsmith and her colleagues find a direct correlation between the rise in migrant deaths and the enhancement of border security. Edison's story renders it clear there are risks to your personal as well as financial security.

Like Mateo and Noe, Edison spent a substantial amount of time in Mexico, but he spent all of it trying to leave. He would try to make it across but would get robbed and swindled and end up back in Mexico. Edison's story is one of struggle and perseverance, with more than a few twists of bad luck. Edison was born in 1976 and grew up in Canalitos, a suburb outside of Guatemala City. Throughout the interview, he mentioned that he had worked hard all of his life, starting at the age of 11. He worked and studied throughout high school. At 17, he left school and worked two or three jobs to save up money to buy a car and a piece of land. He married at age 20 and had two children with his wife. Things were going fairly well for them, but they were still poor by most standards.

Shortly after Edison's second daughter was born in 2001, his uncle came to visit from the United States. He told Edison about all of the opportunities in the United States, and he suggested Edison accompany him on his return trip. Edison thought about it and decided to give it a shot. They didn't make it, however. The Mexican police took all of their money at the Guatemala-Mexico border and they spent the next eight months trying to get across Mexico. Eventually, Mexican immigration authorities caught them in Veracruz and deported them back to Guatemala.

Back in Guatemala, Edison couldn't stop thinking about going to the United States. He was able to find three jobs in Guatemala. Despite working all the time, he still did not have enough money. He became more determined to make the trip to the United States. Edison talked about his dream with his family, and his mother and brother and sister lent him the money to pay a coyote the 40,000 quetzales—about US$5,000—it cost to get to the United States in 2003.

Edison contracted a coyote who helped him make it safely to Los Angeles. A friend of his came to pick him up and took him to his apartment in Oakland, California, where he slept on the floor for a month. Edison worked for the first couple of months as a day laborer. He barely made enough to get by and contemplated returning to Guatemala to be with his wife and kids. But he had the debt to repay. Plus he was already in the United States and figured if he just tried harder he could make it.

One of Edison's biggest obstacles was his lack of English skills. Without English, he had trouble making money to pay off the debt and to help his family at home. He began to study English, and, slowly, things began to get better for him. Soon, Edison was making what felt to him like a lot of money—$18 an hour—which was enough to repay his debt and build his savings. However, he missed his family. He asked his wife to come with the kids. She said she would only go if he came to get them. Edison decided to fly back to Guatemala. It had been three years since he had seen his family. He had made it into the United States once and figured he could do it again.

Back in Guatemala, Edison bought a pickup truck to drive himself around while he prepared to take his wife and kids to the United States.

Two months later, the pickup was stolen while parked in downtown Guatemala City. He bought a taxi to rent out to earn extra money. A month later, it broke down. Nothing was going right for Edison in Guatemala. He had US$5,000 saved, so, before he lost that, he called the coyote who had taken him the first time and told him he was ready to leave—without his family, since he couldn't afford to bring them all. A couple of months later, Edison made it to Ciudad Juárez, on the U.S.-Mexico border. There, the coyote passed him on to someone else and went back to Guatemala. Edison explained what happened in Ciudad Juárez.

The coyote handed me over to a girl. I was there for 15 days, in Ciudad Juárez, waiting. . . . I was bored to be there in that damn hotel room. Finally, they told us that we were going to cross. They told us they would give each of us $200 that we were supposed to pay once we made it over to the other side. Two guys came and they told us they were going to help us cross. There were four of us. When we made it to a certain point the guys told us we needed to give them the money because they had to pay the driver. We didn't know what to do, so we gave them the money. They disappeared right after that. What were we supposed to do? We walked back to the hotel and told the lady that the guys had robbed us. She was like: "How could that happen?" Anyway, so we called our coyote from Guatemala. He had already gone back to Guatemala. We told him, "Look, we are out of money; they don't want to feed us any more. You need to come do something, because we already paid you for the whole trip."

Finally, someone came for us to help us cross. They put us with 10 other Mexicans and we crossed over. But, just before we made it to the freeway, we were already on the other side, we saw a Border Patrol truck. We were already in American territory. We saw the Border Patrol truck and we all threw ourselves down. There were a lot of us. We were lying there for a while, but nothing happened. Finally, I heard some voices. It was really dark so I couldn't see anything. Then, bam! I felt a foot on my back and heard someone say, "Don't move!" I screamed, "They got us!" Everybody started running. I knocked the foot off my back and ran, too. I tried to run away, but we were surrounded. At first, it seemed like I might get away. But there were a lot of Border Patrol cars and officers, and they got me. There were a lot of us, too. Two got away.

After spending a couple of weeks in detention, Edison was deported back to Guatemala. Once home, he sought out the coyote and told him he had to take him again. Coyotes usually give you three chances to get to the United States for the same fee. It took the coyote a few months, but he finally took Edison back to the U.S.-Mexico border. Once they got to the border with Mexico, though, the coyote told Edison he didn't have any more money and that Edison needed US$2,000 to cross over to the United States.

Edison called his wife and she sold the taxi to send him the money. Edison's income in the United States before his return had been sufficient to justify the sacrifice. However, the Mexican coyote lied to Edison and said the money never came. Edison was still in Juárez in a house where migrants stay waiting to cross over. The owner of the house called his wife and told her to wire another $2,000, as Edison was already in Texas and owed the money. If not, she would bring him back from Mexico. His wife sent the money.

When Edison found out, he approached the woman about her lie. She gave him back $1,000 and disappeared. He decided to try it alone. Edison met up with two Mexicans and a Colombian who also wanted to cross over. They went through a tunnel and were picked up on the other side by a coyote. As they were driving on the freeway, four cars surrounded them and pulled out guns. The driver stopped the car and they got out with their hands up. One of the officers threw Edison on the floor and pointed a gun at his head. Each of them was put into a different car and questioned at the police station. The officers told them that if they didn't say who the coyote was, they would be put in jail. Edison spent over a month in prison on a smuggling charge—he was charged with being the coyote.

After a month in prison, the officials came to him and told him that if he admitted that the driver was the coyote, they would put him on a plane to Guatemala the next day. He agreed to make a statement. Instead of putting him on a plane, however, he was confined to a halfway house. From there, he went to immigration detention, where he spent two weeks before being deported to Guatemala. Edison's attempts to return to the United States were foiled by unscrupulous coyotes in Mexico and intensified Border Patrol enforcement in the United States. By 2007, it had become quite difficult to enter the United States.

Edison is not sure if he will make the trip again. In Guatemala, his family has a tenuous future. But they are all together and none of them are going hungry. With him working so much, he can't see them as often as he'd like. For now, he will continue to work hard, so long as his health permits. The dream of returning, however, lingers. He knows he has a job waiting for him in the United States and that he could earn enough money to provide a better future for himself and his family. Returning, however, would likely put Edison in debt. He is likely to be able to work off this debt—as many migrants do. However, we can also see how enhanced border enforcement has raised the cost of illegal immigration, which in turn seems to make migrants even more vulnerable. In my interviews with Brazilians, the economic costs of illegal migration were even more salient.

Brazilians: A Long Trek across the Americas

Like Jamaicans, the Brazilians I met all left their country in airplanes. However, unlike the Jamaicans, most of the Brazilians traveled to the United States on tourist visas or across the Mexican border illegally. The fortunate ones were able to take planes directly to the United States, because they had tourist visas. Those less fortunate took planes to Mexico City and had to make their way to the U.S.-Mexico border surreptitiously from there.

Most of the Brazilians who secured tourist visas did so through travel agencies that helped them fabricate documents that made it seem as though they had many more economic resources at their disposal than they actually had. This strategy was common among deportees I met who traveled to the United States in the 1990s. However, those who went in the 21st century no longer had that option. In fact, after 2005, Brazilians began to need visas to enter Mexico, meaning they first had to fabricate documents that permitted them to enter Mexico and then they had to travel the dangerous route through Mexico.[13]

Sueli was able to travel to the United States before the visa restrictions in Mexico were in place, and she had a somewhat easier time than people who traveled later on. Sueli's goal was to work in the United States for two years in order to earn enough money to establish herself in Jaraguá, purchase a home, and pay for her son's education. She applied for a visa three times and was denied. A friend convinced her to travel to the United States via Mexico. Her friend promised she would not have to walk through the desert and that she would pass through a normal port of entry. She explained they would use a car with false seats and Sueli would travel inside one of the false seats. Sueli would not have to pay the money until she arrived. She agreed. The trip would cost US$10,000.

In 2004, Sueli set out for São Paulo. In São Paulo, she waited for a few days in a hotel for her plane to leave. She took a plane to Mexico City. From there, she traveled for three days, crowded into a hot car, to the border. In Mexicali, Sueli lived for two weeks in a house with only Brazilians. Each day some would leave and others would stay. There were more than 30 people—men and women—in the house. Finally, it was Sueli's turn.

Although they were told that they would go in one of the cars with the false seats, it turned out that Sueli was put into the trunk. The driver was a very heavily made-up Mexican American woman. When they got to the border, the Border Patrol pulled them over and opened the trunk. They found Sueli inside, and she was taken to San Diego to an immigration detention center.

Sueli agreed to be deported and did not contest her case. Within eight days she was deported to São Paulo. There, she met with the coyote again and he said that she could try again. This time, however, she would need to pay a more expensive fee (up $2,500, to $12,500). This trip involved her crossing the border seated in a van with other people.

Sueli went back to Tijuana this time to another migrant house. There were 48 Brazilians in this house. They stayed there for two weeks until it was time to leave. When the moment came, they all got into different vehicles and passed through the border without a problem. From San Diego, they had to make it to Los Angeles past other checkpoints. They made it across and Sueli got on a plane to Danbury, Connecticut. Although this route is one of the most comfortable routes, legally it is one of the most problematic. It could be argued that Sueli misrepresented herself as a U.S. citizen in order to pass through those checkpoints. If found guilty of this offense, Sueli would be permanently ineligible for entry to the United States. However, she was never apprehended or charged with this offense, and she left the United States of her own accord after reaching her targeted earnings goal.

Santiago went to the United States through a different route: He went straight from Mexico to the Texas border and walked across the desert. Like Sueli, he wanted to go to the United States to earn money. Santiago's father passed away when he was 10, obliging him to work at a young age. Santiago's mother sent him to a dairy farm, where he found work milking cows. Eventually, his mother was able to bring him back to the city, and Santiago worked while attending school. He finished the fourth grade, so he knows how to read and write. Despite his humble origins, Santiago was able to establish himself in Brazil. He bought and sold cattle in addition to working as a moto-taxi driver. He was able to get a vehicle because he financed a motorcycle and paid it off in installments.

Santiago was able to get by, but he wanted more out of life. His dream was to go to the United States, where he heard you could earn good money. Thus, in 2003, when a Brazilian coyote came to his town, asking R$32,000 (US$15,000) to get him to the United States, Santiago accepted. He sold everything he had, including the motorcycle, and borrowed the rest of the money. He left his wife and two daughters in Brazil and made his way to the United States. Santiago describes his arduous journey:

> First, we went to Chile, and from Chile to Mexico, where we stayed about five days before going to the border. From there we went to the desert that is at the United States border. There were lots of thorns. It was complicated, very difficult. The coyote told us it would not be difficult, that we would not have to walk, that we were going by car. . . . There were times when I thought I would not make it, that I would never see my family again. We spent 22 days overall getting from Brazil to the United States—six days walking in the desert. We had water, and we found gallon jugs of water at times. We saw many crosses of people who had died in the desert. Then, we had to cross a very big river. . . . There were 30 of us, but by the end, there were only eight. . . . I don't know what happened to them. . . . After crossing the river, we saw two cars. The coyotes told us to run. . . . I couldn't take it anymore and decided to hand myself in. . . . The immigration agents arrested us and took us to a jail, where we stayed for six days. It was cold and uncomfortable, and they barely gave us enough food to eat. Finally, they let me out on bail and told me to come back in six months for a hearing.

Up until 2005, some sectors of the Border Patrol had a "catch-and-release" program, where they released all non-Mexican migrants and told them to come back for a hearing. The reason for this policy is that there was not sufficient detention space along the border to hold non-Mexican migrants, and the Border Patrol could not send non-Mexicans back to Mexico. Thus, the official policy was to release them and tell them to come back for a hearing. Hondurans topped the list of non-Mexicans apprehended along the border, but Brazilians came in at a close second in 2005. Remarkably, the apprehension of Brazilians along the Mexican border increased eight-fold between 2002 and 2005—from 3,100 to 27,396 apprehensions. The apprehension of Brazilians increased at the same time that temporary U.S. entry visas for Brazilians decreased. Whereas the United States granted 500,000 nonimmigrant visas to Brazilians in 1997, that number had decreased to 100,000 by 2002.[14] It thus seems that the smuggling networks were able to figure out that their fraudulent methods of securing tourist visas would no longer work, yet they were able to quickly ascertain that the option of entering through Mexico was a viable route for Brazilians. This is one clear example of how a change in border enforcement policy leads to a change in tactics on the part of migrants and smugglers.

Remarkably, the Mexican policy of granting visas to Brazilians coincided with the U.S catch-and-release program, which made it fairly easy for Brazilians to reach the interior of the United States. Many Brazilians paid coyotes thousands of dollars to help them plan their trips, which involved traveling to Mexico on a tourist visa and then trekking across Mexico only to present themselves to U.S. Border Patrol agents in McAllen, Texas, where they were detained and then released with a hearing date.

Many of the Brazilians I met misunderstood the catch-and-release program and considered their hearing date to be a pass—a *permiso*—to stay in the United States for six months. With his hearing date in hand, Santiago made his way to New Jersey and never showed up for his court date. He would stay in the United States for nearly three years before being deported when Immigration and Customs Enforcement (ICE) agents showed up at his home.

In 2006, the Border Patrol ended the catch-and-release program, and, in 2005, Mexico suspended its visa-waiver policy for Brazilians.

These two decisions made it more difficult, but not impossible, for Brazilians to enter the United States. Some, like Antonio, tried to enter by boat. This turned out to be a long and arduous trip for Antonio, who left Brazil in 2007. Antonio, who never got a pass to remain in the United States, told me,

> All of the coyotes tell you lies. They mislead you. They tell you they have it all planned out, that they have the police and the Border Patrol in their pockets. But it is all lies. They tell you that so that you don't worry, and so that you pay them. . . . The first time I went from Goiânia to São Paulo, from São Paulo to Panama, from Panama to Cuba, and from Cuba to Freeport. I needed a visa to get into Nassau, but the coyote had bribed the immigration agent in Nassau. I stayed in Nassau for 15 days before making the trip across the sea.

The Coast Guard stopped Antonio's boat, and he was detained at sea for several hours before being brought on land. He was detained by immigration agents for a month before being deported to Brazil.

Antonio's payment to the coyote included a second try. This time, they took a different route, from Goiânia to São Paulo, São Paulo to Panama City, Panama City to Guatemala, Guatemala to Mexico, and Mexico to Texas. Antonio spent 27 days traversing Mexico, including a few days waiting in Mexico City. Antonio explained that the coyote in Matamoros was very organized. They were placed in a house that was full of illegal drugs. The coyote first made sure that the drugs were sent to the United States, then sent Antonio along with other Brazilians on the same route. Antonio ended up in McAllen, Texas, where he was promptly arrested by Border Patrol agents. Antonio had a hard time after being arrested. He told me, "We suffered in McAllen. We went three days without eating. We were taken to a prison in New Mexico and I was scared because the police were using excessive force just to show that they could. That was unnecessary."

Antonio was taken to an immigration detention facility, where he ended up spending nine months and thousands of dollars on immigration lawyers. Antonio recounted that the lawyer's secretary advised him that if he lied at his immigration hearing, he would be released. Antonio paid the immigration lawyer $5,500. He had already paid $6,500 to the coyote just to get him to McAllen. The secretary explained to him that if he made up a story about him being persecuted in Brazil, he would be released pending his immigration hearing. Antonio fabricated a story as he had been advised, but his story was not credible, as he had agreed to be deported just a few months earlier. Nine months after being arrested in McAllen, and many thousands of dollars later, Antonio was sent back to Brazil, financially and emotionally devastated.

Geraldo would suffer at least as much as Antonio for the dream of living in the United States, and he would find that dream just as unfulfilled. He was born in 1979 in Jaraguá. His parents owned a small farm. Geraldo worked from a young age, first on the farm, and then he worked sewing garments starting at age 13. Geraldo decided to travel to the United States in 2002 when he was 23. He was not married and was working but not earning much money. His parents were fairly well off, but Geraldo wanted to go and earn cash in the United States as he saw many other people from his town doing. He found a coyote who would charge him $7,000 for the trip. He paid half up front and would pay the rest when he arrived.

Geraldo traveled to São Paulo and from there to Mexico City. They traveled by land to the border. They spent two nights in a border city until one evening the coyotes told them it was time to go. Geraldo and two other Brazilians were told to lie down in the back of a truck. The truck traveled for about four hours until it stopped. When they got out, the coyotes pointed guns at them and ordered them to walk away. They did. Geraldo and his companions had no idea where they were and began to walk in the desert. They walked and walked—never seeming to get anywhere. They had no food or water. They had been left for dead. On the way, they saw three corpses and were sure they would meet the same fate.

The sun was unrelenting and there was no shade. They took off their clothes and tied them to sticks to make shade. Geraldo was wearing thin-soled shoes and had to pull thorns out of his feet several times. They walked and walked, likely in circles. On the fifth day, they finally saw a light in the distance. They walked toward it and came to a river. They used their last bit of energy to swim across the Rio Grande. When they got across the river, they encountered Border Patrol agents. They were in Laredo. The agents asked them if they were hungry. They told them they hadn't eaten in five days, and the agents took them to a stand and gave them some cookies and a soda.

Geraldo's skin was severely burned. He was dehydrated and starving. Geraldo told the immigration agents he just wanted to go home. It took 82 days to deport Geraldo—even though he bought his own ticket so he could go as quickly as possible. In detention, he went hungry again as he found most of the food inedible. The only things he ate were boiled eggs and milk on the days those were available. A hefty man, he lost about 50 pounds through the entire ordeal.

While Geraldo was suffering in the desert and in detention, his parents were being swindled out of more money back home. The coyote called Geraldo's father to tell him Geraldo had arrived in the United States and got $1,000 more out of him. A lawyer promised to free Geraldo from immigration detention although his bail was $30,000. Geraldo's father paid the lawyer $7,000 for nothing.

Geraldo was happy when he saw Brazil again and resolved never to return to the United States. Overall, the fiasco cost his father R$100,000 (US$50,000) and nearly cost Geraldo his life. He was more reluctant to speak with me than most of the deportees I met, perhaps because of the trauma he suffered from the experience—without obtaining any benefit.

Despite these tremendous ordeals that Brazilians suffered attempting to cross after 2006, some deportees told me they intended to attempt to cross over again. I did not interview anyone who successfully entered the United States after 2006 and was subsequently deported. One likely reason for this is that Brazilians who entered illegally after 2006 had to avoid detection by the Border Patrol. With no record of their entry into the United States, noncitizens are less likely to be deported. A noncitizen like Santiago, who enters, is caught, and released with a court date is transformed into a "fugitive alien" once he fails to show up for his court date. This status enhances the likelihood that he will be caught. I explain this process in more detail in chapter 5.

Conclusion

The stories in this chapter show that enhanced border security contributes to a context where people endure extreme hardship, violence, and almost unimaginable deprivation as they enter the United States.

Moreover, I would argue that border security makes migrants more vulnerable. For Brazilians and Guatemalans, as the cost of entry went up from $5,000 to $15,000 to $30,000, the barriers to entry were greater, but heavily indebted migrants are also more vulnerable to exploitation. For example, if Edison ever makes it back to the United States from Guatemala, he will only be able to do so by going deep into debt. His primary goal, once in the United States, will be to earn enough money to pay off the debt and to support his family back in Guatemala. He will not be in a position to complain about any unsafe conditions in the workplace or to demand better wages—for fear of reprisal, which could have severe consequences for him and his family. We see this pattern happen across these different situations, as the price for entry—legal or illegal—skyrockets.

These border-crossing stories show that enhanced enforcement does not stop border crossings but does lead to increasingly dangerous passages. When tourist visas are no longer available, Brazilians find other ways to get to the United States. With increased risks and fewer migrants, Guatemalan coyotes are more willing to accept payment only once the trip is successful—and to offer several attempts at crossing. Enhanced border enforcement has made the trip more costly—meaning people take out loans to migrate. It also means that undocumented parents are less willing to return home for their children. Instead, they are more likely to send money and pay for their children to come with a coyote. My findings thus align with previous reports that U.S. policies that strengthen the border do not prevent migrants from coming; they simply make the crossing more difficult and more costly (Cornelius 2006).

However, there is a twist: Enhanced border enforcement is somewhat effective at deterring economic migrants such as the Brazilians. The Brazilians I interviewed often desired to go to the United States primarily because they could earn money more quickly there than in Brazil. They were not fleeing poverty and violence in Brazil; they simply were looking for ways to earn and save money so that they could return to Brazil and establish secure middle-class lives for themselves. Their stories contrast with the Guatemalans, whose country is plagued with violence and severe poverty. The Guatemalans have stronger reasons to leave and thus are more likely to contemplate returning to the United

States, despite the risk of being kidnapped, sexually assaulted, or killed in Mexico. In addition to being physically closer to the United States than Brazil, Guatemala is also more closely tied to the United States through economic linkages, a long history of migration, and a troubled narrative of U.S. military interventions. These ties make the pull to the United States stronger.

The pull to the United States is even greater when migrants have children in the United States. Department of Homeland Security (DHS) statistics confirm this trend: In 2012, reinstatements of final orders accounted for a third of all deportations and nearly a quarter of all deportees had U.S. citizen children; these numbers point to the fact that, increasingly, many of the people Border Patrol apprehends are seeking to return to the United States to be with their families. The metrics of a cost-benefit analysis change when migrants are calculating more than future potential earnings. Many deportees would risk quite a lot to see their families again. Some migrants are willing to risk federal prison sentences, especially if their only other choice is to never see their loved ones again.

There is nothing "natural" about the risks these migrants face. Their stories render it evident that, by forcing people to take illegal routes, these policies create a situation where migrants are open to a host of other abuses beyond those posed by the natural terrain. Strong borders create an underground economy of coyotes and other people well positioned to exploit vulnerable migrants. Edison was swindled out of his money by a Mexican coyote. Antonio was misled by a lawyer's secretary in Texas and lost thousands of dollars. After being abandoned by a smuggler, Geraldo got lost in the desert and nearly died. Those migrants who traveled across in the past few years spoke of the involvement of drug cartels, which are absent from earlier border-crossing narratives.

There is some debate among scholars about the role of coyotes. In *Clandestine Crossings*, David Spener (2009) argues that coyotes have a worse reputation than they deserve and that they are more likely to help Mexican migrants than to hurt them. My findings suggest that, as Spener argues, coyotes are helpful when migrants acquire them through close personal ties. However, migrants such as Brazilians and Guatemalans who must cross several countries often are handed off from one coyote to another. This strategy greatly increases the risk that they will encounter an unscrupulous coyote, because the links are weaker and the hometown camaraderie dissipates.

Finally, those migrants that crossed most recently made it clear that enhanced enforcement has fundamentally changed the underground border-crossing economy. Brazilians who crossed over after 2006 told me that the Mexican coyotes were involved in illegal drug smuggling. One Brazilian told me that the safe house where he was held in Mexico had rooms full of illegal drugs. The smugglers would alternate between sending drugs to the United States and sending Brazilian migrants. This example shows how enhanced policing along the border has not only increased the physical and monetary costs of crossing the border but also changed the very nature of illegal crossing, through the involvement of international narcotraffickers.

By 2012, there were more than 20,000 Border Patrol agents—mostly stationed along the U.S.-Mexico border. The DHS budget included $242 million to pay for surveillance technology along the southern border, as well as $1.4 billion to enhance the Coast Guard's fleet of ships and aircraft. The overall DHS budget authority is $57 billion; of that, 21 percent goes to Customs and Border Patrol (CBP) and 18 percent to the Coast Guard. These are the two largest units in DHS, according to their proportion of the budgets.[15] At least 39 percent of the DHS budget is directed toward keeping undesirable people out of the United States. A recent report reveals that the United States spent nearly $18 billion on federal immigration enforcement in 2011, an amount that exceeded spending on all other principal federal criminal law enforcement agencies combined.[16] These efforts keep some people out. However, those who are determined to get to the United States come anyway.

Once they arrive, migrants who are deeply indebted and who have experienced danger and trauma are more likely to keep their heads down and serve as a vulnerable workforce. Thus, although border enforcement ostensibly keeps migrants out, its latent function is to keep migrant workers vulnerable. In this way, border enforcement reinforces global apartheid both through keeping out working-class people and poor noncitizens as well as enhancing the vulnerability of immigrant populations already in the United States.

Once in the United States, immigrants settle and find their place in their new homes. This process of incorporation is affected by the neighborhoods they move to, their age at arrival, their legal status, and the opportunities available to them. The next two chapters focus on what happens once immigrants arrive in the United States and their new lives begin. Chapter 3 looks at migrants who arrived in the United States as children. Growing up there, many of them became Americans.

Interlude

Samuel

I was charged for attempted murder.
This is some of the things I hate to talk about. . . .
It's just an unfortunate situation, you nuh.
I'm to be blamed of some of it because
the company or whatever. . . .
I might have caused certain things. . . .
I spent 26 years . . .
half of my life was gone. . . .

When everyone is locked up they always say, "Oh, I didn't do it."
You nuh, it's a common joke.
But . . . for a person who actually is there
and haven't done anything
it's not no joking matter. . . .
Probably I don't explain myself properly
just to let someone really understand. . . .
it's just painful for me. . . .

Well, I'll talk about it.
But you nuh . . .
I just say it's, like, here we go again. . . .
I was charged with attempted murder. . . .
The people that I was hanging out with is friends, you nuh . . .
the night when I got arrested
I was in a stolen car
which I didn't know. . . .

And we got, we got stopped.

And that's where, when I got arrested.

And after, then, that's how I know I was charged with attempted murder. . . .

They found a weapon. . . .

No prints were found.

They say that we don't take fingerprints from a weapon.

3

Becoming (Black and Latino) American

The Impact of Policing

I met Victor in the back of a barbershop in a downtown Kingston, Jamaica, neighborhood. He walked, talked, and dressed like a young man from Brooklyn. Victor told me, with a heavy Brooklyn accent, "I'm from Brooklyn. I grew up in Brooklyn, all my life." Although Victor considers himself to be from Brooklyn, he was born in Jamaica, in a hospital not too far from where we sat. When Victor was four years old, he and his mother took a plane from Kingston to New York City.

When Victor first arrived in Brooklyn, other children teased him because of his accent, calling him a "coconut," taunting him about the "banana boat" on which they presumed he arrived. By high school, no one teased Victor anymore, as he had become indistinguishable from the other black youth in Brooklyn. He graduated from Wingate High School in 1991.

With a high school degree and a legal permanent resident card in hand, Victor was able to secure a job as a messenger. He worked for a couple of years, but the pay wasn't enough for him to move out on his own. His mother had separated from her husband because of domestic abuse and was barely able to make ends meet with housekeeping and babysitting jobs, so his income was a welcome addition to the household. Victor saw his friends earning more money selling marijuana than he did as a messenger and he decided to join them.

As a street-level seller, Victor quickly was caught. His first charge was possession of marijuana, and he was given three years' probation. Victor managed to stay out of trouble for a while after his first arrest. However, in 1996, he was caught with a large quantity of marijuana and was sentenced to four years in prison. He served two and a half years, and, in 1999, was deported to Jamaica. Victor was 27 years old. He had visited Jamaica once when he was about 15 but had no close ties to the country.

Victor is one of thousands of legal permanent residents (LPRs) who have lost their legal status because of drug offenses and have been deported to countries they barely remember. This chapter focuses on the stories of immigrants who arrived as children, whom sociologists describe as the "1.5 generation"—somewhere between native-born (second generation) and immigrants who arrive as adults (first generation). They are both the children of immigrants and immigrants themselves. Growing up in the United States, these children become Americans. Growing up in black communities, many of these children became black Americans. Others grew up in Latino communities and became Latino Americans (see Golash-Boza and Darity 2008).

Victor and his mother traveled to the United States as legal permanent residents. An LPR is a foreign national who both has been granted the privilege of residing permanently in the United States and qualifies for citizenship by naturalization after living in the United States for three to five years. Victor and his mother qualified for U.S. citizenship when Victor was seven. Had Victor's mother become a U.S. citizen herself before Victor's 18th birthday, he could have become a U.S. citizen automatically. Victor's mother never went through the naturalization process. When Victor turned 18, he could have applied for naturalization. Yet he did not. The costs of naturalization, the paperwork, and the time needed to complete the process were all obstacles that Victor was not able to overcome in time to avoid deportation.

Victor grew up in poverty in Brooklyn. His path into hustling was his own choice. Yet it is also the path for many poor youth. In their work with drug dealers in New York City, both Philippe Bourgois (2003) and Randol Contreras (2012) found that selling drugs offers young people a way to earn income while holding on to their dignity and self-respect. Selling drugs in Brooklyn or the Bronx, they don't have to travel to Manhattan to deliver messages or clean toilets for rich white people. In the context of deindustrialization and a hollowed-out job market, there were few other opportunities for low-skilled men such as Victor in New York in the 1990s. Victor saw what life held for the working poor when he looked at his mother, and he didn't feel inclined to follow her example.

In this chapter, I pay particular attention to how neoliberal reforms that created a bifurcation of the labor market, cutbacks in social services, and enhanced police presence in urban areas helped to push migrants like Victor along the path toward trouble. Studies of immigrant incorporation rarely examine the impact of heavy policing in immigrant neighborhoods (Zhou et al. 2008). Many immigrants, however, have to contend with the racialized police state in addition to a limited labor market when they arrive in the United States. Any consideration of immigrant incorporation must take these structural conditions seriously. And an analysis of immigrants who arrive in heavily policed neighborhoods must contend with the impact of heavy policing on immigrant integration.

Victor's mother, similar to the mothers of many of my interviewees, worked in a low-level service-sector job that barely allowed her to make ends meet. Without higher education, Victor's prospects in the formal economy looked equally bleak. Victor's choice between low-wage work and the drug economy was constrained by the racialized opportunity structure in New York City. His choice, nevertheless, had lifelong implications, because it resulted in his exile to the country he and his mother left when he was a toddler.

In 1953, the Presidential Commission charged with reviewing deportation orders had this conclusion: "Each of the aliens is a product of our society. Their formative years were spent in the United States, which is the only home they have ever known. The countries of origin which they left . . . certainly are not responsible for their criminal ways" (quoted in Morawetz 2000: 1961). This sentiment could be applied to Victor—the fact that he was born in Jamaica had nothing to do with his decision to sell marijuana to supplement his income, and everything to do with him having been raised in Brooklyn—where, like many youth, he simultaneously developed a desire for material goods and faced limitations in acquiring them legally (Contreras 2012). Under current U.S. law, however, people born abroad who have spent their formative years in the United States routinely experience deportation. Many of these deportees were in the United States legally and had no intention of returning to their countries of origin.

Deportations of immigrants who arrived in the United States as children were among the most tragic of the stories I heard. These children grew up in the United States, mostly with some form of legal status, and usually never expected to have to leave the countries they called home.

Having grown up in the United States, deportation to the countries in which they were born often seemed like a cruel punishment.

Whereas the previous chapters discussed migrants from each country in its own section, this chapter explores the experiences of the 1.5 generation together to focus on how their experiences in the United States converge. This will be the case for the remaining chapters—until we get to chapter 7, where I discuss deportees' experiences in their countries of origin, where we again see a divergence. The Guatemalans, Dominicans, and Jamaicans discussed in this chapter arrived into neighborhoods where opportunities to get into trouble abounded. I don't discuss Brazilians in this chapter because none of the Brazilians I interviewed had arrived as minors in the United States.[1]

Family Separation, Reunification, and Troubles

Children who migrate to the United States often join their parents, whom they have not seen for several years. In many cases, the mother travels first to the United States to establish herself and later sends for her children and sometimes her partner. It is fairly common for migrant women to leave children with a grandmother when they first venture abroad. As sociologist Nancy Foner (2009) notes, the transition is often challenging. Emigration separates the children from their caregivers and transplants them to a new environment with a hostile climate and a distinct culture. Their mothers' long working hours exacerbate the problems of a reunion after a long separation (Waters 1999; Foner 2009). Many deportees recounted this migration story to me, and they implied that these factors are in part responsible for their involvement in criminal activity. Notably, when children migrated with their mothers, they rarely mentioned any negative consequences of their father having left first. This is similar to what Rhacel Salazar Parreñas (2005) found—that children were more upset by a mother's emigration rather than a father's. It also resonates with Joanna Dreby's (2010) finding that Mexican children more readily accepted the fact that their fathers had to migrate to work than their mothers, because they understood that their fathers needed to work to earn money and they were less accepting of their mothers' need to do that.

Parents who travel abroad to work and leave their children behind do so because of various constraints. In some cases, they cannot afford the visas and tickets for their children and thus have to work in the destination country to get the money together. In other cases, the trip is dangerous and they do not want to put their children at risk. In still other cases, the type of visa or the type of job they have only permits them—and not their children—to migrate (Hondagneu-Sotelo and Avila 1997). In each of these cases, we can see how migration restrictions enforced by the United States create a situation where parents are faced with difficult choices. In these stories, it becomes apparent that, although parents and children dream of reuniting one day, reunions are often challenging.

In the cases of these deportees whose parents left them behind in their original migration, this decision was made in the context of constrained choices. It is important to note, however, that this cycle of migration and separation continues insofar as many of these deportees have now left their children behind in the United States. The 37 Jamaican deportees I interviewed left a total of 101 children in the United States. The 46 Dominican deportees left a total of 77 children in the United States.

For Samuel, the reunion with his parents after living in Jamaica with his grandmother for several years was not easy. Samuel arrived in New York City in 1973, when he was 14. He went to high school in Queens for a couple of years. He found the school much less disciplined than Kingston College, and the schoolwork less advanced. In addition, the students ostracized him because he spoke differently and wore different clothes. Eventually, he couldn't bear the teasing and taunting about his accent and his clothes anymore and dropped out in the 11th grade. When he left school, his tenuous relationship with his parents soured and they kicked him out of the house. He went to live with friends and slowly got pulled into the street life. As I explain below, Samuel's friends got him into trouble.

Freddy arrived in New York about a decade after Samuel, and he entered into a very different situation. Freddy, whose story I told in chapter 1, was born in 1971 in Guatemala City, and he grew up in Zone 1 with his grandmother. His mother abandoned him as a baby, and his father went to the United States to work. Freddy grew up in poverty, with barely enough to eat. When he was 12, his dream finally came true:

His father sent for him to come to the United States. He and his four brothers and sisters arrived in Spanish Harlem with his father, his stepmother, and his half-brother and half-sister.

Things did not turn out as Freddy expected. His father was an abusive alcoholic. Freddy described his life growing up in New York City:

> It was bad. What happened was that my dad was an alcoholic and she was, too. We didn't know that. So, we thought we were going to be, like, better, you know, but it wasn't, because every weekend, you know, he would hit us and everything. Yeah, 'cause he used to get drunk. He is a very nice guy. He is a very hardworking guy, too, because he used to do a lot of overtime. But he would not be the same person after he would start drinking. He would drink alcohol and beer. He never got high; he never used drugs, you know, but the alcohol just changed him and stuff, so he would just, like, pick on us and, you know, hit us and everything.
>
> Like, we thought it was going to be wonderful because we suffered here [in Guatemala], and then over there, it was. . . . We had food, . . . a lot of food. . . . But, clothing, not much, because my father really. . . . He didn't really care about buying us proper clothes for winter.

At school, kids teased Freddy because of how he dressed. He resented his father for not buying him clothes so he could fit in and keep warm; he had to wear his slacks and shirts from Guatemala whereas other children sported new jeans and tennis shoes. As Freddy got older and his older brothers began to earn money, they began to take care of him, buying him new clothes, shoes, and a winter coat—things his father did not provide for him.

Freddy lived in Spanish Harlem. His family was the only Guatemalan family he knew. The other people in the neighborhood were primarily Dominicans and Puerto Ricans. Freddy recalled being the only kid in his class who ate tortillas. Kids used to tease him at school because he was short and dressed and ate differently. Eventually, Freddy tired of all of the abuse in his family and the teasing at school and dropped out of school so he could earn enough money to move out on his own.

Both Freddy and Samuel ended up dropping out of school. This was fairly common among deportees I met, and it is likely related to their subsequent incarceration, because high school dropouts are much more likely to end up imprisoned (Western 2007). Some scholars argue that immigrant children drop out of school because of pressure from native-born peers to resist assimilation into the middle class (Zhou 1997). Freddy and Samuel, similar to other deportees I met, did not openly reject middle-class ideals. Instead, they felt overwhelmed by their life circumstances, and dropping out of school permitted them to provide for themselves and attain the consumer goods they perceived they needed to fit into U.S. society. Unfortunately, leaving school also meant that they would be unlikely to do better in the United States than their parents had.

Cultural Differences and Becoming Americans

Freddy and Samuel both arrived in the United States with the aspiration of doing better than they had in their home countries. Both young men found themselves at the bottom of the totem pole in New York City, as newly arrived immigrants whose parents worked low-wage jobs. Both Freddy and Samuel were able to drop out of school and find work that would enable them to purchase the consumer items that have become requisite for youth to feel as if they belong. Scholars refer to this process of consumption as belonging as "consumer citizenship," which refers to citizenship being redefined through consumer power (Harris 2004: 164). Ultimately, for Freddy and Samuel, the only kind of citizenship that would matter in their deportation hearings was formal, legal citizenship, which they never attained.

For many youth, like Freddy and Samuel, the learning curve for acquiring the requisite apparel and cultural capital to fit in was steep. The cultural shock of arriving in the United States as a teenager seemed particularly harsh in the 1970s, when there were relatively few young immigrants in the United States, as well as fewer transnational flows of information. Jamaican teens who arrived in New York City in the 1970s often did not fit in. They spoke the wrong way, wore the wrong clothes, and did not know the code of the streets. Most of them dropped out of high school, even those who excelled in school in Jamaica. Alberto, for example, told me the following story about his arrival in New York in the 1970s:

I had an accent, which the other students would laugh when I speak, you know. I dressed differently. They were wearing those big bellbottom pants and the boys had high heels. I remember a guy had a fish in his shoe; I remember my shirt was with big old sleeves and the guys were wearing pants looking like girls and no back pockets. Everything was weird, and my pants were English material, Terylene wool. We wear shirts like these, you know, Arrow shirts, very nice shirts, you know. We were well dressed. We were like English. Them was laughing at me, and I was laughing at them.

Like Freddy, Alberto faced taunting for wearing clothes from his country of origin.

Alberto had studied at Kingston College in Jamaica, and, like Samuel, he found the coursework at his new school to be relatively easy. Many of the other schoolchildren asked him for help on tests, and he used his smarts to make friends. His experiences contrast with Mary Waters's (1999) more recent depictions of West Indian immigrants as arriving with weak educational backgrounds, yet are supported by Nancy Lopez's (2003) findings that immigrants from the Caribbean often had better schooling in their home countries than in the United States.

Although Alberto did well in school, like Freddy and Samuel, he had problems at home, partly related to his family separation prior to migration. His parents also greatly disapproved of his decision to grow dreadlocks. These tensions led him to move out of his house, drop out of school, and get a job. His first job was at New York University, working in the blood and urinary analysis lab. At the same time, Alberto honed his skills as a musician and went to trade school.

Alberto made his life in the United States, but he held tightly to his identity as a Jamaican and as a Rastafarian. Alberto told me that he had a "good life" in Jamaica, yet he was not able to replicate that middle-class status in the United States. Other scholars have found that West Indians who identify strongly with their country of origin tend to integrate more easily than those immigrants who identify with black Americans (Waters 1999). Alberto, however, was similar to many other deportees I met whose parents objected to their affiliation with the Rastafarian community, which is very much a Jamaican phenomenon.

Both Samuel and Alberto were on track to middle-class lives in Jamaica. Their parents were not able to make their ways into the middle class in the United States. For them, this was important insofar as their working-class status determined where they lived. Living in a working-class, primarily black, heavily policed neighborhood in New York, Alberto had many encounters with the police: He was arrested for carrying a switchblade once and for a marijuana sale another time. He was unaware that the switchblade was illegal, as he bought it in a store. As for the marijuana arrest, he explained: "I was just there on the sidewalk and everybody got arrested. I was charged for that drug sale. I did not make that sale but I got charged for it." Illegal weapon possession and drug sales are both deportable offenses. Heavy policing of black and Latino neighborhoods increases black and Latino immigrants' likelihood of being arrested for these offenses.

The Context of Reception

Whereas scholars who write about the urban African American or Latino experience often highlight the impact of mass incarceration, those who focus on immigrants rarely mention heavy policing or mass incarceration. This is remarkable, as we can see from Alberto's story that policing immigrants has been going on for decades. Whereas immigration scholars often focus on attitudes and identities, scholars of mass incarceration argue that, regardless of your attitude, U.S. drug laws are so draconian that it becomes difficult for any black or Latino male youth to avoid the criminal justice system, particularly if he lives in a primarily black or Latino neighborhood (Western 2007; Alexander 2010). What, then, is the context of reception for these immigrant youth and how does it affect their incorporation trajectories?

Immigration scholars argue that there are distinct paths to becoming part of society and refer to this process as segmented assimilation. These sociologists argue that the children of immigrants who are born in the United States or who arrive there as youth experience either (1) assimilation into mainstream society; (2) selective acculturation; or (3) downward assimilation (Portes and Zhou 1993; Zhou 1997; Portes and Rumbaut 2001). Researchers maintain that at least three factors influence the incorporation process: (1) individual features such as education, race, and occupation; (2) the context of reception; and (3) family structure. Those immigrants whose families have lower education, who arrive and settle in low-income areas, who lack legal status, who are viewed as nonwhite, and who don't have intact families are more likely to experience downward assimilation (Portes and Zhou 1993; Zhou 1997; Portes and Rumbaut 2001). According to these scholars, downward assimilation refers to the process whereby the children of immigrants are unable to attain middle-class status and identify with the experiences of low-income, native-born blacks and Latinos instead of adopting the optimism of their parents (Kao and Tienda 1995).

Some proponents of segmented assimilation contend that racial prejudice, deindustrialization, and the proliferation of the drug trade in immigrant neighborhoods influence the likelihood that second-generation youth will experience downward assimilation (Haller, Portes, and Lynch 2011). Other scholars focus more on individual factors such as attitudes and oppositional identities (Ogbu 1990; Kao and Tienda 1995; Waters 1999). Min Zhou (1997: 69), for example, argues that marginalized youth develop an "oppositional culture" and are unlikely to see school achievement as a viable path to upward mobility. Similarly, Alejandro Portes, Patricia Fernandez-Kelly, and William Haller (2005: 1008) contend that poor immigrant families often live in central cities, where children encounter a context that "may promote a set of undesirable outcomes inimical to successful integration such as dropping out of school, joining youth gangs, and using and selling drugs." Mary Waters (1994: 802) posits that "some Jamaican Americans, for example, are experiencing downward social mobility while others are maintaining strong ethnic ties and achieving socioeconomic success." The work of these scholars implies that immigrant youth are either protected by their ethnic cohesion or exposed to the norms of marginalized native-born youth around them. From this standpoint, youths' attitudes and orientation will determine their incorporation trajectories. This raises the question of whether youths' attitudes can also protect them from heavy policing in their neighborhoods.

Research by Portes and Rumbaut (2001) and others who study immigrant success and failure primarily focuses on individual-level characteristics such as the human capital of immigrants and their individual ability and aspirations. For example, Ruben Rumbaut (2005), in an important article on the determinants of incarceration for immigrant youth, uses individual-level statistical data to argue that gender, school suspensions, and leaving school are associated with subsequent incarceration. These studies pay attention to the "context of reception," yet they rarely focus on how the enhanced coercive arm of the state also plays a role in immigrant incorporation. Portes, Fernandez-Kelly, and Haller (2005), for example, talk about poverty in inner cities, yet they do not mention failing schools, the lack of social services, or, most poignantly, the heavy policing of neighborhoods where immigrant youth of color live. Similarly, Kasinitz, Mollenkopf, Waters, and Holdaway (2008: 303) argue that black and dark-skinned immigrants "face more systematic and authoritative racial boundaries" than their lighter-skinned counterparts. However, their focus is more on individual-level discrimination than structural racism, although they do point out that Dominican and West Indian males in their survey were as likely to report problems with the police as African Americans. As Jemima Pierre (2004: 114) argued in a critique of the literature on downward assimilation, it is essential to "ground theories of Black distinctiveness within analyses of power relations and ongoing practices of racial subjugation."

I contend that we must pay attention not only to power relations, but also to the structural conditions of the urban neighborhoods into which black and Latino immigrants arrive. In this spirit, I pay particular attention to the impact of heavy policing in immigrant neighborhoods and ask how this policing affects youths' incorporation trajectories.

In the contemporary United States, a working-class or poor youth of color who strays from the straight and narrow path could quickly find himself in serious trouble with the law. The consequences of minor errors in judgment can be enormous when you live in a heavily policed neighborhood and attend a school that focuses primarily on discipline. Whereas middle-class, white U.S. citizen youth are rarely punished for marijuana usage, noncitizens can face deportation for this offense. Any consequent conviction can be life-changing when you are not a citizen. Victor was deported after being convicted of selling marijuana. We can contrast Victor's predicament with the mostly white wholesale vendors of marijuana in Colorado today who face no criminal charges for selling marijuana. The same act—selling marijuana for profit—has remarkably different consequences, and these consequences are shaped by the legal context.

The Legal Context: The 1996 Laws

In 1996, Congress passed two laws that fundamentally changed the rights of all foreign-born people in the United States—the Anti-Terrorism and Effective Death Penalty Act (AEDPA) and the Illegal Immigration Reform and Immigrant Responsibility Act (IIRIRA). These laws eliminated judicial review of some deportation orders, required mandatory detention for some noncitizens, and introduced the potential for the use of secret evidence in certain cases. Six years prior, the Immigration Act of 1990 had expanded the definition of who could be deported for engaging in criminal activity and had made many immigrants deportable for having committed "aggravated felonies" (Fragomen and Bell 2007). The 1996 laws further expanded the definition of an aggravated felony and also made deportation mandatory.

Under IIRIRA, aggravated felonies include any felony or misdemeanor where the court imposes a sentence of at least one year in prison, regardless of whether the sentence is served or suspended. These crimes can be relatively minor, such as shoplifting or a combination of two minor illegal drug possessions. These cases do not require judicial review: In an aggravated felony case, the immigration judge cannot take into account whether or not the person has been rehabilitated, his or her family ties in the United States, or whether or not the person has any ties to the country of birth. Judges have no discretion once a determination is made that a crime is an aggravated felony. Furthermore, the law has been applied retroactively: Any LPR charged with a crime at any time during a stay in the United States, even before 1996, could be subject to deportation. For example, a person could have come to the United States legally at two, been convicted of attempted arson at 18, and—20 years later, after the passage of IIRIRA—could be deported at 38. Even adopted children of U.S. citizens have faced deportation under these laws, in those cases where parents failed to naturalize their children prior to age 18 (Morawetz 2000; Master 2003). Only undocumented migrants can be deported on noncriminal grounds, whereas legally present immigrants can only be deported after a criminal conviction. These convictions can be as trivial as public urination.

Immigration proceedings in the United States are civil, not criminal, in nature and do not include all of the due process protections afforded to people accused of crimes. Noncitizens can be detained without a bond hearing to assess their flight risk or danger to society. They can be deported without due process. The 1996 laws eliminated judicial review of aggravated felony cases. The absence of judicial review in immigration cases means that LPRs who have lived in the United States for decades, have contributed to society, and have extensive family ties in the country can be subject to deportation for relatively minor crimes they may have committed years ago. Judges cannot take their family and community ties into account. Nor can judges take into account weak or nonexistent linkages to their countries of birth. The only recourse for people facing deportation on aggravated felony charges is to hire their own lawyer (often for thousands of dollars) to argue that the charge they face is not in fact an aggravated felony. If the judge determines that the crime is indeed an aggravated felony, the defendant cannot present evidence that, for example, he is the sole caregiver of a disabled U.S. citizen child.

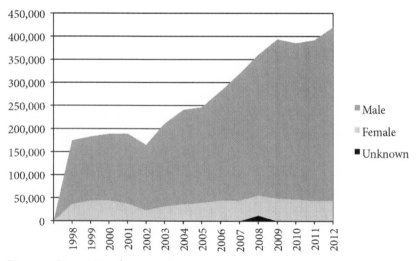

Figure 3.1. Deportations by sex, 1998–2012.

These laws have had a distinctive gendered effect. Prior to 1996, there were about 50,000 removals per year. By 1998, there were 44,000 removals of females alone—accounting for about a quarter of all removals. Unfortunately, I don't have data on removals by sex prior to 1998. However, it is unlikely that females made up even half of all removals prior to 1998—meaning that there was likely a substantial increase in the number of removals of women after the passage of the 1996 laws. However, the number of female deportees has remained steady since 1998 whereas the number of male deportees has continued to increase. Over time, the 1996 laws have had a disproportionate effect on men, with men making up nearly 90 percent of removals in recent years. This pattern is directly related to patterns of gender and racial profiling in criminal law enforcement and is reflective of the ways that deportation reinforces global apartheid.

Legal, but Not Citizens

Many of the deportees I met who arrived in the United States as children arrived as LPRs. They took the "permanent" aspect of their status literally and never intended to return to their countries of birth. However, the passage of the 1996 laws made it possible to lose their permanent status. The 1996 laws transformed these immigrants from LPRs to deportable aliens. By reducing the threshold for deportable crimes, these laws made these immigrants, and many other noncitizens, deportable, and thus, "illegal."

After being an LPR for three to five years, an LPR can naturalize and become a U.S. citizen. This involves filling out an application, taking a test on the U.S. Constitution as well as an English test, swearing an oath, and paying several hundred dollars. The filing fee for an N-400, an Application for Naturalization, in 2014 was $680. There are other costs, including securing transport to the U.S. Citizenship office, obtaining the supporting documents, and taking time off work first to submit the application and later to attend the swearing-in ceremony. Some LPRs never seek out naturalization.

The reasons my interviewees gave for not seeking out citizenship varied and include (1) the belief that citizenship is not necessary to remain permanently in the United States; (2) the processing fees; (3) a lack of

English abilities; (4) no free time; (5) a lack of knowledge about the process; and (6) the fear of losing citizenship in one's country of birth. Other LPRs do not seek out naturalization because they think they are citizens. Still others apply for naturalization but are not able to complete the process before being deported. The risk of deportation has risen significantly since the passage of punitive immigration laws in 1996.

Many of the deportees introduced in this chapter qualified for citizenship based on their status as LPRs and their years lived in the United States, yet they never applied. Although they did not have citizenship in a legal sense, many felt as if they belonged in the United States. This sense of belonging could be called cultural or social citizenship (Marshall 1950; Pakulski 1997), yet the lack of formal citizenship meant that they still could face deportation. This formal, legal exclusion as noncitizens often carried no meaning in their daily lives. It became extremely meaningful, however, when lack of citizenship led to their deportation.

Although many of the immigrants who arrived as children did not perceive citizenship as significant, other experiences of disruption and exclusion were salient in their lives. Many immigrants who arrived as children were separated from their parents before emigrating, and the reunions were often difficult. They often encountered cultural differences when they arrived—especially when they landed in neighborhoods with relatively few immigrants. Low-wage work was also significant in their experiences—both because their parents worked in low-wage jobs and because many had to supplement their parents' income with a part-time job. The prevalence of drugs and gangs in their neighborhoods also shaped their experiences, as did the heavy police presence.

Social Networks

Who you know often matters as much as what you know, the saying goes. Scholars refer to the benefit of knowing particular people as "social capital." Social capital, however, is not always advantageous in terms of integrating into the mainstream: The value of your social networks depends on the people they encompass. Many of the deportees I met got into trouble with the law by virtue of the people they spent time with:

people they met in their working-class, primarily nonwhite, neighbor-hoods in the United States. Most immigration scholars who write about social capital imply that social capital is beneficial insofar as immigrants receive resources and support from their ethnic communities, which facilitates their success (Portes and Schauffler 1994; Zhou and Bankston 1994; Stanton-Salazar and Dornbusch 1995; Sun 1999). Sun (1999: 423) for example, argues that, "just as within a family, tight interpersonal ties within a residential community also enhance academic performance." Zhou and Bankston (1994) contend that ethnic solidarity is particu-larly necessary in communities that are situated in economically dis-advantaged neighborhoods. This ethnic unity protects children from the many distractions in their immediate vicinity. In contrast, many of the deportees I met got into trouble because they were deeply embed-ded in their neighborhoods. The social capital they had access to often turned out to be detrimental, even when it was based on ethnic ties. None of these young men reported having encountered positive or helpful ethnic-based organizations designed to help them succeed.

Social networks are undoubtedly crucial in these deportees' lives. These networks are what led their parents to immigrate to the United States in the first place. Similar to other immigrants, their parents used their social networks to find work and housing in the United States (Model 2008). Whereas these deportees' mothers had networks that helped them find work in the healthcare and other industries, their sons often developed a different kind of network—a sort of under-ground social capital that helped them find work in the drug economy. This underground social capital helps them socially and financially in the short term but often leads to legal troubles. The Jamaican and Dominican deportees I spoke with who were deported on drug charges described their neighborhoods as filled with opportunities to sell drugs.

Most studies of the experiences of Jamaican and Dominican immi-grants pay little attention to two salient aspects of the urban experi-ence in the United States: (1) participation in the drug economy as an alternative to the formal labor market, and (2) the criminalization and incarceration of blacks and Latinos. Of course, most Jamaicans and Dominicans, like most black Americans, do not participate in criminal activity. However, the rate of incarceration of Jamaicans is higher than that of native-born whites (Hagan and Palloni 1999), and Jamaican and

Dominican immigrants often live in neighborhoods with high levels of drug activity and arrests (Kasinitz 1992; Kasinitz et al. 2008).

Dominicans and Jamaicans in the United States are black immigrants, and they often share experiences with African Americans, particularly in under-resourced neighborhoods and schools (Waters 1999). Incarceration has become a common event for black American men: The sociologists Betty Pettit and Bruce Western (2004) point out that in the United States, more black men born in the 1960s have been incarcerated than have served in the army or gone to college. Blacks in the United States are seven times more likely than whites to be incarcerated and Latinos are four times as likely (Alexander 2010).

Dominicans and Jamaicans, like other black immigrants (Brotherton and Barrios 2011), often become ensnared in the criminal justice system. Jamaicans and Dominicans in the United States have become entangled in the War on Drugs in part because Jamaican and Dominican organized crime has played a major role in the distribution of crack cocaine in the United States. In the mid-1980s, prominent Jamaican "posses" such as the Shower Posse and the Spanglers were heavily involved in distributing crack cocaine and marijuana in cities such as New York and Washington, D.C. New immigrants are prime candidates for recruitment to these posses (Kasinitz 1992; Gunst 1995). In a similar vein, a Dominican crack-selling organization in New York City called the Wild Cowboys controlled over $16 million a year in sales during the 1980s (Jackall 1997; Contreras 2012).

Jamaicans who migrated as children had a different experience than those who migrated as teens; elementary schoolchildren tended to be more accepting, and the youth had a longer time to become Americanized while still in school. O'Ryan's story is one example: He moved to the United States in 1984 when he was six. When he first started school, the kids in Brooklyn teased him because of his accent and his hair. However, it did not take much time for him to fit in. By junior high school, there were few noticeable cultural differences between O'Ryan and the other kids in his neighborhood. His neighborhood was culturally diverse, with Puerto Ricans, Dominicans, Guyanese, Thais, Cambodians, African Americans, and Jamaicans.

O'Ryan spoke and acted like a typical kid from Brooklyn. He played sports and was popular in school. O'Ryan graduated with honors from his junior high school and made it into John Dewey, a competitive high school in Brooklyn. He hoped that Dewey would take him away from the friends in his neighborhood who were getting into trouble. O'Ryan told me he tried to stay out of trouble because he hated the look on his mother's face whenever she heard about it.

But it turned out that many of his friends got into Dewey, too. Many of his friends weren't attending school, and he slowly stopped going to school. His mother worked at a hospital from noon to midnight, and he had a lot of unsupervised time. O'Ryan explained to me how he ended up hanging out with the "wrong crowd."

> I get dressed to go to school and everything and I, like, reach out on the block and everybody be hanging out. They be there smoking. Then, you know, they give me a little package, and we be smoking. And we just take it in. And next thing you know, . . . when I look at the time it's like I'm too late . . . they locked the gates. So, if you were not in school on time, there is no getting in.

I asked him what his mother said when she found out he had been skipping school to smoke marijuana. He told me that she was upset and angry, and I asked if she was able to influence him to return. He said, "She tried to, but, I mean, she had, my moms [sic] had to work all the time. . . . It was just me and her. My dad wasn't there and, you know, it was just me and her. She was going through her struggles, too, so she had to work all the time . . . she was working 12 to 12."

Although he dropped out of high school, O'Ryan did go on to earn a GED and eventually enrolled in Mercy College, where he studied computer programming. During this time, he worked part-time at a series of jobs. He had a good job at a trucking company but lost his job after getting into an argument with his boss. Unable to find a new job, O'Ryan had to quit college. With nothing to do, O'Ryan began hanging out again with his friends on the streets in Brooklyn.

One evening, a friend of O'Ryan's called to ask him to pick him up, as his car had broken down. O'Ryan agreed and drove out of the city for his friend. They encountered a roadblock on the way home. At that point, his friend told him, "Yo, I'm dirty," meaning that he had drugs with him and had not told O'Ryan. The police found the drugs and O'Ryan was sentenced to three to nine years for drug trafficking. He chose to do boot camp, so he only spent 18 months in jail.

O'Ryan's mother, his girlfriend, and his newly born daughter came to his graduation from boot camp. O'Ryan saw his daughter for the first time. He was expecting to go home with them and start over.

O'Ryan had been in the country for nearly 20 years and had no family he knew in Jamaica. O'Ryan qualified for citizenship and, in fact, had applied when his green card expired in 1996. His mother and cousin applied at the same time. His mother's citizenship went through, and then his cousin's. So, he went to check on his citizenship. The citizenship office told him he needed to redo his fingerprints. He finally received the letter saying he should go to the swearing-in ceremony in 2001, five years later. Unfortunately, O'Ryan had been arrested a few weeks earlier and was in jail when his letter arrived. So, at the age of 25, when he was released from boot camp, instead of going home, he was sent to Jamaica.

Talking to O'Ryan, it was hard for me to believe that he had been in Jamaica for seven years at that point. He seemed as if he had come from Brooklyn the day before. He reminded me of my students at the University of Kansas. He spoke with a Brooklyn accent and was poised and thoughtful. He wore a red T-shirt and jeans. His simple sneakers were perhaps the best indication that he no longer lived in Brooklyn. New York continued to be his lifeline. He talked to his neighbors, his cousins, his mother, and his seven-year-old daughter every day. He showed me his cell phone. All of the calls he had made recently were to New York.

O'Ryan told me he understands he made mistakes, but he doesn't feel he should pay the rest of his life for those mistakes. He did not see a future for himself in Jamaica, where he felt like a foreigner. It was hard for O'Ryan not to dwell on the "what ifs." What if his citizenship application had been processed just a few months earlier? What if he didn't get into an argument with his boss? What if he didn't answer his phone that day to go pick up his friend? What if there wasn't a roadblock on that evening? What if his mother didn't move to Brooklyn when they migrated from Jamaica?

Like O'Ryan, many Jamaican youth grow up in neighborhoods that are inimical to their success. The poverty, joblessness, crime, school failure, and mass incarceration in their neighborhoods limit their opportunities to join mainstream society (Portes and Zhou 1993; Wilkinson et al. 2009: 945–946). Jamaicans who get into trouble as youth are nearly always males and often live in primarily black inner cities. The experiences of these youth—who traveled to the United States between the ages of 4 and 16—contrast with depictions of Jamaican immigrant youth as relatively immune to the lure of the streets (Kasinitz et al. 2008).

Samuel's social networks in New York City also got him into trouble. After he dropped out of high school and moved out of his parents' house, Samuel was drawn even farther into his peer circles. One afternoon, Samuel was riding in a car with friends, and a police officer pulled them over. Samuel told me he had no idea the car was stolen. When he realized what was going on, he ran. As he was running, Samuel heard shots. He hid in someone's backyard. A police officer cornered him in the backyard and shouted, "Freeze, police!" Samuel says he put his hands up and the officer arrested him. At trial, however, the police officer said that Samuel had pointed a gun at him, and Samuel was charged with attempted murder of a police officer.

I asked Samuel if the officer found a weapon. He said they did but that they did not check the weapon for fingerprints. The police officer's word was sufficient. Samuel was convicted. At age 19, his first conviction turned into a 15-year-to-life sentence in prison. Samuel served 26 years, because the parole board did not release him. He said that was in part because he would never admit guilt and in part because the board was particularly harsh on violent crimes. The fact that the person he had allegedly pointed a gun at was a police officer certainly did not help his case. His case is similar to that of Muhajid Farid, sentenced in 1978 to 15 years to life for the attempted murder of a police officer and who ended up serving 33 years in prison after repeatedly being denied parole.[2]

Before Samuel told me his story, he said it is a common joke in prison that everyone is innocent. It's not a joke, however, he said, when you really are innocent. He sounded resigned, as if he has recounted his story many times and is tired of worrying about whether or not people believe him.

I listened to his story, watching Samuel, a light-skinned man with long dreadlocks, who looks like he has a lot of Asian Indian ancestry, fight back tears. He never let one drop. "Everyone in prison says they are innocent," he said. I looked into his eyes and saw a life wasted. Samuel is calm, intelligent, articulate, poised. He has to sacrifice his dignity every day to get a plate of food and a warm bed to sleep on. When we spoke, he was staying with a childhood friend who was willing to hide Samuel's past from others.

Samuel spent five years—his teenage years—on the streets of New York, and he then spent 26 years in the penitentiary. In 2005, he was deported to Jamaica. Samuel told me that his mother became a citizen of the United States before he turned 18 years old and that he, too, should have U.S. citizenship. Although he was in immigration detention for nearly a year, he did not have a chance to go to court to argue that he was in fact a U.S. citizen and should not be deported. (He would not have been able to win his case, as his parents were married, and both of them would have had to become citizens before he turned 18 in order for him to qualify for derivative citizenship.)

Samuel wishes he had gotten a second chance. In the United States, he was locked up for a long time. When he was incarcerated, his brothers and sisters came to visit occasionally. His parents never came. They were too ashamed to visit him in prison. I asked Samuel if he talks to his father on the phone. He said that when his father gets on the phone, he cries. He can't bear to think of what has happened to his son.

Even if the officer's account of Samuel's behavior when he was 19 years old is accurate, his sentence for a crime in which no one was hurt seems extremely harsh. He spent 26 years in prison and then was deported to a country where it is difficult for him to survive from one day to the next, a country where he has no family and few friends. Nearly 50 years old, he feels as if his entire life has been wasted.

O'Ryan and Samuel both found a place for themselves in New York City. In both cases, their networks of friends led to them getting in trouble. Of course, they could have been more careful about the friends they chose and could have made better choices. However, it is important to keep in mind that the options they had were a product of where they lived in the United States and of the racialized opportunity structure there. As black immigrants, they lived in racially segregated black neighborhoods with poor schools, few resources, and plenty of opportunities to get into trouble. With heavy policing in their neighborhoods, a misstep and being at the wrong place and the wrong time had lifelong consequences for these young men.

In his book *Punished*, Victor Rios (2011) reflects on the fact that the state has not abandoned the poor; instead, the state uses punitive institutions such as police and prisons to control the poor. Rios argues that criminalization and punitive social control had serious consequences for the black and Latino youth in Oakland he studied. We can see this play out for O'Ryan and Samuel. O'Ryan got into trouble both because he gave a friend a ride and because his friend had drugs on his person. Samuel got into trouble because he went riding with friends and ran when the police pulled them over. These youth, similar to the youth in Rios's study, transgressed the law. For both of them, the consequences of this law breaking were life-changing and devastating.

Notably, two decades separate the arrests of O'Ryan and Samuel. Samuel was arrested in 1979 and O'Ryan in 2001. In the late 1970s, tensions between the police and black communities in New York City were high, and Samuel was caught in the middle of this. By the late 1990s, New York City had implemented a series of harsh drug laws and enforcement tactics that led to O'Ryan getting pulled over on the highway and charged for the package his passenger was carrying. Drug crimes are at the root of many of the deportations discussed in this book.

Drugs

The consumption and sale of illegal drugs was a significant aspect of the lives of many of the deportees I interviewed, particularly the Dominicans. The scholarly depictions of Dominican and Jamaican migration recount the travails of hard-working migrants whose primary struggle revolves around resisting discrimination and surviving on low wages. Mary Waters (1999) argues, in her comprehensive study of West Indians in New York City, that black immigrants who come to the United States face difficulties raising children in highly segregated neighborhoods with poor schools and few positive opportunities for their children. Others, such as Suzanne Model (2008), focus on the interpersonal discrimination black immigrants encounter in their places of employment and neighborhoods. However, there is relatively little discussion of how Jamaican and Dominican immigrants live in neighborhoods that are racialized as black and Latino neighborhoods, heavily policed, and drug-ridden. Two recent exceptions are *Banished to the Homeland* by David Brotherton and Luis Barrios (2011), which describes the life trajectories of Dominican deportees—many of whom were involved in the drug economy in the United States, and *The Stickup Kids* by Randol Contreras (2012), which describes the urban blight of the Bronx where many Dominicans live. The Jamaican and Dominican deportees whom I met often described the drug economy as ubiquitous in their neighborhoods, which resonated with the descriptions of New York City in the 1980s and 1990s provided by Contreras.

Scholars of Dominican migration often treat Dominican involvement in the drug economy as primarily a negative stereotype: They point to the media portrayal of Dominican migrants as drug dealers and argue that it is overblown. Jorge Duany writes that Dominicans have been "intensely criminalized and racialized in the popular imaginary of the United States" (2004: 45). Ernesto Sagás argues that the Dominican media often portray Dominican migrants as "rude, ostentatious, and prone to criminal activity" (Sagás and Molina 2004: 68). Peggy Levitt (2001) concedes that there are stereotypical "Dominicanyorks" in the community where she did her research that may have been involved in the drug economy but that she had limited involvement with them. It is likely that sensationalist media reports of Dominican drug activities are exaggerated both in the Dominican Republic and in the United States. However, as Robert Jackall details in his book *Wild Cowboys,* about Dominican drug dealers, and Laurie Gunst in her book *Born Fi' Dead,* about Jamaican posses, the drug trade was very active and profitable in New York City in the 1980s and 1990s. The omnipresence of drugs in Washington Heights, Brooklyn, and Queens was a recurrent theme in my interviews with Dominican and Jamaican deportees and deserves our attention.

Using Drugs

Admitting to drug addiction can be shameful. Thus, it is conceivable that some of my interviewees had used drugs yet did not admit it to me. One exception is the use of marijuana. The Jamaicans I interviewed did not find marijuana use to be deviant and openly admitted to smoking marijuana on a regular basis. Simple possession of marijuana, however, is unlikely to lead to deportation. In contrast, possession of small amounts of narcotic drugs can easily lead to deportation. Some of the people I interviewed who traveled to the United States as children admitted to having been addicted to hard drugs. This addiction eventually led to them getting in trouble with the police, and, as a consequence, they faced deportation.

Ernesto is a dark-skinned, slim man who is balding and is missing a few teeth. When we met in Santo Domingo, he assured me he had a good story for me. We ordered food before we began the interview. When I got to the table with my tray of rice, beans, and chicken, Ernesto had already begun to eat. He apologized, saying he was hungry. As I got to know him better, it became apparent that hot meals were few and far between for Ernesto.

Ernesto was born in 1954 in San Cristobal, Dominican Republic. He is a third-generation immigrant—his grandmother came to the Dominican Republic from St. Thomas, and his grandfather from Dominica. English was the primary language in his house as he was growing up. When he was a young boy, Ernesto's family moved to Santo Domingo. When Trujillo was assassinated in 1961, the country became unsafe for Ernesto and his family. His mother left for the United States, leaving Ernesto behind. When he finished the eighth grade, Ernesto's mother was able to secure visas for the whole family to immigrate to the United States.

They ended up in Manhattan, at 141st Street, in a primarily black American neighborhood. Ernesto did well in high school and was enrolled in the Upward Bound program, a college preparation program for disadvantaged high school students. Because of this, when he finished high school, he already had 21 college credits and enrolled directly in Marymount Manhattan College on a scholarship. He got his degree in political science and economics in 1978. He recounted to me a few of the famous, well-regarded people with whom he went to college.

When Ernesto finished college he got a series of jobs at the public library, at an insurance company, at Bloomingdale's, as a taxi driver, and at a hospital. However, he became involved in drugs. He first began to use drugs recreationally but eventually spiraled downward. "I did have a drug habit. I started experimenting, a little marijuana here, a little acid there, and . . . cocaine. Finally, heroin," Ernesto explained to me in his New York–accented English.

The first time Ernesto was arrested was in 1983, for possession of heroin. When he was released, he got a job as a taxi driver, because that allowed him a flexible schedule and enough income to support his habit. In 1988, Ernesto decided he needed help and enrolled himself in a rehab program, which was to start the following week. Two days before Ernesto was to begin the program, he was arrested. He was coming back from buying heroin for himself and his friends. He got nine months in jail for possession of $250 worth of heroin. He spent a year in immigration detention fighting his case and was deported in 1990 to the Dominican Republic. Although Ernesto had been in the United States since he was 14, he had never become a U.S. citizen and thus faced deportation.

Ernesto arrived in the United States at a fairly young age and had been able to do well for himself educationally. His drug addiction, however, pulled him down. Ernesto was one of the millions of drug users in the United States. Most drug users are never punished for breaking the law. In 2002, for example, 175,000 people entered prison for drug offenses. However, there were an estimated nearly 20 million drug users in that same year—meaning any individual drug user has less than a 1 percent chance of entering prison in any given year. Blacks are much more likely to be punished for drug crimes than whites, even though blacks and whites sell and use drugs at similar rates (Alexander 2010). As a noncitizen, Ernesto faced an additional punishment: deportation. Thus, although it is clear that Ernesto broke the law, it is also clear that his race, gender, and citizenship status affected his ultimate punishment.

Noe, like Ernesto, started out on the right path in the United States. He arrived in the United States from Guatemala when he was seven, after a harrowing journey across Mexico (described in the previous chapter). His family moved from place to place. They spent two months in Texas and then went to Compton, California. His mother didn't like the neighborhood, so they went to South Dakota. Finally, they ended up in Minnesota when Noe was 11. His parents worked in meatpacking. Noe seemed to do fine through all of these moves: "Up until middle school, I was just a regular kid and going to school, doing homework and everything. . . . In eighth grade, that's when I started hanging out with bad kids."

When Noe was about 13, he started to experiment with drugs because many of his friends were using drugs and he was curious. By the time he was 14, he was smoking marijuana on a regular basis. When his parents found out he was using illegal drugs, they kicked him out of the house. This made things worse for Noe, as he went from using drugs to selling them to support himself and his habit. He began using crystal meth along with marijuana. He kept going to school, however, and was able to graduate.

Noe was undocumented, because he and his parents had crossed the southern border without permission. When the police arrested Noe for disorderly conduct a few months after his high school graduation, they were able to use a data-sharing system to check his immigration status. This check revealed that Noe had entered the United States illegally. Thus, the police contacted immigration authorities to ask them to come for Noe. Soon afterward, Noe was deported.

Juan, also Guatemalan, arrived in the United States when he was eight—older than Noe, yet young enough to become fully Americanized. I met Juan in the café of the call center where he works. He was wearing a white Izod three-button shirt with jeans. He has three holes in his left ear but no earrings. Juan told me that when he first arrived in Guatemala, he dressed baggy, had a fade haircut, and wore earrings. Now, he had taken on a more preppy look. "People can change," he told me. Juan is clearly a changed man.

Juan and his mother traveled to the United States in 1987 to join his father, who had been there for a year. They arrived in Los Angeles, and his parents put in an application for political asylum. Years later, they received their legal permanent residency. By that time, however, Juan was no longer a minor and had to apply on his own. Although he qualified as well, he never completed the process and eventually fell out of status.

Juan finished high school in San Fernando Valley, and he obtained an associate's degree in photography at Santa Monica College. Upon graduating, he got a job at Lifetouch Photography, taking pictures of school kids all over California. He enjoyed his job and was doing well financially. Throughout high school and college, Juan stayed out of trouble. He was on the soccer team in high school and did well in school.

However, as he neared the end of college, he went to a party with a friend. At that party, he encountered drugs for the first time. There were all sorts of drugs at the party, and he decided to try crystal meth. Soon, he was addicted. He described how it happened.

> It was one Friday night. I mean, it was the last day of school. We were about to go to spring break and we were throwing a party at my friends' house. And this girl, she's, like, "You wanna come?" I'm, like, "Yeah, sure." I went and picked her up. Everything was like a normal party. And then she's, like, "You wanna go into that room?" I'm, like, "Why not?" There was all kinds of little groups, people doing coke, people doing crystal meth, people doing weed, all kinds of drugs. You name it. They were right there. And I was, like, "Whoa!" I had never seen drugs in my life and I was, like, 21 already, and I had never seen drugs in my life. And she was, like, "You wanna try it?" I didn't want to be, like, a party pooper. I'm, like, "Why not?" And it was crystal meth. That was the first time that I tried crystal meth and that was the end for me. . . . To be honest with you, I liked it a lot. And, I mean, I started missing school. . . . That was at the end of my second year. I was supposed to transfer. I never did. I started missing school. I started selling all my clothes, the nice clothes that I had and doing all kinds of stupid things for drugs. My mom, she find out. She is, like, "You know what? We are going to send you to rehab." And I was, like, "No, I'm not gonna go. I'm already old enough." I mean, when someone's on drugs, they think that they know what they're doing. It's just not true. That's why I'm right here. But, I mean, I don't regret anything that I did 'cause, I mean, I'm learning from my mistakes.

Juan used crystal meth on and off for seven years. He managed to keep his job. But crystal meth is illegal and he risked getting into trouble. Sure enough, in 2007, Juan was caught with crystal meth, and the passenger in his car had stolen credit cards. Juan was charged with both crimes and given 16 months in state prison. At the end of his prison term, Juan was sent to immigration detention, where he stayed for two and a half months before being deported to Guatemala. He arrived in Guatemala in February 2008. By the time he had arrived in Guatemala, his kidneys were in a bad state, likely due to prolonged drug use, and he was forced to go on dialysis to survive.

All of the stories in this chapter have been about men. Women make up about 10 percent of all deportees and are an even smaller fraction of people deported on criminal grounds (Golash-Boza and Hondagneu-Sotelo 2013). In Jamaica, for example, fewer than 2 percent of all deportees are women. However, I did meet one woman in Guatemala who came to the United States as a child and was deported after a drug conviction. Her story is similar to that of Noe and Juan in that she became addicted to crystal meth. However, a gendered dimension to her story is that her addiction is intimately tied to sexual violence and child abuse.

When I met Betty in Guatemala City for our interview, she was wearing a gray off-the-shoulder T-shirt, jeans, and large silver earrings. She had copious amounts of silver eye shadow over her eyes, in addition to eyeliner. Betty told me that people in Guatemala could tell that she was not from there because of the style in which she wore her makeup. Betty also has several visible tattoos. One of her boyfriend's names—Ernie—is tattooed on her hand. She also has three dots—signifying "mi vida loca"—on her left hand. She has Betty Boop tattooed on her leg and the names of her five children on different parts of her body: One is on her breast; one on her arm; and one on her back. The tattoos on her back were visible because of her low-cut shirt. When I asked Betty about her tattoos, she told me she loves tattoos and wants to get more.

Betty arrived in the United States when she was 18 months old. Betty was born in Guatemala to a Salvadoran mother in 1981—she was 32 when we met. Betty's mother remarried in the United States. When Betty was 10, her stepfather began to sexually abuse her. Betty would tell her mother that she did not want to be around him, but her mother insisted that he was her father and that she had to respect and love him. Betty's mother ignored her pleas for help. When Betty was in 10th grade, he insisted that Betty stop going to school because she was finding boyfriends there. He wanted Betty to himself. He continued to regularly rape her until she was 18 and moved out of the house and into her boyfriend's house.

Betty's boyfriend read her diary and found out what her stepfather had done to her. He told her she had to tell the police. Betty said she did not want to be a snitch. He told her it wasn't being a snitch; she was protecting her younger sister, because her stepfather surely would do the same to her. Betty went to the police. The police set her up with a wire kit. She called her stepfather and told him that if he admitted to what he had done and apologized she would come home. He admitted to his actions and apologized. She turned the tape over to the police and they arrested him.

Betty's mother insisted Betty was lying and never forgave Betty for sending her husband to jail. Years of sexual abuse combined with her mother's rejection pushed Betty to drugs. She told me that when she takes crystal meth, she feels powerful. One of the visible signs of her long-term meth use is that she barely has any of her upper teeth. The few upper teeth that do remain appear to be just barely holding on.

When Betty spoke of the abuse, she put her head down in shame. When she talked about her mother's reaction, she couldn't hold back the tears. After all her mother had done to her, Betty still craves love and affection from her mother. Tears streamed down her face as she told me her mother told her she was nothing to her. Betty insisted that, after all of that, she still loves her mother. She has her mother's initials tattooed on her back.

After moving out of her mother's home, Betty lived on the streets. She occasionally had an apartment to call her own—usually with a boyfriend. She worked occasional jobs. But, mostly she sold drugs to support her habit.

Soon after moving out, Betty met and married a white American, Thomas, and she had her first child. As they both were addicted to meth, they handed the baby over to his mother. Betty tried several times to get clean but was unsuccessful. She had three more children and lost each of them to Child Protective Services. When Betty was pregnant with her fifth child, she decided to get clean again. She spent several months in rehab, had her baby, and then moved out into an apartment with her boyfriend and her baby. She resolved to herself that things would work out this time.

Things were going fairly well until one day Betty and her boyfriend got into a fight. He beat her extremely badly. Although she was covered in bruises, he told her that if she told the police, he would call immigration on her. Had Betty known her rights, she could have taken her baby, gone to a shelter, and applied for legalization under the Violence against Women Act (VAWA).

VAWA exists to protect women like Betty who are victims of domestic violence and whose partners hold their illegal status over their heads. Betty and her mother could have applied for legalization under VAWA when she was a teenager because of her stepfather's abuse, but they did not. She also could have applied in the aftermath of her boyfriend's abuse, but she still was not aware of this option.

Betty decided to press charges despite her boyfriend's threats. When the police came to arrest her boyfriend, he was alone with the baby. Thus, the police called Child Protective Services to come take the baby. When Betty found out, she was confused, hurt, and panicking, and she turned to alcohol and drugs, although she had been clean for months. When she went to claim her baby, she was high. The police officer arrested her for public intoxication.

When he arrested her, he said, "You're illegal, right?" Betty imagines her boyfriend must have told them about her status. He did exactly what he said he would do. And the police, instead of protecting Betty, arrested her and put an Immigration and Customs Enforcement (ICE) hold on her.

Betty spent several months in immigration detention. During this time, her case could have come to the attention of immigration lawyers. She qualified for legalization under VAWA. Although she had been on and off drugs for years, she did not have any serious criminal charges. She had one charge for paraphernalia and one for public intoxication and thus still may have qualified for VAWA. Without information or resources to pursue her case, Betty was deported to Guatemala, leaving behind her baby and all that she had known.

Ernesto's, Juan's, Noe's, and Betty's parents brought them to the United States with the hope that they would have a better future than in their countries of birth. Notably, all of their parents came to the United States fleeing tumultuous conditions in their countries of origin—conditions that were exacerbated by U.S. foreign policy. In a study of Guatemalan refugees in Mexico, a public health study found that every single one of them had experienced at least one traumatic event. Fully half reported witnessing the disappearance of others and 40 percent exhibited signs of depression (Sabin et al. 2003). The only person I interviewed who attributed her drug addiction to her relationship with parents was Betty.

However, I think it is important to take note of the fact that these four people, similar to most of my other interviewees who had trouble with drugs and alcohol, are also the children of people who fled their countries of birth.

A few weeks after I returned from Guatemala in 2013, I received a call from Betty, who wanted help regaining custody of her youngest child. I reached out to the Boston Post-Deportation Human Rights Project, and the attorney there put me in touch with a team of people willing to help Betty reunite with her child. But, ultimately, it became clear that, despite her desire to regain custody, and her legal right to do so, Betty was homeless and jobless in Guatemala and, practically speaking, was not going to be able to file the paperwork. She thus likely never will regain custody of her children.

Selling Drugs

Many of the deportees I interviewed arrived in neighborhoods in the United States where selling drugs was part of the neighborhood fabric. Whereas their parents worked long hours to keep the family afloat, these youth saw the easy money their peers were able to make in the underground economy. As Waters (1999) argues, "Part of becoming American for these teens is to expect expensive consumer goods, such as fashionable clothes and jewelry, from parents. . . . This difference between the expectations of the children and the limited resources available for the hard-working parents leads to an increased susceptibility on the part of the teens to the underground economy" (217). Many of the youth I interviewed had some experience in the low-wage economy. However, due to economic restructuring, the kinds of jobs available for young men in the city were limited and low-paying. Moreover, as Philippe Bourgois (2003) posits, the kinds of jobs available—office staff, restaurant work, cashiers, and messengers—are not amenable to the cultural styles and habits that young men learn on the streets. For this reason, black and Latino youth with low skills often find it hard to secure and keep employment. As we will see in the following narrative, Leroy was able to get a job as a cashier while he was in high school, but he preferred the income and lifestyle of the drug economy to that of a minimum-wage job.

Leroy, born in Jamaica in 1971, went to the United States as a child. Leroy arrived in a suburb of Washington, D.C., in 1978, when he was seven years old. Leroy's father came to the United States as an LPR and, a few years after he arrived, was able to legally bring his wife and children as well. When Leroy arrived in the United States, he had been separated from his father for several years but was young enough so that the transition was not difficult.

Leroy recalls being teased when he first arrived. Yet he quickly learned American ways and was able to blend in. Few of his high school friends even knew he was Jamaican. While in high school, Leroy had a series of part-time jobs, first at a liquor store and then at the dining hall at a local university. Then Leroy began to notice that other kids had things he did not. He told me:

> We used to play basketball. . . . You have some guys come across from D.C. over to our community and play basketball. And you see them with the beepers and the phone and yuh wonder how dem get dat. . . . And dem start say, "Mi like yuh game, yuh have a good basketball game" and ting. We start talking and him tell me how what kinda lifestyle he's involved in . . . you know, the fast money and I just got mixed up in it . . . and just started dealing.

Leroy's parents made enough to get by in the United States by working long hours. Initially, Leroy was able to accumulate the material goods he desired by working part-time after school. However, like many children of immigrants, Leroy opted for the "shortcut to the American dream" (Vigil, Yun, and Cheng 2004: 215). Similar to many American youth (Lay 2009), Leroy wanted material goods beyond what his parents and part-time jobs could provide for him, so he resorted to the underground economy to attain them. Once Leroy started dealing drugs, his parents put him out of the house and he was on his own. He moved in with his girlfriend, and they had a baby together.

Leroy was drawn to the allure of fast money and began selling drugs in high school. The early 1990s offered young men plenty of drug-selling opportunities. Leroy owned a BMW, then a Benz, and then a Corvette. Leroy's years of fast cars and money did not last long. In 1994, he sold a half an ounce of cocaine to an undercover agent and was arrested. He posted bail and went back home to his wife and newborn son. His wife was studying at the University of Maryland at the time. Leroy was on the run for a while, but the police kept asking his mother and his wife where he was. Eventually, he turned himself in. Leroy was sentenced to three years in prison for selling cocaine.

Leroy thought he would be released after serving his time. However, deportation laws changed while he was in prison. Even though a three-year drug sentence did not render Leroy eligible for mandatory deportation in early 1996 when he pled guilty, he faced mandatory deportation when he was released later that year.

When Leroy finished serving his time, he was transferred to an immigrant detention facility. He spent six months there and then was deported to Jamaica, a country he had not been to or even thought of for nearly 20 years. Having moved to the United States at the age of seven, he looked, talked, and walked like an American. Once in Jamaica, Leroy could only think of going back to the States. He tried three times through various illegal means but was unsuccessful; he has now resigned himself to remaining in Jamaica.

The stories of Dominicans who migrate to the United States as children make clear the challenges these children face when arriving in poor urban settings. Jay's family migrated to Brooklyn in the 1960s. Jay's grandmother traveled first, then his parents, leaving Jay with his aunt for two years. Jay was six years old when he entered the United States as an LPR in 1968. Jay completed all of his schooling in Brooklyn where he made friends with his Puerto Rican and Dominican neighbors. When Jay was growing up, his parents took him to the Dominican Republic regularly for vacation. But he felt no affinity for the country and stopped accompanying them as soon as he was old enough. Jay did not complete high school but got his GED when he was 19.

Jay told me he had been a "bad boy." He was arrested for the first time when he was 11 years old, for breaking a window. He did not actually serve time, however, until he was in his 20s. He saw his friends making quick money in Brooklyn, selling drugs. In addition, he tried cocaine and liked it. He started selling drugs, and soon after, in 1980, Jay was arrested for drug possession. In 1983, he was arrested again, this time for possession with intent to distribute 125 grams of cocaine. He was sentenced to 5 to 10 years, and he served five years in prison. While in prison, Jay married his girlfriend with whom he had a son, and he began to take college courses. When he was released in 1987, Jay found a job in a sports shop and soon became a manager. A couple of years later, Jay and his wife decided to relocate to Massachusetts to start their lives over.

Jay found a job with Coca-Cola in Massachusetts, and he moved up quickly in the company. However, even though he was out of New York, he still had trouble staying away from alcohol and drugs. When his addiction threatened his ability to do his job, Jay decided to go into rehab. While in rehab, Jay met various community leaders. They recognized his ability to connect with youth and his passion for his community, and they gave him a job at a community organization when he got out of rehab. Around the same time, Jay and his wife had their second son. After many years, things were finally going well for Jay. He became the director of a local AIDS prevention organization, and he counseled youth about drug abuse prevention. He had been clean for three years and had found his passion. Jay loved doing community work and was good at it.

Since Jay had been released from prison in 1987, he had been out on bail from the Immigration and Naturalization Service (INS), pending his immigration hearing. According to the applicable laws in 1987, he was eligible for a hearing where the judge would look at his case and would consider his family and community ties in the United States and the Dominican Republic. Jay felt good about the years of delay, as he was amassing lots of evidence of his rehabilitation and reincorporation into society. His wife and children were U.S. citizens. He was a community leader. He had no trouble with the law since his release. He was drug and alcohol free. He was confident he would win his case when it came up.

In 1996, however, a law was passed—the IIRIRA—that limited the judicial review of certain deportation cases. Under this new law, the judge could not take any of these factors into account. Jay's crime—narcotics possession with intent to distribute—made him automatically deportable. In 1997, 10 years after his release from prison, Jay finally had his hearing, under the new laws. He was deported to the Dominican

Republic, leaving his wife and two kids behind. Jay had moved from the Dominican Republic when he was six years old and had few connections there.

When Jay was deported, he tried to maintain ties with his wife and children. However, his household was thrown into a severe financial crisis with the loss of his income. That, combined with the stress of his deportation, led Jay and his wife to divorce, after having been together for 20 years. He talks to his children on the phone but feels as if his deportation has prevented him from raising his children as he would have liked. They visited him once in Santo Domingo, but their financial circumstances prevent them from seeing him regularly.

Jay had qualified for citizenship when he was 11. But his parents did not apply for him, and he never applied for himself. He told me he was not aware that he could be deported.

Jay's story is similar to that of other Dominicans I met who had arrived in New York City as young children in the 1960s and 1970s. These young men became Americanized and sought opportunities in the local drug economy in order either to consume drugs themselves or to purchase expensive consumer items. Their experiences were similar to those of the deportees that Nina Siulc (2009) recounts in her work with Dominican deportees. Siulc describes the experiences of several Dominican men who were raised in New York yet exiled to the Dominican Republic after being incarcerated in the United States. Siulc explains that Dominican neighborhoods in New York in the 1980s and 1990s were "flooded by drugs and targeted in law enforcement activities" (2009: 160). Siulc conducted an analysis of 500 deportee files and found that more than 90 percent had either an arrest or a conviction for drug-related crimes. Brotherton and Barrios (2011) found that nearly three-quarters of the Dominican deportees they interviewed had been deported on drug charges. Similar to Siulc, they point out that Washington Heights had some of the highest rates of poverty and crime in New York City in the 1970s, 1980s, and 1990s.

These youth arrived in urban areas of the United States, where their parents were able to secure working-class jobs that kept them afloat. In those cases where the parents arrived in the 1970s, their fathers often were able to secure manufacturing jobs that paid a decent wage and had benefits. However, the changes in the economies in the 1980s meant that those immigrants who arrived later, particularly the female immigrants, often had difficulty getting well-paid jobs. By the time their children came of age in the late 1980s and early 1990s, there often were few options for them in the low-skilled job market. Their parents often pushed these youth to go to college so that they would have better job prospects. However, many of these youth wanted to earn money right away and chose to sell drugs instead of following the path of their parents into the low-wage economy or the path of some of their siblings who did go to college.

The sociologist Robert Jackall, author of the book *Wild Cowboys* (1997), distinguishes between gangs, which are organized for protection, and criminal organizations, which are designed to earn a profit and sold drugs as a money-making enterprise. I found a similar trend in my work: The Jamaicans and Dominicans who lived on the East Coast talked about selling drugs to earn more money whereas Guatemalans who lived on the West Coast recounted stories of joining gangs for protection. They may have used their gang affiliation to carry out illegal acts such as car theft, but money making does not seem to have been their primary motivation for joining gangs.

Gangs

The Guatemalans were the only group in my study who mentioned gangs in reference to their experiences in the United States. Most of these Guatemalan deportees had migrated to Southern California as minors in the early 1980s, fleeing the violence in their country of birth. Many of them joined gangs for protection yet quickly found themselves in over their heads.

Geronimo's grandmother raised him in Guatemala City once his mother left for the United States in 1971, when he was three years old. When he was 11, his mother finally sent for him and his grandmother. Geronimo moved into a primarily black and Latino neighborhood in Los Angeles, where he almost immediately began to have problems with local gangs.

When Geronimo was 12, he joined a gang for protection, as many of his family members had done. When he was in 11th grade, he dropped out of high school. Geronimo began working in warehouses, where he was able to earn decent money. However, the lure of the streets was always present, and he and his friends stole cars and robbed people. He was in and out of jail. Geronimo married a woman and had two children with her. However, their relationship did not last very long, as Geronimo was in and out of jail. After his most recent stint in jail, he was deported.

Larry also explained that he joined a gang for protection. Larry arrived in the United States in 1988, when he was nine. He moved in with his mother, who worked as a live-in housekeeper in a middle-class neighborhood in Southern California. He has good memories of this time:

> Actually, it was nice, because she [his mother's employer] had two daughters, and I never had any brothers or sisters, so they were like my sisters, you know. And, I mean, they were like, awesome. . . . They were nice. It was nice. It wasn't, you know, like, they didn't push you away or anything. Like if they went somewhere, they would take me all the time with them. So, I was, like, part of their family also.

Larry and his mother lived with this family for a couple of years until their family was able to get their own place together, along with Larry's father. They lived first in Buena Park, when Larry was in fifth grade, and then in Bell Gardens, a working-class, primarily Latino neighborhood in southern Los Angeles. In this new neighborhood, Larry did not have the same protections he did in the wealthier neighborhood and his family faced a new set of problems.

In the 1990s, when Larry was in high school, gang activity was quite common in Bell Gardens, and most of his childhood friends joined gangs. Larry followed suit, and this got him into trouble. Three days after his 18th birthday in 1998, Larry and his friend were pulled over by police in East Los Angeles because the taillights on their car were broken. The police found 24 rocks of crack cocaine in the car. As a passenger, Larry was found guilty of possession of crack cocaine and was given three years of probation. Despite this felony conviction, Larry was able to get a job at LensCrafters, where he worked for six years. In 2001, Larry got married and lived with his wife and two children. She worked as an insurance agent, and they rented a three-bedroom apartment in Bell Gardens.

Larry was an undocumented immigrant, yet he was able to apply for legalization on the basis of his marriage to a U.S. citizen. To qualify for legalization, however, he would have to get his drug conviction expunged. Larry was in the process of expunging his record when he was arrested and deported in 2009.

Whereas Geronimo continued to get in trouble long after his teenage years ended, Larry had chosen to leave that lifestyle behind. However, immigration law does not distinguish between those noncitizens who have been rehabilitated and those who have not. One criminal conviction can be a deportable offense. When it is, noncitizens often face mandatory deportation.

Conclusion

The lives of the deportees profiled in this chapter were profoundly shaped by the United States legal context. Many of them faced extended separation from their parents due to strict immigration laws. When they arrived in the United States, this long separation affected their relationships with their parents. Many of the youth turned to their peers for support and friendship. However, these friendships often led to them getting into trouble. The problems they experienced and the trouble they got into were both a result of the choices they made and the opportunities they had in the United States. The consequences they faced were a result of the punitive nature of U.S. law enforcement and immigration laws. For these youth, there often were no second chances.

In some ways these youth assimilated to the local subcultures in their neighborhoods. However, their stories diverge a bit from the traditional tales of immigrant children gone awry insofar as these youth did not necessarily adopt an "oppositional pose" (Waters 1999: 307) and "reject the immigrant dreams of their parents." Instead, they sometimes maintained strong ethnic ties (especially the Jamaicans who are Rastafarians) and sometimes did not—as in the case of Leroy who rarely, if ever, thought about Jamaica. Many of them, like O'Ryan, continued to have high aspirations, despite their peripheral involvement in illegal activity.

And, others, like Jay, had reformed. None of this, however, could protect them from the consequences of heavy policing in their neighborhoods and a punitive law enforcement system.

Their ethnic ties also did not protect them. Mary Waters (1999: 302) argues that "some Jamaican Americans, for example, are experiencing downward social mobility while others are maintaining strong ethnic ties and achieving socioeconomic success." However, my interviews reveal that Jamaican youth who maintain strong ethnic ties are not protected from heavy policing because an outward display of Jamaicanness such as wearing dreadlocks does not seem to prevent police from presuming that these young black men are criminals. In fact, it may reaffirm their blackness and thus their presumed criminality. The same could be said of Latinos who outwardly express certain aspects of Latino culture that have come to be associated with criminality.

The U.S. economy relies on the labor of these immigrants' parents. In fact, their labor was essential as the United States made its economic transition from a manufacturing to a service-based economy. However, society must bear the social costs of the low-wage labor that this transition entailed: crime, alienation, and drug addiction. These stories render it clear that the opportunities available to these youth and their parents played a role in the deportees' paths to criminal activity and eventually deportation. However, through deportation, the United States is outsourcing some of the social costs of the low-wage economy to the countries of birth of these migrants—thereby reproducing the global inequality that led to migration in the first place. As we see in the stories of many of these deportees, instead of receiving a helping hand from the government, these children of immigrants encountered an iron fist.

This look at migrant incorporation through the lens of deportees provides a different take on immigrant incorporation patterns than we usually read. Of course, most immigrants, like most of the native-born, never have to deal with the criminal law enforcement apparatus in the United States. A consideration of those who do, however, provides us with unique insight into how the coercive arm of the state affects immigrant communities. It also permits us to see how enforcement is linked to deindustrialization and deprivation in immigrant communities. Youth who are discouraged, disengaged, or dispossessed find that one misstep can lead to arrest, incarceration, and deportation. Those who choose to sell drugs are often given no second chances. And those who fall into drug addiction are faced with punishment instead of rehabilitation.

The United States has spent a tremendous amount of money on the War on Drugs. However, a very small amount of that money goes to treatment and prevention of drug use whereas a lot of money is spent on enforcing drug laws and keeping people behind bars. Many of the deportees profiled in this chapter became addicted to drugs or otherwise involved in the drug trade. The prevalence of drug-related crimes will become even more apparent in the next chapter when I explore another crucial link in the neoliberal cycle: the spillover effects of the War on Drugs on immigrant communities in the United States.

Interlude

Juan Pablo

I was at the gym
On 145th and Broadway
On the second floor.
The police came inside
They arrested me
They put me in the paddy wagon.

They gave me a lawyer.
I asked him, "What are the charges?"
Possession, selling,
That I belonged to a narcotrafficking organization
That I earned more than $250,000 a week
They charged me

I was sure that
They had the wrong person
I thought I was going to leave
That they were going to see
That I had nothing to do
With what they were accusing me of

I was certain
They would realize
That I had nothing to do
With what they were accusing me of
I have nothing to do with that
They need to have some evidence

After being there for six months
My lawyer comes and says,
I got a plea bargain for you
Just plead guilty
If you plead guilty
You will be out in six months.

These people want to charge me with possession
Selling, conspiracy,
That I belong to a narcotrafficking organization
That I earn more than $250,000 a week
And they are going to make a deal
For me to leave in six months?

You know that I had nothing
I have nothing to do
With what they are accusing me of—
No, let's go to court

I am nervous
I am depressed
Because of what is going on with my life
I had little communication with the mother of my children
I don't talk to my kids.

My name was in the paper
That I belong to a narcotrafficking organization
That I earned $250,000
Who knows what else they wrote
In the newspaper.
This worried me.

Who would hire me?
No one wants to hire a criminal

I had faith in God;
I cried and I asked God
To prove my innocence.

The judge came and he told me,
These people have video
They have photos
They have you in a corner
You are going to go down if you go to court
If you still want the offer
I will give you one more chance

I said to the judge,
Mr. Judge
There is a little problem
It's that I can't plead guilty
Of something that I am not
That is the small problem we have

I don't care
If they have video
If they have pictures
They can have what they have
Because I have done nothing

No, Mister,
The mere fact of you being Dominican
Makes you guilty.

It started Wednesday.
Thursday the prosecutor brought his evidence and his witnesses
Friday I made my statement
At 11:00 am the jury began to deliberate
The time went by, went by
The time went by and nothing happened.
They did not reach an agreement on Friday.

I am certain,
I am certain,
I am certain I will be free.

On Tuesday,
The judge comes to me and says
Mister. You think that people
Who belong to a narcotrafficking organization
Can be found innocent?
When I was going to answer
A beep sounded,
The bell rang,
And the jury came out.

When the jury came out
They found me guilty,
They found me guilty of possession
And they found me not guilty of intent to sell.

So the judge gave me
Five years inside,
Five years outside.

4

The War on Drugs

Getting Ensnared by the Criminal Justice System

In 2005, Alex was awakened one morning at 5 am by Immigration and Customs Enforcement (ICE) agents pounding on his door. When the agents entered the apartment, his girlfriend began to scream, which woke the children. Their six children watched their mother cry and their father taken away. Alex told me he never wants to think about that day.

ICE agents raided his home because they had a warrant: A 1998 conviction for possession of four ounces of cocaine made Alex deportable. Alex spent 45 days in immigration detention and was deported to the Dominican Republic.

Why are ICE agents raiding homes in Washington Heights looking for small-time drug dealers? Why would Alex, who led a law-abiding life in the Dominican Republic, turn to selling drugs in New York City? And, why, as we will learn below, does deportation policy target Jamaicans and Dominicans?

Alex was born in Santo Domingo in 1963, in a neighborhood called 27 de Febrero, named for a Dominican national holiday. This poor neighborhood sits precariously on the edge of the Ozama River. Alex attended Catholic school and nearly finished high school, save for one French class. He worked as an electrician until 1993, when he went to the United States—with the hope of improving his financial situation.

The trip on a yola is dangerous and Alex said he would never do it again "even if someone paid [him] to do it." Alex spent 45 days in Puerto Rico before boarding a plane for New York. In a few days he found a job in Manhattan as a messenger.

Alex met and married a Puerto Rican woman in New York. Because she was a U.S. citizen, he was able to obtain legal permanent residency through the marriage. He also could bring his 14-year-old daughter to the United States in 1997, once he became a legal permanent resident (LPR), due to family reunification provisions in U.S. immigration law.

Alex's marriage to the Puerto Rican woman did not last. However, soon after they separated, he met a Dominican woman, with whom he had six more children. When I asked Alex what he missed most about the United States, he told me he missed his kids. He especially missed the weekends, when he would take his whole family out to eat. It was quite an endeavor to take his six kids and partner out to dinner, but it was the highlight of his week. (His eldest daughter, born in the Dominican Republic, had moved to Florida so he saw her less frequently.)

When he first migrated to the United States, Alex found it hard to make ends meet, to have enough money to send home to his family, and to save for his daughter's immigration, which cost him upward of $1,000. Alex decided to sell cocaine to augment his income, something he says "was a serious mistake."

In 1998, he was arrested and convicted of a drug offense. Alex spent one year and four months in jail and was released on parole in 2000. Alex decided he would not put his family at risk again, and he went back to working as a messenger. He was leading a law-abiding life when ICE agents raided his home, took him to detention, and deported him to Santo Domingo.

When a Dominican deported on criminal grounds arrives at the airport in Santo Domingo, Dominican immigration authorities meet him and take him to the police station where he is booked as if he were being arrested for a crime. The police take a picture with a number across his chest, fingerprint him, and record his personal information in a database. Alex is one of a few of my respondents who avoided this. He knew someone who could get him out of the airport, and thus he does not have "deportado" on his police record. As Alex points out, he only engaged in illegal activity in the United States. He told me, "Here, I have always been an exemplary person; here I have never been in prison; I have never been in trouble."

Back in Santo Domingo, Alex was able to work as an electrician, as he had prior to leaving for the United States. Because he was not recorded as a deportee, he has been able to open up a bank account, get a driver's license, and secure employment. He does not earn as much as he did in the United States, but he earns enough to get by in Santo Domingo, where he lives in his mother's house.

I asked Alex if he learned anything during his time in the United States. He paused and said the main thing he learned is that he never should have gone afoul of the law. "I never should have done that; this is what I learned. I should have eaten stones if I had to," he told me. It weighs heavily on him that he made a mistake that separated him from his children. When Alex left his daughter in the Dominican Republic, he did so with the intention of reuniting eventually. He knows he now has no real hope of living with his children again, as they all plan to stay in the United States.

Alex wishes he could bring his children to the Dominican Republic, but he could not afford school fees for the six who are still of school age. In addition, they were raised in the United States, and living in the Dominican Republic would be difficult. Alex has to be content with their occasional visits and frequent phone calls.

Some readers may hear Alex's story and think, "He was a guest in the country, and he violated the rules, so he had to go." Others may think that he served his time for selling drugs, and that should be enough punishment. Still others may find 16 months in prison—let alone deportation—harsh punishment for possession of cocaine. This chapter presents the stories of many other immigrants who have been convicted of crimes. I argue that the guilt or innocence of each deportee matters less than the broader significance of the policies and practices that lead to their punishments. Why is the U.S. government spending billions of dollars arresting, imprisoning, and deporting drug dealers and users?

The previous chapter dealt with immigrants who arrived as youth and considered how their neighborhoods and social networks led to them getting into trouble. This chapter looks at immigrants like Alex in order to develop an understanding both of how the neoliberal cycle transformed them from labor migrants to criminal deportees and of how their deportation reflects that cycle of displaced and disposable labor. This chapter focuses on Dominicans and Jamaicans only for three reasons: (1) They are by far the most likely to be arrested and deported on drug charges; (2) they are concentrated in New York City, which emerges in these stories as a hub for deportations based on drug charges; and (3) they are the groups most likely to be deported after having received legal residency.

Targeting Jamaicans and Dominicans

Mass deportation of Dominicans and Jamaicans is reverberating on these Caribbean islands. In December 2010, when I was in Santo Domingo, I was amazed at how easy it was to find deportees in a city with a population of three million people. One afternoon, for example, I asked my Dominican research assistant to set up two interviews with deportees for me. He arranged to meet two deportees at a park near the edge of the colonial city. When we got to our destination, there were at least two dozen men waiting for us—all deportees who wanted to be interviewed. These men were all from two neighborhoods in Santo Domingo: Maria Auxiliadora and Villa Francisca. I found myself in a very awkward position; there was no way I could interview all of them in any meaningful way. I was able to ask them, as a group, how long they had been in the United States and how they had gotten overseas. Nearly all of them had traveled illegally on yolas or aboard cargo ships, spent a short time in the United States, and had been deported on drug charges. This story provides a glimpse into the prevalence of this situation. Countless Dominican men travel to the United States aboard ships undetected, arrive in New York City, get involved in the drug economy, and are deported.

This chapter focuses on Dominicans and Jamaicans because, although these two groups are similar, they are distinct from other national origin groups in terms of deportation statistics. Only about 10 percent of all deportations involve LPRs, yet the rates are much higher for Dominicans and Jamaicans. Dominicans and Jamaicans are also the two groups most likely to be deported on drug charges. Overall, about a quarter of all criminal deportees are deported on drug charges: For Dominicans, it's about 80 percent and for Jamaicans, it's 40 percent (Headley et al. 2005; Siulc 2009; Brotherton and Barrios 2011). The Dominican Republic and Jamaica are the two countries with the highest rates of criminal deportees. In 2005, more than three-quarters of Dominican and Jamaican deportees were classified as "criminal aliens," compared to 15 percent of Guatemalans and 8 percent of Brazilians. When I chose these four countries as the places to carry out this research, I was curious as to why these differences existed. My interview data suggest that one salient reason is that, unlike Guatemalans and Brazilians, Dominicans and Jamaicans tended to live in primarily black neighborhoods in New York City and other large cities.

My calculations indicate that a Jamaican or Dominican male LPR has about a 1 in 12 chance of facing deportation. Between 1997 and 2006, 27,986 Jamaicans were deported from the United States (Glennie and Chappell 2010). About 10,000 of those deportees were LPRs of the United States, deported on criminal convictions.[1] That amounts to 4 percent of the LPR population of Jamaicans, estimated at 240,000 in 2007.[2] Because nearly all Jamaican deportees are men, this is about 8 percent of the male LPR population. If we look at deportation more generally and include the deportation of undocumented and temporary migrants, the percentage is actually larger. Since 1996, nearly 5 percent of the 637,000 Jamaican immigrants in the United States have been deported, a grave threat to this community as a whole in light of the havoc deportation wreaks on deportees and their families (Glennie and Chappell 2010). Most of the Jamaican and Dominican deportees I met had no intention of returning to their countries of origin prior to being deported. The majority left children, parents, and spouses in the United States. The 37 Jamaican deportees I interviewed left a total of 101 U.S. citizen children in the United States. The 46 Dominicans left a total of 77 U.S. citizen children behind. Deportation has wide-ranging consequences beyond the individual deportee.

Between 1996 and 2007, 87,884 of the 12 million LPRs in the United States were deported. The vast majority (90 percent) of LPR deportees are from 17 countries: These countries are Mexico, the Dominican Republic, Jamaica, El Salvador, Colombia, Philippines, Haiti, Guatemala, Trinidad and Tobago, Guyana, Honduras, Canada, United Kingdom, Portugal, Ecuador, Peru, and South Korea.[3] Proportionally speaking, Jamaicans and Dominicans were the LPRs most likely to be deported. About 10 percent of LPR deportees have been Jamaican, yet Jamaicans make up fewer than 2 percent of all LPRs. About 20 percent of them have been Dominican, yet Dominicans make up fewer than 4 percent of the LPR population. Both Jamaicans and Dominicans are about five times as likely as other legal permanent residents to be deported. The

1996 laws, discussed in previous chapters, made it fairly easy to deport LPRs, even for relatively minor drug convictions.

Deportation and drug laws in the United States are very strict: Anyone who is not a citizen that police catch with illegal drugs faces deportation. This strictness demands selective enforcement. It would be impossible to deport the millions of people who lack the legal right to remain in the United States. And it is not feasible to punish the tens of millions of citizens and noncitizens who use and sell drugs. Because the laws must be selectively enforced, law enforcement agents target the most vulnerable populations (Alexander 2010).

The explanation for why Jamaican and Dominican LPRs are deported in numbers disproportionate to the population is complex, but one clear contributing factor is that, in the War on Drugs, police have targeted neighborhoods where Jamaicans and Dominicans live. My conversations with Jamaican and Dominican deportees make it clear that these men lived in areas with a heavy police presence and they experienced racial profiling. Many deportees recounted a routine stop in which police searched their cars. Others told me they were stopped and frisked on a street corner. The combination of racial profiling and heavy policing renders these two groups susceptible to deportation.

Structural Racism and Mass Deportation

It is well established in criminological scholarship that blacks and Latinos are more often the targets of law enforcement than whites or Asians, and this is due in large part to the War on Drugs (Feagin 2000; Pettit and Western 2004; Western 2006; Alexander 2010). The criminal justice system systematically disadvantages black and Latino men. In a time of skyrocketing incarceration, even though black and white men have similar levels of criminal activity, black men are seven times more likely than white men to be imprisoned, and Latinos are four times more likely than whites (Feagin 2000; Collins 2004; Western 2006).

Racism in the criminal justice system has severe implications for black and Latino immigrants. Many Jamaicans, Dominicans, and Haitians are phenotypically indistinguishable from African Americans and often experience the same set of resource deprivations and racist ideologies and practices that lead to the mass incarceration of black men.

Immigrants from Latin America often live in heavily policed black or Latino neighborhoods. Consequently, immigrants of African and Latin American descent get jailed and eventually deported at higher rates than immigrants of European or Asian descent who do not face the same set of structural barriers, prejudices, and discriminatory actions as blacks and Latinos do. Whereas the immigrant population includes many whites and Asians, blacks and Latinos have an almost exclusive presence among detainees and deportees (Dow 2004; Golash-Boza 2012). Law enforcement criminalizes the behavior of Jamaican and Dominican men living in urban areas. They can be subject to searches on street corners, or they can be pulled over on expressways for almost any reason (Alexander 2010). Their structural location in the United States creates a situation where they are more likely to be involved in the drug economy than the average person, so they are more likely to be caught.

Because law enforcement agents cannot possibly fully enforce drug laws, they must be strategic with their resources and enforcement tactics. Because of stereotypes that drug law violators are black, combined with the relatively little political power of poor black communities, law enforcement agents have targeted open-air drug markets in poor black communities for their enforcement efforts. In her 2010 book, The New Jim Crow, Michelle Alexander argues that

> the clear majority of Americans of all races have violated drug laws in their lifetime. In fact, in any given year, more than one in ten Americans violates drug laws. But due to resource constraints (and the politics of the drug war), only a small fraction are arrested, convicted, and incarcerated. In 2002, for example, there were 19.5 million illicit drug users, compared to 1.5 million drug arrests, and 175,000 people admitted to prison for a drug offense. (101)

The United States sends black men to prison on drug charges at 13 times the rate of white men, yet 5 times as many whites use illegal drugs as blacks. Although whites are much more prevalent among users, blacks are much more likely to end up incarcerated (Alexander 2010).

The United States has not always had harsh drug laws: Most of the current laws are a product of the War on Drugs. When President Ronald Reagan declared the War on Drugs in 1982, fewer than 2 percent of

Americans viewed drugs as the most important issue facing the nation. And crack cocaine had not yet hit the streets. What, then, started the War on Drugs?

Alexander (2010) points out that the War on Drugs took off just as inner-city communities were experiencing economic collapse. Blue-collar factory jobs were disappearing quickly and unemployment was rising. Loïc Wacquant (2009) and Alexander (2010) both argue that mass incarceration is designed to warehouse a low-skilled, expendable, disposable labor force. The criminal justice system is not just about controlling crime; it strives to control people, especially people of color.

I make a similar argument to explain mass deportation. Mass deportation is not designed to remove all unauthorized immigrants; instead it is designed to remove surplus labor and to keep labor compliant. William Robinson (2014: 95) explains that "the neoliberal revolution unleashed by globalization marked a transition from the Fordist-Keynesian social structure of accumulation to a savage global capitalism that entailed 1) a redisciplining of labor through globalization, flexibilization, high un- and under employment, and the dismantling of the welfare system, and 2) the development of vast new social control systems, including prison-industrial complexes and transnational immigrant labor control systems."

A consideration of how mass deportation happens is a critical example of what Robinson (2014) describes. In addition, this analysis allows us to see how the disciplining of labor through social control systems works together with the disciplining of labor through immigration control. Dominican and Jamaican immigrants are often caught up in the crossfire of both systems of control, which have created mass incarceration and mass deportation.

Alexander (2010) points out that there are nearly 20 million drug users in the United States, only a fraction of whom are in prison. Similarly, the United States deports only 400,000 of its 11 million undocumented immigrants each year. Mass deportation, similar to mass incarceration, targets specific populations—those perceived as expendable. When we examine mass deportation alongside mass incarceration, it becomes clear how the War on Drugs and War on Terror work together. The War on Drugs has been carried out in an effort to exercise social control over urban populations. Concomitantly, the rise in deportations in recent years has been folded into the broader project of the War on Terror.

As I explain in *Immigration Nation* (Golash-Boza 2012), mass deportation has been made possible because of an enormous infusion of money into government agencies in the aftermath of the terrorist attacks of September 11, 2001. The U.S. government's launch of the War on Terror involved the creation of the Department of Homeland Security (DHS) in 2003. DHS took over the operations of the Immigration and Naturalization Service (INS) as well as those of other agencies, including the Federal Marshall Service, the Secret Service, and the U.S. Coast Guard, that were not part of the INS. The creation of such an overarching and broad-based agency as DHS was the most significant transformation of the U.S. government's security structure in over a half century. For immigration policy, the transfer of immigration law enforcement from the Department of Justice (DOJ) to the DHS was a critical moment; immigration policy took on new meaning when it became central to the War on Terror. In my interviews, it became clear that mass deportation is also directly related to the War on Drugs.

The term "mass incarceration" has been deployed to explain how and why the United States locks up a higher percentage of its citizens than any other country as well as much more than in the past. The term "mass deportation" draws from the conceptual logic of "mass incarceration."

There are 242 million adults living in the United States and 2 million of them are behind bars.[4] The scale of deportation is much smaller but the comparison is legitimate insofar as there are 11 million undocumented immigrants and another 13 million LPRs, for a total of 24 million noncitizens who live permanently in the United States.[5] Any noncitizen can be removed from the United States, although undocumented immigrants are at greater risk than LPRs.

In 2013, there were 368,644 removals. At least 133,551 of these removals involved people who were living in the United States—so-called interior removals.[6] A very conservative estimate of mass deportation, then, which only focuses on interior removals and takes into account the entire noncitizen population, reveals that 0.56 percent of the potentially removable population was removed in 2013. In contrast, 0.82 percent of the U.S. adult population is behind bars and a much smaller fraction entered prison in 2013. Given the relative similarity between the numbers, as well as the dramatic increase in the raw numbers over the past 20 years, I describe the current moment of immigration law enforcement as "mass deportation."

Scholars of neoliberalism and urban decline, like David Harvey (2005) and Loïc Wacquant (2009), draw attention to the relationship between the growth of the criminal justice system and the rise of neoliberalism in the United States. Wacquant (2009) argues that there is a "close link between the ascendancy of neoliberalism . . . and the deployment of punitive and proactive law-enforcement policies" (1). Wacquant notes that both welfare policies and the War on Drugs are designed not to protect the poor but to transform them into "compliant workers fit or forced to fill the peripheral slots of the deregulated labor market" (101). This argument has great resonance with the experiences of deportees.

As Wacquant and Harvey suggest, neoliberalism requires docile workers willing to work for less than a living wage. Noncitizens in the United States provide this necessary labor force. However, as inequality has increased and real wages have dropped, workers are finding it increasingly difficult to get by. Some choose to make forays into the informal or illegal economy to make ends meet. This choice, however, entails enormous risk. Noncitizens who choose to earn a living wage by working in the underground economy instead of becoming low-wage workers in the formal economy face the prospect of incarceration and deportation. Their deportation serves as an example for other workers who might entertain the thought of eschewing low-wage labor.

Immigrants who keep their heads down, stay away from drugs, and accept work in low-wage jobs rarely get deported. The deportation of those who stray from this path serves as an example to others who might consider fighting for better conditions or seeking out alternative sources of income. The marginalization of people of color in the United States and of deportees in the Dominican Republic, Jamaica, and Guatemala underscores the divide between "good" and "bad" immigrants and contributes to self-imposed social control.

Mass Deportation and the War on Drugs

Dominican and Jamaican immigrants who landed in New York City in the 1980s and 1990s found neighborhoods devoid of opportunities to succeed in the formal economy yet full of opportunities in the informal economy (Brotherton and Martin 2009). Some of these immigrants resisted the temptation to sell drugs, whereas other immigrants, similar to their U.S.-born counterparts, decided to seek out their fortune in the drug economy. Many of these immigrants were subsequently deported as criminal aliens.

In 2012, the United States deported 225,390 people as "criminal aliens," the largest number of criminal deportees in its history.[7] Few scholars have sought to determine why criminal deportations have soared. In 2012, the sociologists Ryan King, Michael Massoglia, and Christopher Uggen published a study that examined criminal deportations between 1907 and 2005. They found that, between 1941 and 1986, criminal deportations correlated well with unemployment rates, yet after 1986 the relationship between criminal deportation and unemployment was considerably weaker. Instead, criminal deportations began to correspond with incarceration rates. King, Massoglia, and Uggen (2012) attribute the rise in criminal deportations since 1987 to "a more general punitive turn in U.S. punishment" (1819). The punitive turn is real. However, King and colleagues likely would have found more of a correlation if they had focused on two aspects of the labor market: gender disparities and inner-city unemployment. Mass deportation may not correlate closely with unemployment generally, but it clearly relates to extreme unemployment in central cities, particularly for young black and Latino men. As Alexander (2010) and others argue, the War on Drugs specifically and mass incarceration generally emerged more as a response to unrest in central cities than in response to problems associated with drug abuse or other crime.

Nearly all of the Dominican deportees I met were deported because of drug-related offenses. They were arrested for a drug offense, charged, convicted, served time, and then deported. Many of these deportees described the Washington Heights neighborhood of New York City as overrun with drugs. The overwhelming presence of illegal drugs in the neighborhood, and the large number of Dominicans involved in the illegal drug trade, facilitated the decisions that led to deportation. When I asked Dominicans what they did in New York City, time and time again they told me, "*Me tire pa'la calle.*" This literally translates as "I put myself out on the street" and refers to the fact that they began to sell drugs. When I asked one respondent if he had a job in New York, he responded, "*No, nada, como todos, trabajas en la calle*" (no, nothing, like everyone else, you work on the streets [selling drugs]). The fact that Dominican deportees could simply say "I worked on the streets" and thereby communicate that they were selling drugs indicates the extent to which this practice is widespread among Dominican men in New York.

In my research, it became apparent that nearly all Dominicans and a large number of Jamaicans deported on drug charges were first arrested in New York City. The disproportionate number of deportees that I interviewed who had been initially arrested in New York City led me to research the New York Police Department (NYPD). It turns out that the NYPD has come under scrutiny in recent years for racial profiling and discriminatory policing.

Deporting Drug Users

The NYPD began an aggressive program in the 1990s to arrest people found smoking marijuana in public. This policy was a fairly big shift from the former policy that had decriminalized the possession of small amounts of marijuana. By 2000, smoking marijuana in public had become the most common misdemeanor arrest in New York City, accounting for 15 percent of all arrests of adults (Golub et al. 2007). Between 1997 and 2007, about 400,000 people were arrested and jailed for possessing small amounts of marijuana. Half of all arrestees were black, even though blacks only make up about a quarter of the city's population and whites are more likely than blacks to smoke marijuana.[8] The arrest and eventual deportation of casual marijuana smokers is part of the NYPD Quality of Life initiative, designed to increase tourism and public safety in the city (Golub et al. 2007).

Racism in these Quality of Life initiatives gains saliency when these policies result in deportation, instead of just a few hours in jail. The combination of punitive drug laws with harsh immigration laws means that any noncitizen caught smoking marijuana in public twice could face deportation, no matter how long they have lived in the United States, no matter how many U.S. citizen children they have, and regardless of their lack of ties to their home country.

Duaine, for example, was deported for smoking marijuana. Duaine traveled to the United States in 1998 as an LPR when he was 35 years old. One afternoon in 2003, he was hanging out in Brooklyn, smoking a marijuana cigarette with some of his friends. The police approached them and found $50 worth of marijuana on Duaine. He was convicted of selling marijuana and sentenced to one month in jail. In 2005, Duaine was caught smoking marijuana again—this time he was sentenced to 15 days in jail. As he had two drug charges, even though they were minor, these constituted an aggravated felony and Duaine was deported.

I asked Duaine if he had ever thought about moving back to Jamaica while he was in New York. He responded, "Not really, you know; I was planning to get my kids back there and my girlfriend as she would be my wife, so that my kids could have a better life." Duaine's plans to settle in the United States and bring his family were foiled when he was deported for smoking marijuana.

Kareem's case is similar. He was also an LPR.

Twice I got caught smoking. One time I was walking with it in my pocket . . . but it wasn't any major amount, just a little smoking portion. But now it's really serious because it doesn't matter like, whatever, they lock you up for if it is a misdemeanor or what, now they add it up. If it is more than one time—like habitual . . . they start putting them together and making them an aggravated felony.

In Jamaica, both Kareem and Duaine had grown accustomed to smoking marijuana on a regular basis. Lax enforcement in Jamaica and widespread acceptance of marijuana smoking in the United States made them unprepared for strict enforcement in New York. Neither realized after the first conviction that a second conviction, however minor, would lead to deportation. In fact, a 2010 Supreme Court decision,[9] *Carachuri-Rosendo v. Holder*, stated that immigrants who are legally in the United States do not face automatic deportation for minor drug offenses. They still can be deported, but they also can apply for cancellation of removal, which would allow them to plead their case and argue that they merit staying in the United States.

Mr. Carachuri-Rosendo, the defendant, was brought to the United States from Mexico by his parents as an LPR when he was five years old. In 2004, he was sentenced to 20 days in jail for possession of fewer than two ounces of marijuana. The next year, he was sentenced to 10 days in jail for having a single tablet of Xanax, an anti-anxiety drug, without a prescription. Because this amounted to two drug offenses, Mr. Carachuri-Rosendo was deemed an aggravated felon and faced mandatory detention and deportation. With this court decision, however, Mr. Carachuri-Rosendo was able to apply for cancellation of removal. Kareem and Duaine, in contrast, were deported before being able to benefit from this decision and thus were ineligible to apply for cancellation of removal, which could have allowed them to avoid their deportations.

Deporting Drug Sellers

In Santo Domingo, the neighborhoods of Maria Auxiliadora, Los Guandules, Villa Francisca, and 27 de Febrero are full of Dominican deportees, many of whom tell a very similar story. They grew up in poverty, dropped out of high school, were unable to find work that allowed them to make ends meet, and thus decided to try their luck overseas. These four neighborhoods abut the Ozama River, which has a direct outlet to the sea. These young men watched their friends, neighbors, and relatives stow away on cargo ships or venture aboard yolas, make it to Puerto Rico, then go to the mainland United States. Eventually, they would work up the nerve to go themselves. Some tried time and time again before making it. Once they made it to Puerto Rico, they would work there just long enough to get the airfare to New York City. In New York, these young men would either go straight into the drug economy or work for a few months at a bodega or other low-wage job before being lured to the higher wages and flexible schedules of the drug economy. After a few months to a few years in the drug economy, they would be arrested, jailed, and then deported to the Dominican Republic, with nothing to show for their travails except stories of life in New York.

The Dominican deportees described their occupations to me in Santo Domingo prior to emigration: They were electricians, construction workers, handymen, among other jobs. They were not drug dealers in Santo Domingo. There, they worked in the formal or informal economy, scraping out a living as best as they could. Many risked their lives to get to the United States. Why, then, would they risk everything by going straight into the drug economy in New York?

Edison, for example, had worked in the formal economy in Santo Domingo and in Puerto Rico, his first destination in the United States. However, when he arrived in Washington Heights in 1987, he did not look for work in the formal labor market. His Dominican friends steered him directly to the informal economy, where he sold cocaine and marijuana. I asked Edison why he did not look for a job. He responded, "Because I did not know much about that, about life over there; it is not easy to find a job." Peggy Levitt (2001) attributes the concentration of Dominicans in the low-wage sector of the labor market in Boston to their social networks. In New York's Washington Heights, we can see a parallel process: Dominican friends and relatives often steer new migrants directly into the drug market after their arrival.

Other Dominican deportees told me a similar story: They had arrived as undocumented migrants in Washington Heights, then immediately began to sell drugs. None of my respondents sold drugs in Santo Domingo prior to leaving or upon returning. "Selling drugs is what you do in New York," deportees would tell me. Many of them pointed out that, as undocumented migrants, they had few opportunities in the formal labor market, yet opportunities to sell drugs were abundant. Many worked in the formal economy at first and then turned to selling drugs because it seemed more lucrative.

Jamaican respondents described a similar path from the legal to the illegal economy. Delroy, for example, arrived in the United States in 1970, when he was 16. His mother enrolled him in high school in Harlem, but he dropped out after just three months. "It wasn't no picnic," he told me. "The kids back then used to tease you, you know, and tell you, 'Go back to your country, you coconut.'" To avoid teasing about his clothes and his way of talking, Delroy dropped out of high school and went to trade school. He learned welding and got a job in Massachusetts, where he worked the third shift at night, and it was cold. He stayed there for a few months and then got a job at a shipyard in New York. That work was also hard and cold, and he eventually turned to selling marijuana. He explained how he was lured into the black market:

You could work yourself and all that, but . . . seeing all this glitter. This glitter, flashy cars. You hafta be real strong. I ain't gonna lie. You gotta be real strong. . . . People that don't travel, they don't know that you got poor people in America. You got people that can't afford stuff in America. . . . Because once you travel and, you know, you come back to the islands it's, like, you know, you some king of the hill. It's like my mom used to tell me, "Everyone could own a house."

Delroy didn't stay in the drug economy consistently, however. He went back and forth from selling drugs to working in the formal economy. "A lot of people got jobs but still got to hustle to make ends meet. I worked in a laundry. I didn't stay there too long but most of the time I was dealing. 'Cause the money was good." Delroy was eventually caught and deported in 1999, after serving time for selling drugs to an undercover agent. When he was deported, he left behind his partner and their 16-year-old daughter.

Walter moved to New York City from Kingston in 1991 when he was 26. He worked as an electrician for a while. However, he saw that his cousins were making more money in the drug trade and Walter decided to get involved. Walter began to move large amounts of cocaine and made quite a bit of money. He was convicted on drug conspiracy charges in 2000 and spent five years in prison. In 2005, he was deported back to Jamaica. I asked Walter why he chose to sell drugs in the United States, even though he was a skilled electrician. He responded:

It was a much more faster way for me at the time to accumulate a certain amount of wealth fast. And, you know, putting things together and then, you know, the sort of life when you get involved in that, you know, the fast life, the celebrity style lifestyle, you know, in America. You know, with all that you get caught up in with some of that and the rapper style and most of those, you know. So you get caught up in some of that, you understand me; so it's just really the bling world.

In the Dominican Republic and Jamaica, stories of abundance in the United States circulate. When migrants arrive in New York, the illegal economy offers their only path to the American Dream as they had imagined it. And, unlike working a low-wage job, it further permits them to send money home to their families who are expecting remittances.

Many Dominican deportees told me similar stories; they worked for years in the legal economy before deciding to sell drugs. Fermin, for example, told me, "Yeah, I left work in the supermarket because they paid very little; I began to work on the streets, selling drugs." All of the deportees who transitioned from the formal to the informal economy did so for the same reason: They wanted to earn more money. Most of the time their desire to earn more money was fueled by the need to send money home to the Dominican Republic. Dominican men often feel obliged to be providers, for their families both in the Dominican Republic and in the United States. As they were not able to earn enough money to achieve their material desires in the traditional economy, they turned to the drug economy.

Jose Carlos, for example, worked for over a year in carpentry in Puerto Rico before selling drugs. I asked him about his experience in Puerto Rico:

> T: How did you like Puerto Rico when you arrived?
> JC: Well, at first, everything was great. Then I had to hit the streets.
> T: Why?
> JC: Because I was not making enough to send home and to have some-
> thing for myself over there. I had to hit the streets.

Like many migrants, Jose Carlos felt compelled to send money home and the drug business allowed him to do that. As Pedro describes it, "I was impressed by my friends, people I was born and grew up with, who were over there, selling drugs on the corner. I saw them with gold chains, nice cars, with money." Pedro turned to selling drugs, was caught, arrested, convicted, and deported.

Dominicans in Washington Heights tend to see street-corner drug selling as a man's job. Female migrants receive no encouragement to stand on the corner and sell drugs. Women have roles in the drug economy, but they are often protected from being arrested (Anderson 2005). The one female Dominican deportee whom I met who was deported on criminal charges got into trouble via her white American spouse. Federica's husband was addicted to drugs and engaged in robbery to support his habit. When he was arrested, Federica was arrested as well because the stolen goods were in their home. She was convicted as an accomplice.

I often asked Dominican deportees what their girlfriends or wives thought about their illegal activity. They insisted that they kept those two lives separate, and they made sure that their female partners were either unaware of their involvement or kept completely separate. One deportee, for example, told me he lived in Brooklyn with his wife and kids, yet he carried out his drug-selling activities in a separate location in Washington Heights. Women benefit from the profits of drug selling through their partners' household contributions. By the same token, their partners' arrest, prison time, and deportation affect them severely.

Not all Dominican and Jamaican male deportees deported on drug charges were selling or using drugs. In the next section, I turn to the stories of those who only worked in the legal economy yet found themselves implicated in the drug economy.

Deporting People on the Fringes of the Drug Economy

Many black and Latino immigrants in New York shun the drug economy and work honest jobs. However, associating with anyone in the drug economy may result in arrest. Several deportees insisted to me that they never sold or used drugs, but they were picked up in police raids because of their friends' or neighbors' activities. Some were found in houses or cars where drugs were stored. Others were implicated because they told undercover agents where they could get drugs. Like Evangelio, they proclaimed innocence.

A deeply religious man, Evangelio took his time to tell me his life story, enunciating each word, and sounding as if he was preaching a sermon at times, especially when he spoke of his childhood poverty and perseverance. But when he began to tell me how he was arrested and deported, his speech pattern quickened and it became evident that these events had deeply scarred him.

Evangelio made his living in New York selling clothes door to door. This required him to visit people in their homes and to spend time walking the streets of Washington Heights. One afternoon, Evangelio went with a friend to another Dominican's house. The police arrived just after they did. The police found drugs and a scale in the apartment. Everyone was arrested. Evangelio explains that the police, the judge, and the lawyer all wanted him to plead guilty. As they saw it, he was guilty, as it was clear that both he and the drugs were in the apartment. But, Evangelio, for moral and religious reasons, did not want to plead guilty when the drugs were not his. He became more and more agitated as he recounted this story to me. He felt a severe injustice had been committed against him. He lived in the United States for 12 years without getting into any trouble with the police, without ever touching drugs. He had a U.S. citizen wife and three U.S. citizen children. Despite his claims to innocence, he was convicted, served time, and deported.

Juan Pablo, whose harrowing border-crossing story I told in chapter 2, and whose words make up the Interlude to this chapter, also told me he had never touched drugs in his life. Juan Pablo stayed for a few years in Puerto Rico, before moving to Washington Heights, where he got a job in a bodega. Soon, Juan Pablo got a better-paying job in construction, through people he met at the bodega. He began earning $15 an hour and was able to support himself in New York. In 1996, he met a Puerto Rican woman. They had a daughter in 1998 and a son in 2002. In 2001, they got married and Juan Pablo applied for legalization. Juan Pablo's residency application was approved, but he never actually received his green card. Juan Pablo eventually was able to start his own small construction company, and he began to earn good money with this business venture.

Juan Pablo told me that he had few friends in New York. Mostly, he worked and spent time with his family. On weekends, he would go with his wife and kids on the ferry or to the park or the movies. Juan Pablo also went to the gym on a regular basis. At the gym, Juan Pablo had a couple of buddies and they would help each other lift weights. One day, one of his gym buddies asked him to hold a set of keys for him while he went to do something. Juan Pablo agreed. Not too long after, the police came into the gym and arrested Juan Pablo and charged him with possession, selling, and narcotrafficking. He was confident it was a case of mistaken identity and that he would be cleared. Juan Pablo's bail was set at half a million dollars. Unable to pay the bail, Juan Pablo spent 14 months in jail awaiting his trial. This experience was very stressful.

I began to get depressed about what was happening to me. I had little communication with the mother of my children or with my children. And my work had gone up in smoke because I wasn't answering calls. And surely my name had appeared in the newspaper that I was a major drug trafficker. I was worried about all this—who was going to give me work after all of this? Who would want to hire a criminal to work in their house? All this time, I had faith in God. I cried and asked God to prove my innocence. . . .

In court, the prosecutor showed pictures of Juan Pablo knocking on a door on Broadway. Juan Pablo explained that the house was where a woman who cooked his lunch lived. They showed a video of him walking to the gym on Broadway, where Juan went after work. Finally, it came to light that the main piece of evidence they had was a key. The key that Juan's gym buddy had asked him to hold was the key to a major stash of drugs.

I didn't have a lot of friends, but there were two guys at the gym who I used to chat with. On that day—February 27, 2006—one of them asked me for a favor, to hold a key for him. When the police arrested me, I had the key with me. But the police never asked me about the key so that I could tell them that the key belonged to someone else. . . . When the trial was over, after they showed all the evidence, and the two police witnesses spoke, the jury began to deliberate. That was at 11:00 am on Thursday. Time went by, more time, and nothing. They couldn't come to a conclusion. They deliberated all day Friday and still didn't come to a conclusion. My lawyer told me they would return on Monday. Monday was a holiday, so it had to wait to Tuesday. . . . At noon, they finally called me. . . . They found me guilty of possession of cocaine. The judge gave me five years in prison, and five years of parole.

Juan Pablo spent hours explaining to me each detail of what happened to him, but it seemed like he still was not sure of how it all went down. It was unreal. His case was still being appealed when he was deported.

The excruciating details that Juan Pablo was able to provide with regard to his case render his story believable. However, holding the key made it possible to charge him with drug possession. The judge and jury have no way of confirming whether or not he knew what the key was for, and thus they could convict him on a possession charge because they could prove that he in fact had the key in his possession and that the key was to a place where drugs were stored.

Several Jamaican men also recounted a similar story: They were arrested on drug charges right in their neighborhood because of their association with people who sold drugs. Living in heavily policed, primarily black neighborhoods makes Jamaican and Dominican men a target for law enforcement. As a counterexample, the Brazilians I interviewed ended up in Danbury, Connecticut; Marietta, Georgia; and in small towns in Massachusetts. These places—like many places in the United States—do have drug economies. However, Brazilians were not networked into this drug economy and therefore were rarely presented with the opportunity to sell drugs and did not find themselves surrounded by drug dealers. The arrest narrative of Marcos, who is originally from Jamaica, makes it clear how immigrants who live in primarily black neighborhoods can easily be susceptible to arrest.

Marcos, an LPR who worked as an electrician, was living with his girlfriend and their children in Washington, D.C., in a rented room in a shared house in a primarily African American neighborhood. One afternoon, Marcos and his girlfriend were inside the house and Marcos heard a person outside asking if anyone in the house was selling drugs. Marcos went outside to ask him to leave. This person, whom Marcos suspected to be an undercover police officer, asked Marcos where he could buy cocaine. Marcos told him he didn't know anyone who sold drugs. Marcos explained what happened next:

> After that I heard a knock on my door and it was one of the guys. The guys outside sold the police coke and one of the guys ran past my door shouting, "Police!" . . . When I came outside the house, the police said, "Freeze and don't move, put your hands up." I didn't have nothing. The only thing in my pocket was my phone, wallet, and driver's license. After I was out there for a long time waiting for them to finish searching the house. They did not find what they were looking for.
>
> When we went to Supreme Court, the judge told us that they could not do anything because the warrant they had was outdated. When the

judge asked them what they found, the police said no drugs, no guns. The judge told me that I was free to go. You are your kids' father. Go ahead. They told me I can't get back my passport until the case is finished. I was at my house for three weeks, then I saw a letter come to my house saying I must return back to court. When I went back to court, they said I was charged for aiding and abetting in trafficking.

Marcos was sentenced to five years in prison and was deported after serving his time. According to Marcos, he was not involved in the drug trade and was simply a victim of circumstance. I have no way of knowing whether or not Marcos divulged the entire truth to me. But racial profiling, heavy policing in black neighborhoods, and a woefully inadequate public defender system in Washington, D.C., conspire to make black immigrants like Marcos vulnerable to such victimization while whites and Asians of any nationality often are not. Had Marcos lived in a primarily white neighborhood, it is extremely unlikely that he would have been subject to a similar police raid targeting his neighbors.

Drug laws and drug enforcement make it entirely possible to be found guilty of drug crimes without any active involvement in the drug trade. Many deportees told me that they were not guilty of the drug charges that prompted their deportation. Most deportees who asserted their innocence explained to me that they were riding in a car where drugs were found or they were in an apartment where drugs were found. I am not in a position to verify their statements. In fact, even while protesting their innocence most admitted that they were in a car or apartment where police found drugs, which could render them guilty in a U.S. court of law. Who owned the drugs or meant to use or sell them has little legal importance, which means that just living in a neighborhood flooded with drugs that is heavily policed raises these men's risk of being arrested, charged, and convicted of drug crimes even if they have no personal involvement. Their families in the Dominican Republic and Jamaica who would no longer benefit from their remittances and their families left in the United States who have to carry on without them pay dearly for these laws.

Of course I wonder whether Juan Pablo, Evangelio, and Marcos were wrongly convicted, but they illustrate the way the neoliberal cycle conspires to control the workforce, regardless of their guilt or innocence. Stories like theirs circulate in the Dominican and Jamaican communities. The circulation of this story—that you don't have to actually use or sell drugs to be convicted and deported—creates a situation where the line you have to walk to avoid being deported is increasingly straight and narrow. To avoid deportation, you have to be sure to never associate with drug users or sellers. For many Dominican and Jamaican immigrants, this can be an extremely difficult task.

Jonathan Inda (2013: 294) argues that, under neoliberalism, people

> are expected to adopt an entrepreneurial disposition toward life and insure themselves (using market mechanisms) against the vicissitudes of ill health, accidental loss, unemployment, and anything else that could potentially threaten their contentment. Significantly, in placing such a strong emphasis on individual responsibility, neoliberal rule has tended to draw a rather marked distinction between the proper neoliberal citizen who secures his/her own well-being through prudence and active self-promotion and the deviant subject—the criminal, the poor, the homeless, the welfare recipient—who is deemed incapable of managing his/her own risks.

This idea of neoliberal self-rule and self-control is part of the current system of social control, and it came through clearly in some of my interviews. Many of the people I interviewed spoke of their desire to have a second chance and to go back to the United States and do things the right way. Alex, for example, introduced at the beginning of this chapter, longed for another chance in the United States and regrets having sold drugs as a means to earn more income. As I mentioned earlier, he told me he should have eaten stones instead of selling drugs. Like many other deportees, he believes he should have taken a low-wage job and pinched pennies in order to make ends meet. His story shows that the idea of neoliberal self-rule works: None of the people I interviewed said that they should have organized with their coworkers to demand a living wage instead of turning to the drug economy.

In her study of black and Latino entrepreneurs, Zulema Valdez (2011) found that her interviewees often believed in the "American Creed": the idea that if you work hard you can get ahead. Even when black and

Latino entrepreneurs perceive structural barriers to their success due to their race, class, or gender, they still often believe that success is possible if they work hard enough.

Many of the interviewees bought into the idea that the American Dream was possible with hard work. Deportation rarely caused them to change their mind. Maxwell, for example, was deported after police found him in a car with cocaine, which he said he had no idea the other passenger was carrying:

> Many of us immigrants are innocent. They deport us for almost anything—for public urination, for having a beer, for nothing. The federal government has to change its laws. If it does, this would be a victory for immigrants and for poor countries because the United States is a rich country, not rich in money, but in abundance, in teachings. Over there, you can have the good life. I know because I lived it.

Like many deportees, Maxwell still believed in the American Dream, despite his incarceration and deportation. Maxwell was born in 1972 in the 27 de Febrero neighborhood, like Alex, whose story was discussed earlier. His father worked as a painter, and his mother was a housewife. Maxwell finished the eighth grade in Santo Domingo before he decided to stow away on a boat to Puerto Rico, when he was 16. He lived and worked in Puerto Rico for seven years before traveling to New York, where he heard he could earn more money. He arrived in Puerto Rico in about 1988, then left in about 1995.

In New York, Maxwell went to his sister's house in the Bronx. In 1998, Maxwell married a U.S. citizen and became an LPR through a family-based petition. In New York, Maxwell worked for a food bank, loading and unloading nonperishables onto trucks for distribution throughout New York. He was proud of his work, which provided food for disadvantaged families.

Maxwell's wife, a white American woman, is in the military. She was relocated to Denver, Colorado, and Maxwell traveled there often to visit her when she was not deployed. When he stayed in New York, he often went to visit friends in Washington Heights. One day, a Dominican friend of his asked Maxwell to go with him to his sister's house in New Jersey. Maxwell agreed.

Soon after they crossed over into New Jersey, their car was stopped. The police officers found half a kilo of crack cocaine in the car. Although Maxwell denied that he had any idea there were drugs in the car and told me he never had sold drugs in his life, he also was found guilty. Maxwell served 18 months in prison before being deported to the Dominican Republic in 2008. Maxwell continues to dream of returning to the United States and joining his wife, who is in the Army. Despite this trauma, Maxwell still believes you can have the good life in the States.

Valdez (2011) ties the American Creed to colorblind racism by showing how entrepreneurs continue to espouse the idea that if you work hard, you can overcome racism. This discursive strategy works to blame minorities for their failure to succeed in this land of opportunity. The concept of neoliberal self-rule, as described by Inda (2013), works in a similar fashion. Those who work hard and stay on the right side of the law can benefit from the opportunities made available to them. Both Alex and Maxwell seem to believe in the American Creed insofar as they expressed that they would like to return to the United States to have another shot at the good life.

Conclusion

This chapter began with the question of why a law-abiding Dominican or Jamaican immigrant would turn to selling drugs after migrating to New York City. As I described, my respondents arrived and discovered that the formal economy would not give them their version of the American Dream. This dream included supporting their families and sending remittances to their home countries. Because these men lived in neighborhoods that offered opportunities to sell drugs, it was hard to resist the lure of earning more cash.

I also asked why deportation policy targets Jamaicans and Dominicans. The prevalence of involvement in the illegal economy among these groups supplies some answer. However, the heavy policing of Jamaican and Dominican neighborhoods also plays an important role.

Jamaicans and Dominicans often get entangled in the criminal justice system in similar ways as African Americans do; however, unlike African Americans, Jamaicans and Dominicans are subject to deportation in addition to incarceration. The aggravated felony provisions in immigration law mean that these deportation cases do not take into account individual circumstances—length of time in the United States, lack of ties to the home country, the severity (or lack thereof) of the crime, and number of children in the United States—as they once did.

Deportation laws contribute to structural racism in the United States insofar as they disproportionately affect black and Latino immigrants and the children and spouses they leave behind. Coercive law enforcement in urban areas in the United States operates as a form of social control where black and Latino male immigrants learn that they must walk a very straight and narrow line to avoid deportation.

Scholars, such as Wacquant (2009) and Alexander (2010), who study mass incarceration argue that it is designed to warehouse a low-skilled labor force and to repress the potential for dissent among these marginalized populations. They further contend that mass incarceration took off just as urban areas were undergoing economic restructuring. By considering the experiences of deportees, we can see that many black and Latino male immigrants were also affected by mass incarceration. In addition, we can see that their deportation is an extension of this system of social control. And, as I will continue to argue, the criminal and immigration laws that allow the United States to deport black and Latino men play a critical role in the functioning of 21st-century global capitalism. Deportation creates docile laborers in the United States, and it also disposes of workers who have become expendable in the current economy.

The Jamaicans and Dominicans profiled in this chapter traveled to the United States with high hopes of earning cash and being able to reap the benefits of global capitalism for themselves. Moreover, their family members back home expected they would quickly earn dollars and send them home. When they arrived in New York, however, they found that earnings from a low-wage job were barely enough to survive on and not nearly enough to live large and send cash home on a regular basis. Some of them chose to keep working, to slowly move up the economic ladder, or to work as many hours as they could to augment their incomes. Others, however, decided that they would never achieve their goals by working for $8 an hour and turned to the drug trade.

Law enforcement in New York City has not been able to keep drugs off the streets. After more than 30 years of the War on Drugs, illegal drugs continue to be abundant. The stories in this chapter render evident some of the other functions of the War on Drugs. Aggressive law enforcement keeps many people away from the drug economy and in the formal economy, providing the labor necessary to keep the formal economy functioning, at a wage that enables workers' survival but little else. Many people who use and sell drugs are never caught, but the constant cycling of black and brown men through the prison system sends a message to the others that only absolute compliance will avoid harsh penalties. Those who stray from this path face arrest, imprisonment, and—for some—deportation.

Interlude

Katy

My house was big.
My dad's room had a Jacuzzi.
It was wonderful.
We thought we were fine.

When I came home from school,
My dad told me,
"Immigration came.
We have to leave."

From day to night everything changed.
We didn't want to leave,
so we moved
to another place.

I was waiting for the bus to go to school
when immigration came.
They were, like,
"We have to go."

They handcuffed me
outside, in front of other students.
It was so embarrassing.
I was only 15.

They took my sister and my dad to jail.
And my sister,

while she was in jail,
she almost got raped.

I didn't go to school here
because I didn't know how to write or read Spanish.
So I couldn't.
I only knew English.

Why did this happen to me?
Why am I here?
It really changed our life.
It really did.

5

Getting Caught

Targets of Deportation Policy

At least since the early 1990s, Latino and Caribbean men have been the primary targets of deportation policy. Today, about 90 percent of deportees are men, and nearly all (97 percent) are from the Americas, even though about half of all noncitizens are women and only 60 percent of noncitizens are from the Americas (Golash-Boza and Hondagneu-Sotelo 2013). As the last chapter described, immigration law enforcement is selective: Even with mass deportation, a fairly small portion of unauthorized immigrants is actually deported. Deportation law renders millions of immigrants deportable, yet the vast majority remain in the United States undetected. How are deportees caught? Why are Latino and Caribbean men the primary targets of mass deportation? How does the selective deportation of these groups create a system of racialized and gendered social control?

Thus far, I have argued that neoliberal economic policies in the country of origin push migrants out; that the enhancement in border enforcement has made the passage to the United States more difficult, and at times deadly; that immigrants have been channeled into low-wage jobs; and that certain immigrants have been targeted by law enforcement. Through these analyses, I am building my argument that mass deportation is part of a global cycle of neoliberal capitalism and that these enforcement techniques are part of a system of racialized and gendered social control. Daniel Kanstroom (2007) describes deportation as "post-entry social control." I would add that the racial and gendered dimensions of this social control further illuminate mass deportation's connection to global capitalism and to global apartheid.

Cecilia Menjívar and Leisy Abrego (2012) characterize the complex web of laws that control migrants' lives as "legal violence" (1381) insofar as these laws and practices create new hierarchies and delimit the lives of immigrants in tenuous legal statuses. These scholars and others, such as Nicholas de Genova (2002, 2005) and Joanna Dreby (2012), show how illegality and the threat of deportation affect immigrants' lives and enhance their vulnerability. In this chapter, I build on this scholarship by focusing on deportees who are actually caught. This focus allows us to move beyond the possibility of being caught to the reality of apprehension. These stories render it evident that immigrants are apprehended in very specific situations: Most are arrested in their homes or driving their cars. Moreover, men are much more likely to be caught in the deportation dragnet than women, and this creates a system of "gendered racial removal" (Golash-Boza and Hondagneu-Sotelo 2013).

The stories of apprehension I tell in this chapter are the same stories that circulate in immigrant communities. The deportees I met told me their stories in detail, based on what they remembered. In some cases, their memories may not be completely accurate, or they may not have a complete understanding of what happened. I did not double-check their recounting by looking up police reports, for example. Instead, what is important for my purposes and my overall argument is that these are the stories that circulate in immigrant communities. Immigrants know that *la migra* can come into your home and that a traffic stop can turn into a deportation. As Meghan McDowell and Nancy Wonders (2009–10) argue, both the surveillance itself and the internalization of the security gaze work to regulate how migrants move through public spaces. The circulation of these apprehension stories adds an additional layer of social control to the immigrant population insofar as migrants begin to self-police. In this way, mass deportation works to ensure the self-regulation of immigrants (McDowell and Wonders 2009–10).

Teresa Miller (2008) argues that the criminalization of undocumented workers causes them to have to live below the radar to avoid apprehension, and this in turn increases their vulnerability to economic exploitation. One way that we can see this criminalization of immigrants is in the fact that police officers cooperate with immigration authorities. Another way is that immigration agents raid the homes, workplaces, and neighborhoods of immigrants, using tactics such as handcuffing and the use of heavy weaponry that we traditionally associate with the apprehension of criminals. This criminalization produces fear in immigrant communities, as now millions of people are subject to arrest in the course of carrying out mundane tasks such as driving, working, and sitting at home watching television.

A recent study of dairy farmers in Wisconsin found that high levels of immigration policing in communities created a pervasive fear of deportation that made workers more compliant. The authors, Jill Lindsey Harrison and Sarah E. Lloyd (2012), argue that "increasingly militarized and spatially expanded immigration policy enforcement practices are not just oppressive but also tremendously 'productive' in that they serve two key functions of the state: ensuring capital accumulation in industry and maintaining the political legitimacy of the state in the eyes of the public" (371). My findings support the argument that intensive policing is designed not to remove all immigration offenders but to control labor and legitimize the state.

This chapter will focus on immigration law enforcement to develop an understanding of how it targets particular immigrants for deportation. This inquiry will clarify the racialized and gendered nature of the system of social control that immigration law enforcement has become. As I describe, immigration law enforcement operates without the basic protections we take for granted in criminal law enforcement. Under U.S. law, violations of immigration law are civil, not criminal, offenses, and deportation is technically not punishment but an administrative procedure. This distinction has become increasingly blurred as criminal and immigration law enforcement agents have begun to work together more consistently.

The Merging of Law Enforcement Functions

Eric Boehme (2011) argues that much of the immigration debate revolves around making individuals pay for having broken the law. He contends that this stance weaves together three typical neoliberal discourses: (1) the importance of being tough on crime; (2) the idea that immigrants are a drain on the state; and (3) xenophobic and racist fears about why "aliens" cannot become part of the United States. These same discourses have been used to justify the merging of criminal and immigration law enforcement in the United States. The stories of immigrants who are deported, however, often show that immigration law enforcement is doing little to decrease crime; that deportation poses a burden on the state; and that many deportees were well on their way to becoming integral parts of the United States prior to their apprehension.

Alfonso's story illustrates some typical features of immigration law enforcement as it has been practiced of late, and it demonstrates how deportation practices are not making us safer. Alfonso is from Escuintla, a city south of Guatemala City, where he grew up with his grandparents. When he was eight years old, his father, a truck driver, was murdered in a robbery in Petén, Guatemala's northernmost state. Alfonso's mother decided to immigrate to Miami so she would be able to provide for her three children. Alfonso's mother traveled illegally to the United States, and his older brother and sister followed. He stayed behind. However, like many children left behind, Alfonso decided to immigrate to the United States when he was old enough to do so independently.

When he was 20, in the year 2000, Alfonso's mother paid a coyote $4,500 to cover the costs of his trip to the United States. Alfonso secured a visa to travel through Mexico. When he reached the border of the United States, he had to walk three days through the mountains of Arizona before arriving in a city where he could take a bus to Miami to join his mother and siblings.

In Miami, Alfonso started out mowing lawns but quickly found a more stable job in a recycling plant. His first position was on the floor, but, once he learned how to operate the heavy equipment, he was able to get better jobs. At his last job, he earned $16.50 an hour, meaning his hourly wage was twice the daily minimum wage in Guatemala.

Little by little, Alfonso made a life for himself. He married a Cuban woman, and, in 2006, they had their first baby together. In 2007, their second child was born. Alfonso focused his energy on working and enjoying time with his family. His wife was a legal permanent resident (LPR) of the United States, but not a citizen. Alfonso may have qualified for legalization on the basis of his marriage, but they never looked into applying; they were busy trying to make ends meet and caring for a growing family. Applying would have cost thousands of dollars, and Alfonso had no expectation of being deported.

In the summer of 2009, Alfonso's mother fell seriously ill. He went to the hospital to see her on his day off from work. As he was pulling into the hospital parking lot, a man talking on his cell phone hit his car.

Alfonso got out of the car and saw that, although his car was damaged, the other car was not. He tried to explain to the man, in his limited English, that it was not necessary to get the insurance companies involved or to call the police. Alfonso did not have a driver's license and knew that he would get in trouble if the police arrived.

As Alfonso was explaining this to the other driver, the hospital security guard showed up and asked Alfonso for his registration and insurance papers. Alfonso gave them to him, and as they were going over the details of what had happened, the sheriff arrived.

Alfonso explained what happened:

> The sheriff showed up at the scene of the accident and asked me for my registration, insurance, and driver's license. I showed him my consular ID. He asked if it was real. I told him it was and that I had my passport as well. He asked if I was legal, and I told him the truth, that I was not. He asked how long I had been in the United States, and I told him nine years. Next thing I knew, he was calling the Border Patrol and everything went downhill from there.

Border Patrol arrived on the scene and took Alfonso into custody. Alfonso was in immigration detention for 72 days. His mother died while he was detained. Alfonso feared he would not be able to go to the funeral. However, immigration authorities allowed Alfonso to go to the funeral.

Two Immigration and Customs Enforcement (ICE) agents took Alfonso in a van at 11:00 am to the funeral home where his mother lay. There were no other people there, as the service would not start until 6:00 pm. Alfonso was allowed to change out of the orange prison jumpsuit into gray pants and a sweater, but he did have to wear handcuffs and his feet were chained together. Alfonso spent 45 minutes praying with his mother before it was time to go back to the detention center. Ten days later, he was deported to Guatemala, even though his wife was an LPR, he had two U.S. citizen children, and he had been in the United States for nine years.

When the police cooperate with Border Patrol, any minor interaction with police can lead to deportation. Knowing this, many undocumented immigrants take extreme measures to avoid interactions with police. Some of my interviewees told me they stopped driving and some even went so far as to try and avoid leaving their homes except when absolutely necessary.

The merging of immigration and criminal law enforcement tactics has meant that police officers are often the first step in the deportation pipeline. Merging immigration law enforcement and criminal law enforcement creates a situation where the immigration status of any noncitizen who comes into contact with law enforcement authorities may be checked to determine their eligibility to remain in the country. These programs—which are in place in most but not all police jurisdictions—ensure that convicted murderers and rapists are deported after serving their time in federal prisons. However, they also make certain that when Latinos are driving down the highway and are stopped by the police for a traffic violation, the police officer will do a routine immigration check while writing a citation. This is what happened to Philip, whose story I began discussing in chapter 1.

Philip was born in Jamaica, is married to a U.S. citizen, and has five U.S. citizen children. Philip, like Alfonso, qualified for permanent residency based on his marriage. Philip submitted the initial paperwork but never completed the process. Philip and his wife had their first child in 1998 and their second child the following year. Their second daughter was born severely disabled. She was born unable to see or hear, is confined to a wheelchair, and only eats from a feeding tube.

Philip opened a small vegetarian restaurant in New York and also worked as a musician. With the money he made, he was able to support his family. He had three more children, all girls. When I spoke with him in 2009 in Kingston, his youngest child was two years old.

While on a road trip through Louisiana in 2008, Philip was pulled over:

> I got pulled over because I had Florida State paper plates on the car. My friend's car, you know, it was brand new. . . . I saw [the officer] go in the car and come back and say that I have a deportation order. . . . Then they took me, first, to a county jail. Second, to another county jail that immigration rented out. And then the third one is like a federal detention [also] in Louisiana.

Philip had a deportation order because he had never completed the paperwork for his permanent residency. He did not receive the letter indicating that he had a court date to determine his residency. When he did not report, a deportation order was issued.

Philip most likely qualified for relief from deportation, based on the facts that he had lived in the United States for 13 years, was married to a U.S. citizen, and had a daughter who was severely disabled. However, Philip was taken to a detention facility in an isolated part of Louisiana, which made it very difficult for him to gain access to an immigration lawyer. After three months in immigration detention, he was on a plane back to Jamaica, without ever having the opportunity to consult an immigration lawyer. The police officer who pulled Philip over used his out-of-state paper plates as a pretext to stop him. It is possible that the police officer also noticed before pulling him over that Philip is black. It is clear that the officer surmised he was not a U.S. citizen based on his Jamaican accent.

Tools of Mass Deportation

Philip was declared a "fugitive alien" and deported. Anyone released from ICE custody who failed to report back to their immigration hearing would be subject to this label. Had Philip had a criminal record, not matter how minor—such as a marijuana possession conviction from decades before—he would have been declared a "criminal alien" and deported. If he had overstayed a tourist visa, he would have also faced deportation as an "illegal alien."

In its reports and budgetary requests, ICE uses this dehumanizing language to suggest that removing noncitizens makes America safer. There is little evidence, however, that these noncitizens are actually dangerous. In fact, more than 80 percent of all criminal deportees are deported for nonviolent crimes; fugitive aliens and illegal aliens have broken the law, just as anyone who's driven above the speed limit or executed a kitchen remodel without having the required permits. Moreover, a recent paper by Thomas Miles and Adam Cox (2014) shows that the enhancement in interior enforcement of immigration laws since 2007 has had no meaningful impact on violent or property crime.

TABLE 5.1. How 147 Deportees Were Arrested, by Nationality

	Jamaicans	Dominicans	Guatemalans	Brazilians
ICE	9%	9%	21%	7%
CBP	0%	4%	26%	66%
By police as a suspect	11%	0%	15%	17%
After prison/jail release	79%	87%	53%	10%
n	n = 37	n = 46	n = 34	n = 30

Table 5.1 provides a broader view of how deportees get caught, showing the agencies responsible for carrying out immigration enforcement priorities and how the 147 deportees I interviewed were arrested.
These deportees are not a random sample. Nevertheless, the trends in
the table reflect the range of immigration law enforcement and indicate
that there is variation by nationality. In the overall sample, local police
officers made the initial arrest that led to deportation in the majority
of the cases. ICE made the initial arrest for a relatively small portion
of the overall sample. Customs and Border Patrol (CBP) also made the
initial arrest for a small portion of the overall sample, but these arrests
accounted for two-thirds of the Brazilian interviewees. The Jamaicans
and Dominicans were the most likely to be funneled through the criminal justice system prior to encountering immigration law enforcement.
The Dominicans who were funneled through the criminal justice system were all convicted of crimes whereas 17 percent of the Brazilians
were arrested by the police and eventually deported without ever being
convicted of a crime. The Department of Homeland Security (DHS)
does not release full information to the public, but my sample provides
a foundation for some preliminary conclusions from these data about
how certain immigrants are targeted. The vertical columns do not
always add up to 100% due to rounding.

The available data show that the selective enforcement of immigration law leads to a select group of people facing deportation: black
and Latino men. There are clear racial and gendered dimensions to
this enhancement in the coercive arm of the state. In my research with
deportees, I also found patterns that reflect this selective enforcement.

The majority of Brazilians were apprehended by CBP as they
attempted to enter the United States either via land or air. In contrast,

none of the Jamaicans were apprehended by CBP. Thus, although Jamaicans and Brazilians are both among the top 10 nationalities of deportees, their deportations occur in distinct manners. Whereas Brazilians are apprehended primarily at the border and other points of entry, Jamaicans are much more likely to be deported after a release from prison. Guatemalans were the most likely to have been arrested via an ICE home raid, likely because they had applied for asylum, and thus ICE had their home addresses on file. Brazilians were the most likely to be arrested by police during routine traffic stops. The primary reason for this is that the Brazilians I interviewed lived in places where the police cooperate with ICE. Whereas the New York police will contact ICE if a person actually serves time for a criminal conviction, police in places such as Marietta, Georgia, will contact ICE if they encounter a person who appears to be undocumented—even if the police do not plan to press criminal charges.

The likelihood of being deported is directly related to where you live. Even though large numbers of Brazilians live in New York City and in Boston, none of the Brazilian deportees I interviewed had lived there. Instead, they were deported from two places where police cooperate with immigration authorities: Marietta, Georgia, and Danbury, Connecticut. A close look at how noncitizens are arrested and end up in the deportation dragnet will help us to understand the mechanisms that underlie this system of racialized and gendered social control.

DHS does not make explicit its targeting of black and Latino immigrants. Instead, DHS purports to be carrying out policies that make the nation safer by targeting specific kinds of immigrants. This tactic of using gender- and race-blind language while implementing policies that primarily target specific groups is typical in a colorblind society (Alexander 2010; Bonilla-Silva 2013). Through a language of security and public safety, DHS carries out an agenda of racialized and gendered social control. This agenda need not be intentional to operate effectively.

The fiscal year (FY) 2011 DHS budget request stated that "ICE makes America safer by identifying, apprehending, and removing criminal and other illegal aliens from the United States." ICE budget reports and requests indicate that they are deporting people according to their priorities: convicted criminals, immigration fugitives, repeat violators, and border removals, with convicted criminals as their highest priority.

In 2013, ICE conducted a total of 368,644 removals. Of these, 133,551 were interior removals. The remaining were people apprehended within 100 miles of the border. Of the interior removals, 52,935 were Level 1 criminals, those who, as discussed in chapter 1, have the most serious criminal record. Notably, of the 235,093 people who were deported at the border, only about 65,000 had never attempted to enter the United States before. The remainder were people who had either lived there before or had attempted to enter before and gotten caught.[1]

This chapter will focus primarily on interior immigration law enforcement—the deportation of people who are living in the United States when apprehended by immigration law enforcement. Four programs are designed to locate criminal and fugitive aliens: They are the 287(g) Program, Secure Communities, the Criminal Alien Program (CAP), and the National Fugitive Operations Program (NFOP). These programs rely on a shared fingerprint database that allows local police to identify people who are in the United States without authorization.

1. *The 287(g) Program*: A police officer pulls over a person for an alleged traffic violation. If that police officer is deputized to work for ICE, she can run the driver's fingerprints through a database that contains FBI and DHS information. If the fingerprints reveal that the driver is illegally present in the United States or has an immigration hold, the police officer can arrest the driver and hand them over to ICE.

2. *Secure Communities*: A police officer arrests a person and charges him with a crime. She takes him to the police station, fingerprints him, and then runs his fingerprints through the database. Even if the police decide to drop the charges, if the person turns out to have an immigration hold, they will detain him until ICE comes to pick him up.

3. *CAP*: A police officer arrests a person, charges him with a crime, and the person serves time. Before being released from jail or prison, the police officer can call ICE to come and check his eligibility to remain in the United States. In some cases, the CAP can also function like Secure Communities insofar as it also identifies unauthorized immigrants at booking.

4. *NFOP*: The police provide ICE with the criminal history of a non-citizen. If ICE determines the noncitizen is a fugitive or criminal alien, ICE sends out a team of federal agents to the noncitizen's home and arrests him. A fugitive alien is a noncitizen who failed to appear in immigration court, whereas a criminal alien is any noncitizen convicted of a crime.

Congress appropriated $690 million for these four programs in 2011—up from $23 million in 2004. This 30-fold increase in funding led to an increase in annual arrests through these programs from 11,000 to 289,000 during that time. The shift toward targeting criminal aliens has thus involved a shift in how we talk about immigrants as well as large-scale funding of these initiatives.

The CAP is the largest of the initiatives. In FY 2011, ICE issued 212,744 charging documents for deportation through the CAP. In 2011, 78,246 people were removed or returned through Secure Communities and 1,500 people through the NFOP (the only program where ICE agents are actively on the ground arresting unauthorized residents). In 2010, 26,871 people were removed through the 287(g) Program. Between 2010 and 2012, about half of the 400,000 deportations that DHS realized happened through the CAP. The majority of the remainder of deportations were carried out by CBP (Simanski and Sapp 2012; Golash-Boza and Hondagneu-Sotelo 2013).

The NFOP has come under severe criticism. The budget of this program has increased dramatically since its inception in 2003—from $9 million to $218 million in FY 2008. A 2009 report by the Migration Policy Institute criticizes the NFOP, primarily because of its failure to arrest dangerous fugitives: "NFOP has failed to focus its resources on the priorities Congress intended when it authorized the program. In effect, NFOP has succeeded in apprehending the easiest targets, not the most dangerous fugitives" (Mendelson et al. 2009: 2). Although the NFOP is designed to deport dangerous criminals, nearly three-quarters of the people they apprehended through February 2008 had no criminal records. In 2007, the NFOP, with a $183 million budget, arrested only 672 fugitive aliens that ICE considered to be dangerous. The other 30,000 people arrested were people with deportation orders (15,646), undocumented migrants (12,084), or noncitizens who had been convicted of nonviolent crimes, such as shoplifting (2,005). The Migration Policy Institute report points out that "the number of fugitive aliens with criminal convictions arrested . . . remained relatively constant between FY 2004 and FY 2008. Congressional allocations to NFOP, in contrast, grew 17-fold over the same period" (2009: 15).

The Racial Implications of Key Policies

ICE claims that the primary purpose of the CAP, Secure Communities, the 287(g) Program, and the NFOP is to find criminal aliens. However, ICE detains many people who have not been convicted of crimes through these programs. I found this to be true in my research: Any encounter with law enforcement could lead to arrest and deportation.

A substantial body of research and legal cases concludes that police racially profile people who drive while brown or black (Johnson 2004), and the racial implications of using traffic stops to identify deportable aliens are clear. In September 2012, the Justice Department released a report subtitled "Findings Show Pattern or Practice of Discriminatory Policing against Latinos."[2] This report found that deputies in Alamance County, North Carolina, stopped Latinos at least four times as often as non-Latino drivers, consistently stopped Latinos at checkpoints, and arrested Latinos for minor traffic violations while issuing citations or warnings to non-Latinos for the same violations. (Arresting Latinos enabled officers to process them in the county jail and, in doing so, check their immigration status.) During the period under study, Alamance County participated in both the 287(g) Program as well as Secure Communities. Immediately after the release of the report, DHS rescinded the 287(g) agreement and restricted access to Secure Communities in Alamance County.[3] A study in Davidson County, Tennessee, revealed that officers in this county apprehended 5,333 immigrants through their 287(g) Program, and all but 102 were from Latin America (Lacayo 2010).

Guatemalans were the most likely to be arrested directly by ICE agents, usually because they had outstanding deportation orders and ICE showed up at their houses. In one case, an entire family—Mariluna, Rafael, and their two daughters—was deported this way.

I met Rafael, whose story I began in chapter 2, in his hardware shop in Guatemala City. He came across as a very pleasant and open man, who did not hesitate to talk about his life. When I told him I was writing a book about people who had been deported from the United States, the first thing he wished to clarify is that he did not enter the country illegally. Rafael had traveled to the United States on a multiple-entry visa for years before abruptly deciding to settle there after witnessing a political assassination.

Once in the United States, Rafael applied for political asylum. As he was waiting for his application to be processed, a legal representative advised him not to work until he received a work permit. The family survived on their savings for more than a year before ending up on the streets, homeless. Eventually, Rafael realized that, although he was not authorized to work, he could start a business. He found a business partner and started doing touch-up paintwork on cars. His brother, who was in the same business, taught him the trade. As such, technically, Rafael was not employed but simply conducting business in the United States. Rafael's self-employment strategy is part of a broader trend—8 percent of undocumented immigrants are entrepreneurs, and there are likely others who realize they can avoid breaking the law and feed their families this way (Mastman 2008).

Rafael's plea for asylum was denied on the basis of lack of sufficient evidence. His lawyer told him he would appeal the case, and Rafael and his family continued to live in the United States. Rafael's business grew. One of his daughters, Katy, who had lived in the United States from the time she was two years old, described her neighborhood and her friendship network in Louisiana as primarily white. Katy emphasized that she had a "normal" upbringing: "I grew up with American people all my life. . . . We went to the movies. We went to the mall. We went to, like, the zoo and stuff. It was, like, normal kid stuff." Tears streamed down her face when she recalled her luxurious life. "My house was big. We had, like, two living rooms, two floors, a walk-in kitchen. My dad's room had a Jacuzzi. We had, like, a ten-car parking lot. It was wonderful, actually, you know. And it was funny because my dad and my mom always paid bills, taxes and everything, you know. We thought we were fine."

Katy excelled in school, was popular with her friends, and never got into trouble. She had dreams of becoming a veterinarian, and her sister had plans to become a doctor. "My last Christmas in the United States, I couldn't even think of anything to ask for; I had everything," Katy told me.

Early one morning, however, it all came crashing down. At 6 am, when Mariluna was still sleeping and Katy was getting ready for school, they heard a loud knock on the door of their home and someone shouting: "Does Rafael Gutierrez live here?" Mariluna told me, "They came in, as if we were criminals, as if we were murderers."

The immigration agents decided not to take the family into custody. Rather, they told them they had 30 days to leave the country. Instead of leaving, Rafael and his family decided to move with the hope that they would be able to evade deportation. This was a reasonable expectation, because in 1999 immigration agents did not have the resources to check up on the vast majority of deportation orders. However, the agents returned a month later.

When Mariluna recounted to me the story of what happened the second time immigration agents came to her house, her voice broke and tears streamed down her face. The immigration agents were upset that they tried to flee and told them that this time they would have to take at least two of them into custody to ensure that they would depart. Rafael surrendered, and they had to choose whether to send 20-year-old Alejandra or Mariluna to immigration detention. Alejandra volunteered and was taken to a county jail.

The immigration agents took Rafael to an immigration detention center. However, there was not a center for women close by, and Alejandra had to spend four days in the county jail. She still has nightmares about the experience. Another inmate tried to rape her when she was inside, but she waited years before telling her parents about the incident, as she did not want them to feel guilty. Mariluna wept again, telling me of this.

Mariluna was in shock. Her friends helped her pack her things, but there was no way to ship all of the family's belongings to Guatemala. She was able to pack eight suitcases, only six of which she was able to take with her. They left their house and five cars in Louisiana.

Nine years later, this family still suffers tremendously from what happened to them. Rafael believes his brother, upset by the competition Rafael's business posed, called on the governor of Louisiana at the time, who was a friend of his, to make sure immigration agents knew his application for asylum had been declined and that Rafael and his family were deportable.

Katy was 15 when she was deported and was never able to finish high school, because she did not have the proper papers to register in Guatemala. The Guatemalan educational system has distinct requirements from that of the United States, and the school officials said that Katy would have to start school over again by entering the third grade. Rafael was never able to get a job in Guatemala, as potential employers said he was too old. Thus, he did the same thing he did in the United States: He started a small business. However, he has been much less successful. Today, they have enough money to eat and keep a roof over their heads. But deportation destroyed the lives they had made for themselves in the United States.

Assessing Criminal Aliens' Threat to U.S. Society

Rafael and his family were deported as fugitive aliens because they failed to leave the country after a deportation order was issued. Another top priority for ICE is apprehending criminal aliens, and being a criminal alien also means that you can be subject to a home raid. As Melvin's story illustrates, not all criminal aliens pose a threat to U.S. society. He was deported as a criminal alien for a hit and run.

In 1986 when Melvin was 18, he moved to the United States as an LPR. Melvin went to Arlington, Virginia, to live with his father and stepmother. He stayed there for a few months before moving out on his own. Melvin first worked in hotel maintenance yet later found a better-paying job working on hardwood floors. He worked in that business for about five years. In 1996, his boss encouraged him to set up his own flooring business. It worked out very well for Melvin, and by 1998 he made up to $15,000 a month. He married and had two children: one in 1999, and the second in 2001. He had a house, several cars, and a successful business, and the family took frequent vacations.

Prior to Melvin's trouble with ICE, Melvin had trouble with the law once in 1995. Melvin hit a dead body that was lying in the highway but drove away because he was scared—a decision he acknowledges was poor. The police found him and charged him with involuntary manslaughter and hit and run. The manslaughter charge was dropped when forensics revealed the body was already dead when Melvin ran over it, but Melvin served a year in jail for the hit and run.

Melvin was an LPR and never expected immigration agents to bother him. He had lived lawfully and productively for 10 years when they did.

> They came and knocked on my door. My wife answered. They go, "Mr. Gonzalez?" And I was reading a book to my little boy. And she goes, "Yeah." "Can we speak to him?" So, they called me. I was ready to go to bed. "Are you Mr. Gonzalez?" I said, "Yeah." "So, you're under arrest." I said, "For what?" They said, "We're immigration and you're going to be deported." I said, "For what?" I said, "I got a green card." "Well, you are eligible for deportation because you have problems with the law back in 1995." I was like, "Why do you guys wait so long to do this to me?" I said, "I'm married. I got kids. I got a family. I got a business. Why are you doing this to me?" They said, "Well, all we're doing is our job. Come with us." So that was a big deal, because my wife, she jumped on them and said, "You don't have no right to come and just pick him up. He already did his time. He did what he did. He paid for it." And they actually had to pull a gun on her because she was getting aggressive: "So, you're gonna leave me with my kids here? He's the head of the house. You're gonna take him." I mean, she was pretty bad. They said, "I'm sorry. We're just doing our job."

Melvin spent $15,000 on legal representation, but the law was inexorable: He served several months in immigration detention, and then ICE sent him to Guatemala.

Jodie Lawston and Martha Escobar (2009–10) link the War on Drugs to the criminalization of Latina migrants through the Immigration Reform and Control Act (IRCA) of 1986. Melvin's story shows how the Illegal Immigration Reform and Immigrant Responsibility Act (IIRIRA) deepened the criminalization of Latinos. With the passage of IIRIRA, immigration agents were given license to raid the homes of migrants who had prior convictions. Both the emphasis on border control in the 1980s and the turn to interior enforcement in the 21st century have been justified through discourses of criminality and under the pretense of ending the "imagined crisis of national disorder" (Lawston and Esco-bar 2009–10: 13). Immigration enforcement extends the logic of the U.S. prison regime (Lawston and Escobar 2009–10). These enforcement techniques heighten the threats felt in migrant communities (McDowell and Wonders 2009–10).

The Effect of ICE Street Raids

Street raids are even less common than home raids, but they inspire ter-rible fear.[4] In 2007, hundreds of heavily armed federal agents descended on the Little Village Discount Mall in a predominantly Mexican neigh-borhood in Chicago, in an operation designed to find people who were producing fake permanent residency cards. The use of force instilled great fear in the people present in the mall, and rumors about the raid circulated in the community long after it took place. Community mem-bers were outraged by the raid and felt strongly that such a raid would have never taken place in a middle-class, white neighborhood (Golash-Boza 2012).

A recent study of how immigrants in Lowell, Massachusetts, deal with the environment of increased threat of deportation found that when ICE raids happen, rumors of the raids spread and people become scared. In addition, immigrants develop distrust for local authorities, which leads many people to fear even reporting crime to the police. These researchers also found that immigrants fear going to the hospital, as rumors circulate that health workers may report them to ICE (Slád-ková et al. 2012).

Raids are also detrimental to people who experience them directly. Tamara witnessed a street raid in her Brazilian neighborhood in Geor-gia. She, her husband, and her 20-year-old son had immigrated from Goiás, Brazil, where they had owned a nightclub that made enough money to survive but not thrive. A Brazilian coyote convinced them that they would meet their financial goals if they traveled to the United States.

The coyote helped them get to Mexico and then to Texas in early 2005. In Texas, they were arrested and detained by the Border Patrol. After three days, they were released with a court date and made their way to Marietta, Georgia. Like many Brazilians who were released from immigration detention with a court date, Tamara and her husband never went back to immigration court, making them "fugitive aliens."

In Marietta, they moved in with a Brazilian friend from their hometown. The next day, Tamara was working as a housecleaner. It was hard work with toxic chemicals in the cleaning liquids, chemicals that gave 50-year-old Tamara frequent headaches. Tamara said she enjoyed the work, even though the women whose houses she cleaned barely acknowledged her existence.

Tamara described her life in the United States as *a vida do rico* (the lifestyle of a rich person). She had a modern apartment with new appliances and nice clothes. However, she and her family barely left their apartment, for fear they would be caught by immigration agents. They lived in Cobb County, where authorities work closely with ICE. Since 2008, more than 8,000 people have been deported from Cobb County through the 287(g) Program. That is a fairly high rate for a county with just over 700,000 people and is actually higher than the rate for Maricopa County, Arizona, which is well known for its harsh deportation tactics.

One morning in 2006, as Tamara left her apartment for work, there was an immigration raid in her neighborhood. Immigration agents accosted Tamara in front of her home and asked her for her documents. When she produced her Brazilian passport, she was handcuffed and arrested. She had to spend 42 days in immigration detention before she was deported. Tamara expressed pain at being treated like a criminal, and she was angry about the terrible food in prison and not being allowed outside. She managed by purchasing instant soups in the commissary.

Tamara's husband joined her in Brazil two years later; their son stayed in Georgia, where he has an infant daughter. Although Tamara and her husband have established a more comfortable lifestyle in Brazil than they had before immigrating, she still misses the life she had in Georgia. When we met, she called her husband to come see me, "an American in Brazil."[5] She couldn't believe that I was living in Brazil, when I could live in the United States.

Tamara enjoyed living in the United States. However, she remains bitter about her experience of being arrested, detained, and deported.

She also was diagnosed with cancer upon her return—an illness she attributes to her exposure to chemicals in the United States. I asked her if she would go back. She shook her head and clucked her tongue twice—a very typically Goianian way of saying "no way."

With just over 6,000 agents for the entire country,[6] ICE does not have enough agents to conduct street raids with any frequency, and perhaps they recognize that use of the technique might lead to unwanted attention from civil rights groups.

The Criminal Alien Program

Aside from border apprehensions, the CAP is one of the primary ways in which deportees are apprehended and subsequently deported. This program deports people upon release from prison after they serve time for a criminal conviction. The CAP is a direct extension of the system of mass incarceration that many scholars have referred to as a system of social control (Alexander 2010; Wacquant 2009; Garland 2012).

The crimes committed by "criminal aliens" range quite a bit. The top three categories of criminal offenses for deportees are immigration crimes, drug crimes, and traffic offenses. The previous two chapters explored drug offenses extensively; the next two sections will examine immigration crimes and traffic crimes, respectively. Immigration and traffic crimes are similar insofar as they both can either be administrative or criminal offenses, depending both on the severity of the infraction and on prosecutorial discretion.

Immigration Fraud

Walter was convicted of immigration fraud. He is tall, brown-skinned, in his early thirties, and has a shy smile that seems out of place on a man with such an imposing physical presence. Although he smiled a lot, the pain in his eyes was clear when he recounted to me that he had been deported back to the Dominican Republic, leaving his two children behind.

I interviewed Walter in Santo Domingo, where he lives with his mother, his brother, and his two sisters in a large second-floor apartment in an old building in the Colonial City. The house was nicely furnished, with a new sofa and chairs in the living room and a large wooden dining-room table, covered with a lace tablecloth. Most of the other rooms in the house were bedrooms, which were all tidy, yet small, with just enough room for a bed in each. Walter's sisters were mopping the floors while we were there. Walter told me that his mother had 14 children, and he was the youngest.

Walter played basketball as a youth for the school and the local teams. When he finished high school, he won a basketball scholarship to attend a private university in Santiago. He went to college for two years and majored in business administration. However, in 1994, he decided to take his chances and leave for the United States. Two of his brothers were already there, and they promised to help him get to the States. Walter got a visa to go to Mexico, and then crossed the border illegally.

Shortly after arriving, Walter met and married a U.S. citizen and was able to obtain permanent residency. In 1996, their first child was born, and in 2002 they had another child. Walter had a good job, and he won custody of his children when he and his wife divorced. He left the children with a babysitter in the building where he lived when he went to work each day. Walter and his children lived in the Bronx, and his ex-wife lived close by.

Walter was involved with his local church. He especially enjoyed activities designed to help children. He spent weekends with his children, going out to parks or restaurants whenever they could. Walter never had any trouble with the law, and he thought that he had it made in New York. He had permanent legal residency, two U.S. citizen children, and a stable job.

However, in 2004, an old mistake came back to haunt him. In 1990, when Walter was 13 years old, he had taken a boat to Puerto Rico illegally and been deported back to the Dominican Republic. When Walter applied for legal permanent residency in 1998, he did not mention this previous deportation from Puerto Rico. That amounts to immigration fraud, and it rendered Walter eligible for deportation on criminal grounds. Walter did not know that it was possible for ICE to access this record, but an investigation revealed the history after he was granted legal permanent residency.

Fourteen years after Walter failed to disclose the earlier deportation on his application for permanent residence, police stopped him for a traffic violation on his way to the airport in 2004. This police officer, who was deputized by ICE, was able to run Walter's license through a database and discover that Walter had an immigration warrant. The officer arrested him. At the time, Walter had custody of his three-year-old daughter as well as his eight-year-old daughter. His ex-wife was able to take the children back and care for them, although, similar to many other families I interviewed, his ex-wife had to rely on public aid once he was deported.

Walter spent four years fighting his deportation order. He spent the first two years fighting his case from inside immigration detention. Eventually, he was released, and he continued to go to court to appeal the order, but he was deported in July 2008.

Manuel was also deported for what amounted to immigration fraud, though technically he was convicted of identity theft. One of only three Brazilians I met who were deported on criminal grounds, Manuel was born in 1964 in Goiânia. He fell on hard times after he lost a job he'd held for years in 2001 and a business he tried to start failed. Manuel knew many people from his hometown of Jaraguá who had gone to the United States and who had returned with lots of money. He set out for the United States in 2003, intending to stay two years, and then return to his wife and children with enough money to pay their debts.

Manuel stayed in the States for four years, but he found he did not earn money as quickly as he expected. He took three months to find work, and he then spent a year paying off debt he'd amassed while he looked. His wife wanted him to stay long enough to pay off their house, so he decided to stay two more years, then return to Brazil.

When Manuel first arrived, he worked primarily with Brazilians. However, he soon realized that if he learned English and worked with Americans he could make more money. However, such jobs required him to have a social security card. Manuel told me that the hiring manager in a granite factory where he wanted to work let him know that the social security card need not be real. So long as Manuel presented them with a card, they could claim that they did not know it was fake, and the employer would avoid any sanction. Thus, Manuel did what the vast majority of undocumented immigrants do: He purchased a fake social security card.

Manuel's employer contributed social security payments from his wages into the false account. Such fake accounts use random numbers. Sometimes, however, these random numbers turn out to belong to real people. This happened to Manuel: His number belonged to a child. Thus, unbeknownst to him, Manuel was contributing money each month to a child's account. Manuel would never be able to withdraw this money, of course. Immigrants like Manuel who use fake social security numbers contributed about $2 billion to Medicare and $8.7 billion for social security in 2010—funds they will never see.[7] Nevertheless, when the child's father discovered the payments, he reported it to the police as identity theft.

One afternoon around 2 pm, when Manuel was at work in the granite factory, he was called into the office. He thought they were calling him in to talk about his pending departure, as he had told them he would be returning to Brazil within the next few weeks. When he arrived at the office, the police were there. The police officers asked him if he was using the social security number in question. He said he was. They asked him where he got the number from and Manuel told them he got it in Miami three years before. The officers told him they had to arrest him because he was being accused of a federal crime: identity theft. Notably, if the number had been unclaimed he would not have been charged with a federal crime, because using a fake number that no one owns is not a criminal offense, whereas it is a federal offense to use an actual number that belongs to someone. One month later, he was taken to trial. Manuel pled guilty to identity theft. All told, Manuel spent three months in jail and was deported to Brazil as a criminal alien.

While ICE uses the term "criminal alien" to conjure images of violent threats to public safety, Manuel clearly presents no threat. Moreover, he had every intention of returning to Brazil and could have saved the U.S. government some money had they decided not to pursue his case.

Driving under the Influence

Legal permanent residents are rarely deported for drunk driving because a single DUI conviction it is not an aggravated felony. However, driving under the influence can land you in jail, which can trigger immigration consequences. This is what happened to both Diallo and Ben, migrants from Guatemala.

I met Diallo in the cafeteria of the call center where he works, after his shift ended. Diallo is in his late thirties, has light brown skin, almond-shaped eyes, and curly, short hair. He spoke English with a strong Boston accent. Diallo was born in 1972 in Escuintla, and he moved to Guatemala City when he was six months old. He moved to the United States when he was eight. He is not sure exactly why his family moved, but it was related to the fact that his stepfather was killed in the employ of Interpol, an international policing organization. His mother, who owned several restaurants in Guatemala City, had begun receiving threats. Shortly after they left, armed gunmen came to one of her restaurants, demanding to speak with the owner. Fortunately, they were already in Boston by that time.

Diallo enrolled in the third grade in Boston. His mother achieved legal permanent residency status for Diallo and for herself. He lived in a primarily white suburb west of Boston called Newton, and he graduated from high school there and went to work with his uncle in shipping and construction.

Diallo and his mother bought a house, and things were going well. However, he developed a drinking problem and began to have trouble with the law. In 1999, after 19 years in the United States, Diallo was arrested for the first time. He served a year of probation for driving under the influence. In addition, the police found a few seeds of marijuana in his car, and he had to pay a $50 fine for marijuana possession. In 2000 he served six months in prison for another DUI charge and paid another $50 fine for possession of a marijuana cigarette. Then, in 2004, he received a third sentence, a 300-day sentence for driving while intoxicated.

Diallo had been an LPR for nearly two decades, but any sentence that lasted for more than a year could lead to deportation. On this third occasion, Diallo had been intoxicated but not driving when arrested; his car was parked on the side of the road and he and his passenger, a black man, had gone to get gas for the car. Someone in the primarily white neighborhood had called the police to report suspicious activity: a black man and a Latino man walking down the road. Diallo might have been able to beat this charge had he gone to court, but he accepted the 300-day plea bargain his lawyer negotiated in order to avoid deportation. With no family ties in Guatemala, Diallo preferred the 300 days to that risk. Nevertheless, he was ordered deported—not because of the DUI but because of the two marijuana charges. Under the 1996 laws, two drug charges constitute an aggravated felony, no matter how small the charges are.

In a similar case, Ben, a young, athletic man, was deported to Guatemala in 2008. He had lived in the United States from the time he was six months old, and a DUI charge ultimately led to his deportation. He was only given three years' probation for the charge, which was imposed in 2005 when he was 20, and while he knew any parole violation could lead to jail time, and that his parole officer had the right to search his room, he did not know that he might be deported for any infraction.

When Ben returned from playing basketball with a friend one night in 2008 and realized his parole officer had searched his room the night before, he had no notion that he had anything that could violate his parole. She had scoured the place, creating such a mess that he spent hours cleaning it up the next day. He'd forgotten about a set of brass knuckles he'd owned and a souvenir bullet his cousin, who is in the Marines, had given him. While neither was illegal, the combination violated the terms of his parole.

Ben was charged with having a dangerous weapon while on probation and with possession of ammunition. He was sentenced to six months in prison. When his prison term was over, Ben was handed over to immigration and he spent a year in immigration detention before deportation. "I pretty much thought that I couldn't get kicked out because I lived all my life there, you know. I don't know anything about here [Guatemala, where I met him]. I've never been here, you know. At least, not when I was old enough to remember." Like Diallo, Ben admits he made a mistake. Diallo admits to having a drinking problem and Ben drove a car while under the influence.

Ironically, immigration law represents an area of the law that, perhaps, punishes drunk driving in better proportion to drug crimes than any other. As Michelle Alexander (2010) argues, the disparities between penalties for drunk driving and those for illegal drug possession do not reflect the fact that in 2010 drunk-driving accidents killed more than 10,000 people in the United States.[8] While numerous states now have mandatory sentencing for first offenses for drunk drivers—two days in jail for a first offense and two to ten days for a second offense— possession of crack cocaine carries a mandatory minimum sentence of five years in prison. Alexander (2010) argues that this disparity is due to the fact that drunk drivers are mostly white (78 percent of all arrests in 1990), whereas nearly all people arrested for crack cocaine are black. Drunk driving carries a much less harsh penalty than crack cocaine possession, even though more than 100,000 people die each year from alcohol-related causes, as compared to 21,000 illegal drug–related deaths each year.

Notwithstanding the overall treatment of drunk driving in the United States, deportation extends the logic of a neoliberal society, which places the blame for all actions on the individual (that is, people like Diallo and Ben). This neoliberal logic of crime control uses a discourse of personal responsibility (Passas 2000). Under this logic, Ben and Diallo should be punished. And they have been through the forcible return to their countries of birth.

Assault, Guns, and Police

DHS's suggestion that mass deportation makes the United States a safer place by removing dangerous criminals misrepresents the vast major- ity of deportations. However, I did interview some deportees who were convicted of violent offenses. Alberto had been convicted of involuntary manslaughter in 1984, before such offenses usually led to immediate deportation upon release from prison, and he was subjected years later to a home invasion in which 20 officers surrounded his house. Again, this standpoint relies on the neoliberal logic that the United States is a dangerous place because of a small number of individuals who are unable to control themselves, rather than focusing on structural reasons for crime. The reaction of the state to these lawbreakers is to mete out harsh punishment. When they are noncitizens, an additional punish- ment is deportation.

Fewer than 10 percent of people deported on criminal grounds have convictions for violent offenses. I interviewed very few people with such convictions. One of them, Alberto, was mentioned earlier. Chris is another example. He was deported after an assault conviction.

Chris was an LPR who had been born in Jamaica. He got into trouble after living many years as a law-abiding person in the United States. Chris told me that one of his neighbors, a crack addict, stole some goods from his apartment. Chris confronted him about the theft, and they got into a fight. The addict pulled out a knife. Chris wrestled the knife from him and stabbed him. Chris was convicted of assault and sentenced to one year in jail. He served eight months and was taken directly to immigration detention from Rikers Island. He spent five months in a detention facility in Texas and was deported. This was Chris's first time in jail. When he was deported, Chris had been in the United States for 38 years, was married to a U.S. citizen, and had three U.S.-born children. While the logic of removing people from the United States who pose an ongoing threat to society has some validity, the point of sentences as short as the one imposed on Chris is that society did not judge him an ongoing threat.

Under U.S. law, deportation is not an additional punishment for a crime but is a civil penalty for violation of the Immigration and Nationality Act, which stipulates that noncitizens convicted of certain charges face mandatory deportation.

Emanuel's story involves guns, a controversial issue in the United States. Emanuel had lived in the United States since he was a teenager but was deported to the Dominican Republic on a firearms charge. Emanuel finished high school in New York in 1980, and he decided to join the army afterward. He said that the streets were getting dangerous and he preferred to join the military. Emanuel served in the army for two years. When he finished, he got a job in a factory. Working there, he was able to go to night school to complete a technical degree at DeVry Institute of Technology. When he finished, he got a job with a company that fixed security cameras within supermarkets.

When Emanuel was in the army, he purchased a gun for his personal use. When he acquired it, he lived in North Carolina, where it was legal to own guns. However, he took it with him to New Jersey, where it is illegal for civilians to carry firearms without a permit. One day in early 1996, Emanuel was driving his car in New Jersey. A police officer pulled him over and asked to search the car. Emanuel agreed. The officer found the gun and arrested Emanuel. He was sentenced to one year in prison for illegal possession of a firearm. He served nine months and was released back to his family. Emanuel began working again but had to report to the parole officer each month. During this time, immigration law enforcement set up programs that enabled them to check the citizenship status of parolees. On one occasion, when Emanuel showed up for his meeting with his parole officer, immigration agents were waiting for him. He was deported to the Dominican Republic in 1998.

Like Chris, Caleb had children in the United States. Like Emanuel, he is a U.S. military veteran. Like Ben, he was ultimately deported for a parole violation. Caleb got into an altercation at a nightclub, and this fight earned him two years of probation. While he was still on probation, a police officer followed Caleb to a friend's house. When he parked, the police officer asked him about his car's tags. Caleb asked the officer if he was under arrest; the officer said he was not, so Caleb went into his friend's house. When he came out of his friend's house, the car was gone. The next morning, Caleb went to the police station and found that the Lexus had been impounded and severely damaged in the process. Caleb believes that the police officers wrongly presumed that he had drugs in the car and thus subjected his car to an extensive search. A jury found Caleb guilty of resisting arrest without violence, a charge that specified he had not resisted violently, because he went into his friend's house, for which he received a sentence of nine months in jail. Receiving the conviction meant that Caleb had violated his probation, and the judge sentenced him to 46 months in prison. Caleb was deported to Jamaica, the country he had left 20 years earlier.

Caleb expressed more outrage about the deportation, which separated him from his two daughters, than his imprisonment. When we spoke, he was in the process of appealing his case. His prospects for an appeal are slim. Moreover, even if his case is overturned, he would need the assistance of extremely skilled lawyers to be able to return to the United States. As far as I know, there are only two agencies—one at New York University and the other at Boston University—that operate postdeportation clinics.

A pattern we can discern in the cases described here is that the deportation of each of these men is related to their race, class, and gender. How likely is it that a white, middle-class woman would find herself in a situation where she is being attacked by her neighbor who is high on drugs? How likely is it that she would be arrested after getting into an altercation in a bar or serve time in prison for illegal possession of a firearm? Given residential segregation patterns, white women are less likely to live in neighborhoods where their neighbors might burglarize their homes. Even if arrested and charged with an offense, white women are significantly less likely to be convicted. If convicted, their sentences will be shorter (Mauer 2007).

On the one hand, we can blame individuals for their deviant behavior. However, it also makes sense to ask what structural conditions were involved. In Chris's case, his experience was closely related to where he lived, because his neighbor initiated the dispute. For Emanuel and Caleb, the event that led to their deportation involved being pulled over by a police officer. Even if we can't uncover individual acts of racism by state agents in each of these cases, the trend is apparent. Finally, it is conceivable that, with adequate legal representation, Chris may have been able to have claimed self-defense and Caleb may have been able to have been found not guilty of resisting arrest.

The NFOP: ICE Home Raids

Whereas the CAP is the largest immigration enforcement program, ICE home raids account for a fairly small percentage of deportations. However, they are significant insofar as they create extreme fear for any family that experiences them. Additionally, stories of these raids circulate in immigrant communities, leading to more fear and self-imposed social control, similar to what we have witnessed in the aftermath of large-scale workplace raids (Golash-Boza 2012). As these stories circulate, undocumented immigrants feel compelled to live under the radar as much as possible, and they experience a pervasive fear of deportation, which enhances their economic and social vulnerability (Miller 2008; Harrison and Lloyd 2012).

ICE agents that conduct home raids will enter private homes in search of suspected undocumented migrants or "criminal aliens." A typical raid is usually conducted in the following way. Very early in the morning, when most occupants are sleeping, ICE agents surround a house and pound on the door and windows. I heard stories of 20 officers or more descending on a house and terrifying occupants not yet dressed for the day.

When the occupant opens the door, the agents enter the home, frequently without properly identifying themselves or gaining the consent of the occupant. They may do so under false pretenses—I heard of a case where officers claimed to be responding to reports of a robbery. Once the agents enter the house, they order all of the occupants—including children and the elderly—to a central location. Though often looking for a particular person who is suspected to be a fugitive or criminal alien, they frequently interrogate all occupants of the house and will arrest anyone whom they suspect to be unlawfully present in the United States. Imagine if law enforcement agents could raid homes for tax evasion and then could arrest anyone else in the home unable to provide immediate proof of having filed their taxes. ICE refers to these literally "unwarranted" arrests of suspected undocumented migrants as "collateral arrests." Evidence suggests that markers of a Latino background have been used as the only substitute for nonexistent markers of not being documented, because many U.S. citizens and legally present people of Latin American origin have been arrested in these raids (Azmy et al. 2008).

ICE home raids since 2003 have involved a series of violations both of people's constitutional rights and of ICE's own policies. According to a recent report, aptly titled "Constitution on ICE,"[9] ICE agents routinely fail to observe constitutional rights during home raids. The fourth amendment to the U.S. Constitution implicitly protects citizens and noncitizens from unreasonable searches and seizures, and ICE agents who enter private homes without permission act in violation of this. These protections contrast with ICE protocol, which allows them to arrest any person they suspect not to be a citizen of the United States.

Maximo told me of a violation of just this kind. A Dominican citizen who lived in Puerto Rico, Maximo shared an apartment in San Juan with two other men, a Venezuelan and a Puerto Rican. Early one morning in January 2010, they heard loud banging on the door. Maximo tried to sleep through it, but the banging got louder. Finally, he got up to answer the door. Just before he reached the door, the people knocking decided to break it down. Maximo found himself surrounded by 40 armed officers, some of whom had jackets with ICE stamped on them. The agents did not indicate that they had a warrant for the arrest of a specific person. Instead, they demanded to see all occupants of the house, then pointed guns at them and ordered them to sit on the floor. When they asked Maximo for identification, he gave them his Dominican passport. They asked if he was in the country illegally, and he said he was.

Once the search was over, Maximo was arrested and taken to an immigration detention center. He signed a voluntary departure form and was deported to Santo Domingo two days later. A voluntary departure allowed Maximo to be deported quickly. He could have asked for an immigration hearing, but he would have spent months in detention awaiting his hearing and his chances for gaining legalization were slim to none.

If Maximo's story is accurate, his constitutional rights were violated. Immigration agents have administrative warrants that do not permit them to enter houses without the consent of the occupants. They definitely were not looking for Maximo, as he had never had any previous encounters with immigration agents, so he could not have had a deportation order. He just happened to be there and was arrested when he revealed that he was undocumented. Maximo's arrest is one of the many collateral arrests made by ICE agents during home raids. These sorts of arrests account for a substantial portion of arrests during home raids.

Unlike Maximo, ICE agents actually had an arrest warrant for Vern, a fugitive alien from Guatemala. Vern fled an abusive family situation in Guatemala when he was 10 years old and had lived for 10 years in Mexico. In 1991, when he was 20 years old, Vern traveled to the United States, where he applied for political asylum. The Immigration and Naturalization Service (INS) issued him a work permit while his case was being processed, and he began to work in a frozen-food plant in Ohio. He met and married a Honduran woman, Maria, who was also applying for political asylum. They received work permits every year that allowed them to continue working legally, and their first child was born in 1996. Similar to many other Central American immigrants, Vern and Maria lived in a status of "liminal legality" (Menjívar 2006: 1008), where their status is temporary and contingent, somewhere between the statuses of LPR and undocumented immigrant. Liminal status can expire and people like Vern can easily slip back into being undocumented.

In 1998, Vern received a notice that he should leave the United States—his asylum application had been denied. Vern was devastated; he had established a life in the United States, and he had few ties to Guatemala. He decided to stay, in the hope that his wife's application would be approved, so she could apply to legalize his status. They had another child. Vern lived in fear that immigration agents would come for him. He did everything he could to avoid problems with the police—he never drank, avoided traffic violations, and abided by the laws at all times. He learned English, took his kids on outings every weekend, and tried to blend in as much as possible.

It was not enough. One Sunday morning, two immigration agents came to Vern's house and arrested him in front of his children, aged 12 and 9. Vern was put into detention and, eight days later, he was in Guatemala, the country he had left nearly three decades before. Vern's arrest was part of the NFOP, which has been given the money and the authority by Congress to search homes for dangerous criminal fugitive aliens that threaten national security. Vern was a fugitive alien, and that is why he was deported. It is easy to make the case that Vern did not have the legal right to remain in the United States. That he presented a threat to national security, however, is a hard case to make.

Conclusion

The stated goal of criminal law enforcement is to enhance public safety. The stated goal of immigration law enforcement is to enhance public safety and national security. Prisons serve the purpose of locking people away and preventing them from committing crimes against people who are not incarcerated. Deportation removes people from the United States, with the ostensible goal of making the country more safe and secure. Both of these institutional practices are based on the idea that the country would be safer if they could only get rid of bad people. Long gone is the idea that people could be rehabilitated.

The deportees I spoke with are not simply bad people. Most of them made mistakes, but even those convicted of violent crimes probably do not pose an ongoing risk to society. By being removed, they are separated from their families and communities. Their children, brothers, sisters, parents, and other friends and family suffer the loss of a loved one. The argument that none of this would have happened had they obeyed the law is based on an individualist understanding of lawbreaking and social disorder. From a critical perspective, we can see that laws are made to be broken, that lawbreaking is common across all racial, gender, and class divides, and that the selective enforcement of laws leads to a racialized and gendered system of social control. We can also perceive a long history of devaluing the family ties of nonwhite families in the United States—going back to the era of slavery. As Patricia Hill Collins (1998: 72) points out, "Members of some racial families receive full benefits of membership while others encounter inferior treatment." Because of the devaluing of some families, the "family values" discourse of the 1990s has been primarily applicable to white, middle-class families.

ICE reports its numbers each year, showing the number of Level 1, 2, and 3 offenders. The stories in this chapter show that even if someone is convicted of a Level 1 offense a deportation is not always a win-win situation. Caleb, for example, was convicted of resisting arrest, assault, and violating parole. However, it is far from clear that he poses a constant danger to society. It is very clear that his deportation means that his children will grow up without a father physically present in their lives and that his children and their mother will be much less financially stable than they would have been had he not been deported.

As a consequence of the deportation of the people profiled in this book, hundreds of children are growing up without their fathers present, single mothers are struggling to make ends meet, and parents have effectively lost their sons and daughters. Moreover, the effects reverberate throughout the community. People who hear about or witness deportation live in fear that it could happen to them.

In this chapter, I provided details of the lives of several deportees in order to develop a more nuanced understanding of their lives and to think about the relationship between lawbreaking and deportation. These apprehension stories help us to parse out how people are caught in the deportation dragnet. Once arrested, people are placed in jails, prison, and detention. In the next chapter, we take a look at what goes on behind bars.

6

Behind Bars

Immigration Detention and Prison Life

The incarcerated population in the United States reached a peak at around 2.2 million in 2009. The rate of incarceration of 767 people behind bars per 100,000 in the general population was five times what it had been in 1972. Since 2010, the incarceration rate has shown signs of decline, meaning the era of prison growth may be over (National Research Council 2014). But significant decreases seem far off. More than two million people continue to be behind bars. Seven million people are under criminal justice supervision. Twelve million felons in the United States, many of them released from prison, face lifelong stigma and economic deprivation (Pager 2007; Alexander 2010). Incarceration not only influences the lives of these 19 million people directly involved in the criminal justice system: It also affects their children, spouses, and communities (Comfort 2007).

Many people in the United States are unaware that, in addition to the incarcerated population, there are thousands of people behind bars who are not serving time for a crime or waiting for a trial. Instead, they are in immigration detention and are awaiting an immigration hearing or their deportation. On an average day in 2009, there were about 33,000 immigrants in detention centers around the country.[1] Similar to incarceration rates, there has been an uptick in the rate of immigration detention. In 1973, Immigration and Customs Enforcement (ICE) detained a daily average of 2,370 migrants. In 1994, this rate went up to 5,532. It was up to 20,000 in 2001 and has gone up another 50 percent since (Dow 2004; Golash-Boza 2012).

Nearly all of my interviewees spent time in immigration detention. Some of them only stayed a few days, whereas others were in detention for over a year appealing their deportation orders. Many of the deportees I interviewed spent time both in prison and in immigration detention. Their experiences behind bars help us to understand this integral part of the criminalization of immigrants.

Mass incarceration is a relatively new phenomenon in the United States, and it marks a divergence from attitudes of the mid-20th century, when Americans tended to view incarceration as an ineffective means of controlling crime and sought other solutions to secure public safety. Prison was seen as a last resort, and in the mid-1970s, the Federal Bureau of Prisons planned to close large prisons in Kansas, Washington State, and Georgia. In 1970, Congress voted to eliminate nearly all federal mandatory minimum sentences for drug offenders, because most Americans viewed drug addiction as a problem of public health, not criminal justice (Alexander 2010).

Just ten years later, this mindset—that drugs are a public health problem and prisons are barbaric—was pushed to the margins as mass incarceration took off. The U.S. incarceration rate was about 1 per 1,000 residents for almost the entire 20th century, up until the 1970s. According to the data from the Bureau of Justice Statistics, the rate doubled between 1972 and 1984, then again between 1984 and 1994. By the end of the 20th century, the United States had an unprecedented number of inmates: over two million, more than 10 times any number of U.S. inmates prior to the 1970s. In 2009, more than 7.2 million people were on probation or parole or were in jail or prison: This statistic affects 3.1 percent of all U.S. adult residents, or 1 in every 32 adults. The increase in incarceration cannot be explained by a rise in crime, because crime rates have not fluctuated with incarceration rates (Wacquant 2009; Alexander 2010). Incarceration rates have soared because the laws have changed, lengthening prison sentences and making a wider variety of crimes punishable by incarceration. By the beginning of the 21st century, the United States had built a massive system of incarceration that seems to have little chance of dissipating.

The ease with which the U.S. government puts people behind bars is quite remarkable: Despite the putative importance of liberty, U.S. citizens accept the deprivation of freedom for anyone convicted of a crime. The nominal reasons for imprisonment are punishment (retribution, prevention of future harm, rehabilitation, or deterrence). These ideas of punishment and the moral authority of the state to punish go back to ancient times (Golash 2005). However, the United States is unique insofar as it puts far more people behind bars than any other country does. A consideration of the political economy of mass incarceration helps us to understand why this is the case. It also helps us to see where mass incarceration fits into the story of mass deportation.

The Political Economy of Incarceration

Mass incarceration in the United States is directly tied to neoliberal economic reforms. At the same time that the federal government began to cut funding for social programs, it began to open the doors of its prisons. "Reaganomics," a brand of neoliberalism launched in the 1980s, involved heavy cuts to a wide variety of social programs. As the welfare system shrank, the prison system grew: The number of inmates in federal prison expanded from 25,000 in 1980 to 219,000 in 2011. This dramatic rise in federal imprisonment rates primarily reflects increases in the numbers of people prosecuted for drug and immigration offenses. However, the most substantial increases have happened at the state level. California led the states in a prison buildup.

Between 1977 and 2007, the California Assembly passed more than 1,000 laws extending and toughening prison sentences (Wacquant 2009). The California State prison population increased five-fold between 1982 and 2000, even though the crime rate peaked in 1980 and declined thereafter. Notably, California's incarceration rate increased after the crime rate had begun to decrease. California had built only 12 prisons between 1852 and 1964, yet it built 23 major new prisons between 1984 and 2004 (Gilmore 2007). What happened? Why did California engage in this massive prison-building project? Why did the legislature pass so many anticrime laws?

Economic restructuring in California during the period holds the answers. During World War II, much of California's prosperity had been tied directly to defense contracts; people from across the country flocked to California to secure well-paying jobs building defense machinery. After the war, California invested in education and technology to ensure that defense contracts would continue, and it endeavored to make itself uniquely able to provide research, development, and manufacturing for the Department of Defense (DoD). DoD contracts continued to come in until the 1980s, but these contracts contributed to the bifurcation of the labor force into well-paid, technology jobs on the one hand, and low-skilled, poorly paid jobs on the other (Gilmore 2007). As you will recall from previous chapters, this economic restructuring was a national trend. And although this trend meant a loss of jobs in the manufacturing sector, it opened up jobs in the service economy, which immigrants often filled.

As in other states, the restructuring of California's economy led to increases in unemployment, poverty, and inequality. By the 1980s, California was a highly unequal state, with high poverty rates, high housing costs, and high unemployment rates alongside some of the wealthiest people in the nation. Over the next 15 years, its economy would continue to change, with more and more low-paid manufacturing and service jobs and fewer high-paid manufacturing jobs. Childhood poverty rates increased 25 percent between 1969 and 1979. These rates continued to soar, increasing another 67 percent between 1980 and 1995, such that by the end of the 20th century one in four children in California lived in poverty (Gilmore 2007). Beset with social problems, the California legislature used mass incarceration to address poverty, unemployment, and inequality. Prisons serve the double purpose of providing employment to tens of thousands of Californians who work in the prison system and locking away a good proportion of the surplus labor force.

The economic restructuring and cuts in government spending in California mirrored those in the rest of the country. Christian Parenti (2000: 41) explains: "In 1982 alone, Reagan cut the real value of welfare by 24 percent, slashed the budget for child nutrition by 34 percent, [and] reduced funding for school milk programs by 78 percent, urban development action grants by 35 percent, and educational block grants by 38 percent." These enormous cuts in social spending disproportionately affected low-wage people of color in urban areas. As is typical in these sorts of reforms, the state simultaneously enhanced its repressive capacities. As David Harvey (2005: 77) argues, "In the United States incarceration became a key state strategy to deal with problems arising among discarded workers and marginalized populations. The coercive arm of the state is augmented to protect corporate interests and, if necessary, to repress dissent."

As these cuts to government spending on social welfare spread across the country, companies began to outsource manufacturing jobs, sending jobs once held by blue-collar Americans overseas where cheaper labor could be found. Deindustrialization led to the impoverishment of cities such as Chicago and Detroit. Detroit was hit particularly hard: It lost half of its population in the 1980s. The beginning of the War on Drugs coincided with deindustrialization. Well-paying, stable, blue-collar jobs disappeared, leaving unemployment, as well as social unrest, in their wake (Alexander 2010). The possibility of social unrest led to the expansion of the criminal justice system, designed to manage and contain the underclass created by neoliberal economic policies (Wacquant 2009). Racialized fears of crime have meant that the prison buildup has had public support: People with negative biases toward African Americans are more likely to support punitive policies (Bobo and Thompson 2010).

In 2009, after 30 years of prison building, California found itself with a massive prison system it was no longer able to finance. It is remarkable that the first cuts in California's prison system came not because the prison system was failing to reduce crime but because the state could no longer afford to finance a state prison system larger than that of most other countries in the world. Facing similar economic pressures, the state of New York closed four prisons in 2013.[2]

Mass incarceration served a political purpose insofar as politicians were able to present themselves as tough on crime. It served an economic purpose insofar as it provided jobs in rural areas. And it served an ideological purpose. In a neoliberal society, the state takes limited responsibility for the well-being of its citizens, expecting each individual to be entrepreneurial and independent. It celebrates people who succeed in this environment. When a threadbare safety net fails people who cannot support themselves and who turn to the illegal economy, the state places them behind bars. By doing so, the state sends the message that it is protecting society and also sends a warning message to others who might consider falling out of line.

The effects of incarceration, moreover, are far-reaching. Nearly all prisoners will eventually be released (Petersilia 2003). And many prisoners emerge from prison deeply scarred by their experiences.

Life on the Inside

The deportees I spoke with experienced incarceration as demeaning, stressful, and dangerous. Hector, for example, never expected to end up behind bars. He came to the United States from Guatemala as a toddler. He completed a degree at the University of California and was on track to middle-class success when he was convicted of credit-card fraud. He was sentenced to two years in prison.

When he was initially booked into Los Angeles County Jail, the bailiff inquired about his sexual orientation. Hector told him he was a gay man, and the bailiff placed Hector in the LGBT section of the holding cells. Hector's first cellmate was a transgender woman who explained to him that there are segregated cells in county jail but not in state prison. In L.A. County Jail, Hector was issued a powder-blue uniform, as are all of the other LGBT inmates. L.A. County Jail is unique in that it has a separate facility for gay men and transgender women. This unit, created in 1985, is also distinctive insofar as it is relatively free from threats of physical or sexual violence—quite different from the dangerous conditions in the rest of the jail (Dolovich 2012).

County jails are designed as holding cells and are not for long-term incarceration. The conditions in these jails vary dramatically. Some of the deportees I interviewed expressed frustration about the conditions in county jail. For example, Manuel, a Brazilian deportee charged with identity theft, told me that jail is

> one of the most terrible, dark places you could ever go. There, you don't take a shower; you don't eat properly, because of the enormous stress. Also, they only give you sandwiches, and we Brazilians are not used to eating sandwiches. You will be hungry in there. It is also a claustrophobic place. I suffer from claustrophobia, and when they closed that cell door, that was it for me.

Manuel spent only seven days in county jail before being taken to prison, where he found the conditions a bit more tolerable. In contrast, Hector stayed in L.A. County Jail for three months before being transferred to a state facility. When Hector arrived at the state prison, he told the receiving deputies, "I am gay and I need protective custody." They responded, "You're a big boy. Deal with it." Unlike L.A. County Jail, the state prison had no separate unit for gay and transgender people.

The officers then asked Hector if he was white, black, or Mexican so that they could place him with the right group. Hector, who was born in Guatemala, chose Mexican. He explained his rationale:

> The Mexicans sleep with the Mexicans. The blacks sleep with blacks. The whites with the whites. And if you're Asian, you gotta pick one or the other. Some prisons will let you pick other. . . . I get to state and I walk in and I'm forced to choose a race. I choose Mexican because I'm not black and I'm not white. And the whites are really . . . skinheads.

Racial tensions within prisons are high. Some California prison systems have responded by separating black, Latino, and white inmates into different groups. Manuel also found racial tensions in the Florida prison where he was housed. Manuel explained that the African American prisoners bothered him because they thought he was a "yellow black" (an African American with light skin) and were troubled that he chose to make friends with white prisoners. Although Manuel has African ancestry, in keeping with social norms in Brazil, he does not identify as black. The African American prisoners, however, saw him as black and Manuel had to learn to deal with the racial dynamics of the prison in which he was housed. Similarly, Hector's fellow prisoners pressured him to choose an affiliation with one of the prison gangs.

Hector describes his first Mexican cellmate as a "lifelong gangbanger":

> [He was] this guy with tattoos all over his face. You know, a scary-looking guy. And I tried not to say a word because I know if I open my mouth, I'm gonna give myself away. So I'm keeping it as short and sweet, to the point. And he is asking me if I gangbang and I'm just, like, "No, no, no, yes, no." I lived with him tenuously for a while. I had to choose one of the two Mexican gangs. . . . Well, my cellmate, once he realized I was completely fresh and had absolutely no idea what I was doing, he took a very kind attitude. He was a nice guy. It kind of helped me figure out what I was gonna do and he said he was a Southsider.

Gangs run many California state prisons, and prisoners often feel obliged to choose an affiliation. Most gangs conform to racial categories. U.S.-born Latinos in California state prisons align with one of two gangs: the Northsiders or the Southsiders. Foreign-born Latinos typically join Paisas (Dolovich 2012). As a 1.5-generation Latino with a Southsider cellmate, Hector chose to join the Southsiders. He explained why he did so:

> I chose to be a Southsider because of my cellmate and because of the people that I knew. So, the first time that you go to yard, that's that next morning, you are in the midst of really ground zero. Race tension, violent, race-related violence. It's scary. I remember the first time I saw somebody get stabbed. I saw somebody get sliced seriously, probably where like that person is dead. I know that person is dead. This person sitting next to me just got stabbed and that person is dead. Or the first time that you see the tower shoot somebody. The guard's towers. It's a scary feeling. When lights go out and all the Southsiders have to take care of a problem with another Southsider who has done something bad and then all of a sudden I get caught up in the stuff. I have to or it's my life on the line. At that point it's survival: me or this person. And it broke my heart to do anything, I had to do it. And it's not in my nature and I'm not proud of it.

Prisons may be designed to reduce crime. However, as Hector's story makes clear, prisoners often are vulnerable to violent crime while inside prison. Donald Sabo, Terry Allen Kupers, and Willie James London (2001) argue that many young, nonviolent offenders are thrown into overcrowded prisons and must learn both to toughen themselves up and to become numb to the pain of others. Hector witnessed several acts of violence within prison, and he even admitted to engaging in violence himself for his own protection. Hector was not convicted of a violent crime and had not engaged in violence while he was a free man. In prison, however, he found it difficult to avoid violence. In prisons controlled by gangs, gang members are obliged to get involved in any altercation involving members of their group. If two black inmates were to attack a Southsider and Hector was around, he would have no choice except to jump in the fight. If he didn't, he would surely face a violent reprisal from fellow Southsiders later on, as well as a loss of respect.

The hypermasculinity of men's prisons creates this environment. It requires men to prove their prowess through physical acts. However, prisons also restrict access to heterosexual partners, thereby limiting a key part of men's masculinity. Inside prisons, men do have access to same-sex relationships, and these relationships do occur, both consensually and through rape.

In prison, Hector was fearful of being forced into nonconsensual same-sex relationships. One solution to this potential problem was to develop an intimate relationship with someone inside the prison who would also protect him from unwanted sexual overtures. Hector found an intimate partner and explained that finding a partner was crucial to his protection:

> Obviously, it is very difficult for me to hide the fact that I'm gay. I ended up meeting one of the other Southsiders who was a young guy like me, about the same age. . . . So this guy comes up to me and he is like, "Listen, I can tell that you're gay." And he said, "Why don't you move in with me and be my cellie?" He is one of the carnales, the big homies. He is running the gang on this yard in this building for the Southsiders. He said, "Just move in with me and you're going to avoid a lot of problems." And it turned out that he and I ended up getting along really well. He is heterosexual but we ended up getting into a relationship and as a matter of fact, we were in a relationship for a really long time. The entire time that I was at that prison with him, we were in that relationship. And it got to the point where we chose to stay together.

Hector's partner was able to work things out so that they could share a cell.

> Because he had been there so many times he had a lot of juice with the officers. So, he said, "I want that guy moved into my cell." The officer is, like, "Sure, tell him to pack his stuff. I'll have his cell changed later today." He walked over, helped me pick up my stuff, and moved me into his cell, moved his cellie out of there. And we actually ended really getting into a

relationship really is what it is. For each traditional gender role, he was very much the man. I was very much the woman and I am going to leave it at that because I'm demure. . . . I took care of the cooking, the cleaning, and the washing, really is what it was. I don't mind playing house. I mean, I love it. And he took care of everything else. Right? We shared everything, obviously, and we lived together.

Like any first-time prisoner, Hector had to learn the rules of prison, which are rooted in a patriarchal society but have their own manifestation in prison. Inside prison, it is often acceptable for men to enter into a relationship and for a dominant male to claim possession of another man (Sabo et al. 2001).

Hector was distinct from my other respondents in that he talked at length and in great detail about his experiences behind bars. It seemed that others' reticence reflected trauma and perhaps shame. Most of the other deportees only spoke briefly about their experiences behind bars. No matter how long they spent in prison, it was not an experience they wanted to dwell on. They wanted to forget about it, just as most people on the outside would rather not think about the fact that millions of people live without freedom. Jose Carlos is another deportee who was willing to talk about his prison experiences.

Jose Carlos, who is also Guatemalan, was a tattoo artist and found a niche for himself by making tattoos in prison. Jose was able to make a homemade tattoo machine with a motor from another electronic device along with ink that was smuggled into the prison. He charged inmates $75 for each tattoo, and they paid him by asking family members to put money into his account. Jose Carlos had quite a different experience from Hector. Jose Carlos spent eight months in state prison for drug possession, yet, unlike Hector, he did not experience pressure to join a gang. Jose Carlos explained that he did not have to join a gang, but he was obliged to follow the informal rules and only hang out with Latinos.

Whereas Jose Carlos felt he was able to lay low and just do his time, Hector had to become a different person to survive. Prison transformed a middle-class college graduate into a gang member. Hector's open homosexuality shaped his experience. Hector describes his relationship with his cellmate as consensual and based on mutual respect. Perhaps because of this, other gang members decided to test Hector's partner, to see if he had gotten too soft. The other gang members asked him to kill someone in the prison.

Hector's partner had only two choices: commit the act and risk a greatly lengthened sentence, or break the prison rules and get himself in solitary confinement for his own protection. He elected to seek solitary confinement. Hector decided to follow suit, because his partner's confinement would leave him vulnerable to reprisal.

As Hector's story reflects, violence is an integral part of the incarceration experience for men. In a recent article, Mika'il DeVeaux (2013), who was incarcerated for 25 years, argues that incarceration is traumatic because of the constant threat and reality of violence.

When prisoners are released, many are placed on parole or probation and have access to reintegration programs. These programs are designed to ease former inmates' transition back into society. Noncitizens who are incarcerated and face deportation, however, are not put into reintegration programs. Instead, they are sent to immigration detention and then to their home countries.

Immigration Detention

When Hector finished his time in state prison, he was transferred to immigration detention, where he was to await his deportation to Guatemala. Detention facilities do not have the same level of organized crime and violence as do state prisons. However, they come with their own set of challenges.

The immigration detention system is a complex of Department of Homeland Security (DHS) detention centers, county and city jails, and privately owned prisons used to hold noncitizens awaiting immigration trial or deportation. In 2009, DHS detained about 380,000 people at 350 different facilities, at a cost of more than $1.7 billion.[3] These detainees are not serving time for any criminal law violations. Instead, they are civil detainees awaiting trial or deportation. Unlike in prison, you cannot be sentenced to a fixed amount of time in immigration detention. In contrast, immigration detention is where noncitizens go once they have completed their prison or jail sentences and where noncitizens await immigration hearings.

The recent expansion of immigration detention has created a profitable market for the private prison industry, especially the Corrections Corporation of America (CCA) and the GEO Group. The CCA is the largest ICE contractor, with 14,566 detention beds. The second largest, GEO, has more than 7,000 beds. These two companies have a history of lobbying legislators in efforts to expand detention and of reaping tremendous profits in the era of mass deportation. Between 1999 and 2009, the CCA spent $18 million lobbying Congress as well as DHS.[4]

Privatization of public services is a key aspect of neoliberal reforms. Insofar as neoliberalism involves unleashing the free market from the shackles of government, the idea that private companies do a better job at providing services than the government is central to neoliberal ideology. In the case of immigration detention as well as incarceration, we have witnessed the private sector reaping profits while costing the government billions of dollars.

The law protects criminal suspects and convicted prisoners in a range of ways not available to immigrant detainees. People arrested and charged with criminal offenses in the United States have the opportunity to challenge their imprisonment before a court and the Department of Justice (DoJ) provides them with legal counsel if they cannot afford it. The Fifth Amendment of the U.S. Constitution provides for the right not to "be deprived of life, liberty, or property without due process of law." A Supreme Court decision in 2001 noted that "freedom from imprisonment lies at the heart of the liberty protected by the Due Process Clause."[5] People held by DHS, however, do not have the same rights and safeguards as criminal suspects do in the United States, even though immigrant detention is preventative. DHS can detain people only in order to ensure their deportation or their appearance at a removal hearing. DHS does not have the authority to hold anyone punitively.

In *Demore v. Kim*, Chief Justice William Rehnquist ruled that "the Government may constitutionally detain deportable aliens during the limited period necessary for their removal proceedings." *Demore v. Kim* revolved around the question of whether the government could detain noncitizens who awaited their deportation proceedings or whether it had to give these noncitizens individualized bond hearings to determine whether they posed a flight risk. Kim, who had been a legal permanent resident (LPR) of the United States since he was a small child, argued he should have had the right to a hearing before an impartial official, to determine whether or not he posed a flight risk. In the Court's opinion, Rehnquist concluded he did not require a hearing and that detention during removal proceedings is acceptable, in part because these proceedings are typically not lengthy.[6] Justice David Souter's dissent stated that noncitizens are persons before the law and should be afforded due process. Souter cited a 1987 Supreme Court decision, in which the Chief Justice wrote, "In our society liberty is the norm, and detention prior to trial or without trial is the carefully limited exception."[7] For noncitizens subject to removal from the United States, however, detention has become the norm, and bond hearings are the exception.

Despite the centrality of due process and habeas corpus protections to legal frameworks in the United States, the current system of immigration detention violates these procedural protections in three critical ways: (1) Detainees bear the burden of proof; (2) the state can deny bond hearings; and (3) the judge and the jailer are sometimes the same. DHS justifies the detention of noncitizens as a measure necessary to ensure they appear at immigration trials and leave the country when ordered to do so. With this justification, DHS detains people who are very likely to win their cases against deportation, people who have served in the U.S. armed forces, people who have lived in the United States for most of their lives, people who own homes and businesses in the United States, people who are ill, and people who have U.S. citizen parents, children, and siblings.

Under U.S. law, immigration detention is not considered incarceration. Erving Goffman (1961) described prisons as "total institutions" insofar as they have these four characteristics: (1) Inmates are obliged to sleep, play, and work in one space and cannot leave; (2) inmates are required to live with other inmates, and they all have to do the same things; (3) the day's activities are tightly scheduled according to specific rules; and (4) the various aspects of prison life are supposed to fill the official aims of the institution. Immigration detention facilities also qualify as total institutions under this definition and share many characteristics with prisons.

My respondents who had served time in prison and in detention described the experiences as being similar. Some suffered more in detention than prison, others a little less. Like incarcerated people, they lost touch with their families, experienced violence, and suffered financial jeopardy due to imprisonment. While U.S. law states that immigrant detention cannot be punitive, my respondents experienced immigrant detention as punishment.

Elias spent nearly a year in detention, until he ultimately gave up on the appeal process so that he could get out of detention and be deported back to Jamaica. At first, Elias thought he had a chance to win his appeals. However, after spending 18 months in jail on a controlled substance charge, and 11 months in detention, he was tired of being behind bars. I asked Elias about his experiences in immigration detention, especially insofar as it compared to his experiences in state prison:

Terrible! Oh my God it was worse than the state 10 times. . . . The food is terrible, the place is not clean, and it's just terrible. MRSA staph infection was running rampant though there . . . and the food was terrible. . . . This guy named David . . . they beat him up for nothing and put him in a cell with feces and blood all over the wall. . . . They beat him up terrible. His back was fractured.

Many of the deportees complained about the food, lack of exercise, violence, and unsanitary conditions. Philip, for example, is a vegetarian, and he had trouble getting adequate food. Philip also described unstable conditions inside the detention center, largely due to overcrowding. Many other deportees found immigration detention to be uncomfortable. Alberto, for example, complained it was too cold. He said it was

disgusting. I hate that place; it was icy cold in there and that place even in the winter they have the air conditioning operating the same way. They take all your clothes; they had me in [a] jumper without a t-shirt and they would take you out in the freezing cold to court, without a jacket. The minute I got in I said, "Bring my papers and sign it right now. I want to leave; I can pay my own fare," because I did not want to be in here two years like some guys. I wanted to buy my ticket and then the whole

United States army could escort me to the airport. I didn't want to be in no jail—not even for a second.

Alberto was detained for five weeks and he said the cold environment prevented him from sleeping. A recent report in the Los Angeles Times corroborates Alberto's claim that immigration detention centers are kept cold. Immigration activists say that freezing cells—colloquially referred to by guards and detainees alike as "iceboxes"—are used to pressure detainees to agree to deportation.[8] Melvin, also Jamaican, explained that detention is worse than prison because you don't have the same freedoms you have in prison.

> To me, immigration is, like, you don't commit crimes like a criminal . . . , so you should get better treatment. If you have money in your account, you should be able to buy stuff that you really need. In prison you're free, you can buy your stuff, you could buy your jeans, your shower shoes, your little snacks, so you don't eat all that they give you; you don't have to eat that.

It is remarkable that Melvin said that "in prison you're free" insofar as you are able to purchase some consumer items while incarcerated. In contrast, in immigration detention, Melvin did not have the freedom to purchase items he needed and desired. Melvin didn't feel there was adequate food in immigrant detention.

> When you're in immigration [detention], you have to try to force yourself to eat what you don't even want to eat, you know what I'm saying. Because you have money in your account, and you can't even buy what you need to buy 'cause they don't sell it, you're not, you're not existing, you're not in their world, you know what I'm saying? . . . They don't give us free air, they don't, they, they lock us up, they, they everything is inside, you know what I'm saying?

Prison allowed outdoor recreation and commissary purchases. Detention often did not provide these options. In this way, for Melvin and others, detention involved more of a loss of freedom than prison.

Antonio, a Brazilian deportee, recounted harsh conditions in a detention center in McAllen, Texas, where he says he did not eat for three days because he found the food unpalatable. From there, he was taken to a detention center in New Mexico, where he was "scared because the police used excessive force" even though he followed their every order.

Hector also told me that there were no recreational activities in detention, which compared unfavorably to prison.

> It was two months of absolutely no program. We call it program when you do things, when you go out to yard, when you take a class, when you have a job, whatever. There is no program at all. Only a television and you are stuck in the same room about this big with 50 other people besides the dining room. It's mind numbing and it's really boring. And so I started to feel like a caged lion, and I'm pacing back and forth all day going, "Get me out of here." Every INS [Immigration and Naturalization Service] officer that walked in, I said, "Why am I still here? Send me back home. I don't want to be here. I'm not fighting my case." Because if you fight your case, you're looking at a year. Because even if you win your case at the end of that year, the U.S. attorneys are going to appeal it and you're still gonna get deported. So, I knew that wasn't gonna be the case. I didn't want to be locked up for another 18 months. I just got through doing 18 months. I'm done with this. I'm really done with this. I'm done with the lifestyle. I'm done with it.

For Hector, Elias, Alberto, and other detainees, the conditions of detention centers were a great motivator for them to not pursue any appeals so that they could get out as soon as possible. Unlike prisoners, however, detainees often cannot predict when they will be released. They are not "doing time." Instead, they are waiting for their deportation date, which they have little control over. Hector, however, did point to one positive side of detention: Gangs do not run detention in the same way they do California state prisons. His affiliation with the Southsiders from his prison term worked to his advantage without bringing the dangers it had in prison, even though immigration detention involves people from all over the country. "Once I got to the first INS facility, you know, you see the other Southsiders who were there and I tried to keep my mouth shut as much as I could but eventually they see the 13 on the side of my leg, they're gonna know. And they asked, 'Are you a South-sider?' And I said, 'Sure am, homie.'"

Hector didn't tell anyone that he had run afoul of the Southsiders by choosing solitary confinement over following a gang order, so no one knew. He was transferred to another detention facility and again found his affiliation only an asset.

> What I was afraid of was the gangs in immigration were going to be really active like they are in state prison, but they are not. They are actually inactive. Because they are trying to stay in the country, they are trying to get in as little trouble as they can. So the entire time that I was in that facility for those two months, there really was only one incident of gang-related violence. . . .

At the end of two months in detention, Hector was deported back to Guatemala, the country he had left when he was a toddler. With freezing temperatures, unappetizing food, no recreational activities, and an entirely mundane existence, detention centers are clearly designed to cause suffering and make people seek an exit.

The appeals process for deportation cases can take years, and mandatory detention during the process is a major disincentive to continue with the appeals. While detained, people cannot continue working, which puts tremendous stress on their families and makes it impossible to retain a lawyer. DHS has no obligation to provide counsel. Several deportees told me they stopped appealing their deportations even though they had strong cases.

Diallo, a Guatemalan citizen, was among my most tenacious respondents. He spent over two years in detention fighting his case before giving up. I met Diallo, who speaks with a strong Boston accent, in the cafeteria of the call center where he works in Guatemala City. His voice broke and his eyes filled with tears as he explained to me that he spent more time behind bars fighting his immigration case—two and a half years in the prime of his life—than he had for his original sentence. Diallo, who had lived in the United States for nearly 30 years, was deported for being caught with marijuana seeds on one occasion and a marijuana cigarette on another occasion, a decade later. As I explained in the last chapter, Diallo moved to the United States when he was eight years old in 1980 but faced deportation after serving prison time for a DUI.

After 300 days in prison, Diallo was sent on a plane to Louisiana to an immigration detention facility. Diallo fought his deportation order but was forced to do so from behind bars. After two and a half years, and more than $15,000 in legal fees, Diallo discontinued the appeals process. He and his mother had exhausted their resources. His mother had diabetes and custody of Diallo's daughter, who had been in his custody since she was an infant. In 2008, Diallo was deported to Guatemala, a land he barely remembered, leaving his mother and daughter behind.

Elias, a Jamaican national, gave up on the appeals process after 11 months. Elias moved to the United States when he was 13, to join his mother, who had lived in the United States as an LPR for eight years. Elias arrived in Brooklyn in the early 1980s. He enrolled in the eighth grade and continued to go to school until he finished high school in 1985.

In 1986, Elias was arrested and charged with selling marijuana. He did not have to go to jail but was ordered to pay a $50 fine. He had no more trouble with the law until 2006, when he agreed to take a diaper bag across town for a friend. Elias got into the cab with the bag and, within moments, a police officer pulled the cab over and asked to see the bag. The diaper bag turned out to have 14 rocks of crack cocaine in it. Elias was arrested, convicted, and sentenced to 18 months in prison. Elias appealed the charge, claiming the bag was not his and that he did not know that there was cocaine in the bag.

The criminal justice system didn't hold Elias while his case was under appeal—DHS did. As a noncitizen facing deportation, he was subject to mandatory detention. After 11 months in detention, Elias gave up his appeal. He had lived in the United States for over 20 years. He had 11 U.S. citizen children and no ties to Jamaica. He agreed to be deported because he grew tired of being in detention.

Elias and Diallo did not exhaust their appeal options. Instead, they ran out of money to pay immigration lawyers to help them pursue their claims, and they tired of their lengthy detention. Thus, they decided to give up the appeals process and agreed to be deported. There are many noncitizens currently in detention who have meritorious claims and may be able to overturn their deportation orders. However, the length and cost of the appeals process as well as the conditions of immigration detention prevent many noncitizens from fully pursuing the revocation of their deportation orders. No system of custody hearings evaluates prolonged detention and detainees have to pay for their own counsel. As Mary Bosworth (2014) explains, the uncertainty with regard to how long one will spend in detention creates extreme stress, especially for long-term detainees.

Conclusion

Prisons are the underbelly of global capitalism; these institutions change people on the inside and lead to fear of imprisonment on the outside. They also mirror the larger society, especially the ways in which racial domination and patriarchy play out.

Michel Foucault (1977: 303) argued that "the carceral 'naturalizes' the legal power to punish, as it 'legalizes' the technical power to discipline." The existence of a massive system of incarceration in the United States naturalizes punishment. The disproportionate application of incarceration to black and Latino men makes it easier for Americans to accept the fact that there are more than two million people behind bars. In immigration detention, nearly all detainees are nonwhite.

Prisons are a key aspect of neoliberal reforms. In California, we saw how the buildup of the prison system came at the same time as the state cut back social services and manufacturing jobs disappeared. Mass incarceration allowed politicians to appease voters' concerns about the economy by diverting voters' attention from the economy and focusing on crime. Politicians promised voters they would be tough on crime. These promises led to policies that lengthened prison sentences. More prisons needed to be built, which provided much-needed jobs in rural areas. Mass incarceration, however, has had an array of collateral costs and the United States now has one of the largest prison populations in the world.

Both detention and incarceration work to warehouse undesired populations. Deportation putatively gets rid of them—although in reality deportees continue to exist. While my respondents often willingly chose freedom in their home countries over detention in the country they had come to think of as home, as the next chapter describes, most experienced hardship in the countries of their birth upon their return.

7

Back Home

Disposable Labor and the Impacts of Deportation

Thus far, I have argued that the United States uses deportation as a strategy to keep labor compliant and to get rid of people whose labor the economy no longer can use. What happens to this discarded labor—to these 400,000 people who are deported each year?

Although everyone I interviewed regretted his or her deportation, it would be misleading to paint all deportations with the same brush. The woman who tried to enter the United States on a tourist visa to visit her son and was processed as an "expedited removal" at the airport had a dramatically different experience than the deportee who was arrested in a home raid in front of his children and sent to his country of birth after living in the United States for decades. Deportation always involves a financial hit—from lawyer fees to lost earnings to unrealized financial goals to wasted travel expenses. Deportation nearly always involves an emotional cost. This cost, however, varies tremendously, depending on the circumstances of the deportation and the strength of the deportees' ties to the United States and to their countries of birth. Many of my interviewees shed tears as they recounted all they had lost.

My fieldwork revealed that the context of reception in the deportees' homeland influenced the impact of the deportation. In the Dominican Republic and Jamaica, deportees met with open scorn, making their reintegration nearly impossible. In Guatemala, deportees who have tattoos find themselves victimized by police and gang members. Although thousands of deportees now live in Brazil, Brazilians attach little or no stigma to deportation, viewing it as an unfortunate incident, not a life-changing event.

This chapter describes and analyzes narratives of deportees' reintegration in their native countries. These stories reveal the role deportees play in supporting global capitalism. In many cases, they serve as convenient scapegoats for rising crime. Instead of blaming crime on years of repression, on tremendous inequality, or on poverty, governments blame crime on deportees, who are expendable, stigmatized subjects. This occurs in Jamaica, the Dominican Republic, and Central America.

In the Dominican Republic, Jamaica, and Guatemala, like in the United States, a neoliberal mindset of controlling crime and criminals is pervasive. In each of these countries, the state takes limited responsibility for the well-being of its citizens in terms of health care, education, nutrition, and housing. Instead, it treats individuals as subjects who must take care of themselves (Inda 2013). People who are able to provide for themselves through the formal market are distinguished from deviants—the homeless, welfare recipients, and criminals—who cannot.

Apart from stoking fear and compliance by representing a threat to public safety and justifying governmental control, deportees serve as ideal laborers for transnational call centers, an outgrowth of global capitalism. As bilingual, bicultural people with few options for survival, these stigmatized subjects make capable, compliant workers. Call centers in Guatemala and the Dominican Republic are heavily staffed with deportees. Call centers are places where U.S. customers call the toll-free numbers on the back of their credit cards. Instead of having people in New York or Atlanta answer the phone, many of these operations have been offshored. Deportees who have lived several years in the United States are ideal employees. They speak English and are familiar with the "American" way of doing things. The U.S.-based callers have no idea that the call-center workers are deportees, often earning less than $100 a week.

The proliferation of call centers in Latin America is part of a growing trend of outsourcing labor to cheaper locations. Under global capitalism, the "race to the bottom" means companies can search around the globe for the most exploitable labor. The call centers increase their profits and the deportees are employed. Their forced displacement, however, is often painful.

From the U.S. perspective, deportees are sent "home," thereby ending the story insofar as U.S. law enforcement is concerned. For deportees, however, a new chapter in their life is just beginning. And for their families left behind, deported relatives often continue to play important roles in their emotional lives.

Jamaica: Financial Hardship and Gendered Stigma

I learned firsthand of the negative perception of Jamaican deportees before I even arrived in Jamaica. Waiting for the plane, my daughter Raymi, who was then five years old, began to chat with a Jamaican couple seated next to us in the departure lounge. She told them we were going to Jamaica for 60 days. They were impressed and asked me what I planned to do there. I told them I was going to do research with people who had been deported from the United States. The gentleman politely responded that I was brave, because deportees can be an unsavory lot.

Jamaica could have welcomed back its citizens when deportations started to rise in the United States. Instead, Jamaican government officials and the media found in deportees a convenient scapegoat for crime and poverty on the island. Traveling there, I frequently heard some version of the perception that Jamaican deportees are the source of problems in the country. Media buttresses these fears. An article published in 2010 in Jamaica's largest newspaper, The Gleaner, begins with this sentence: "Kingston, St Andrew, St James, St Catherine and Clarendon—which accounted for the majority of the 1,680 murders last year—were the final destinations for most of the people sent back to Jamaica, sparking more concern about the link between deportees and crime."

Although no evidence links these murders to deportees, the article posits that deportees live in places with high rates of crime. It states that out of nearly 1,500 people deported from the United States to Jamaica in 2009, 62 (fewer than 5 percent) were linked to murders and manslaughter in the United States. This article is typical of Jamaican news reporting about the connection between crime and deportees insofar as it hints that deportees could be responsible for crime in Jamaica, yet it does not provide hard evidence of any connection. The article does state that "senior members of the Ministry of National Security and the police force have long blamed deportees for the upsurge of major crimes in Jamaica, although there is no solid data on the number of deportees arrested or convicted over the past four years."[1]

In spite of this, the article's headline, "Statistics Fuel Deportee-Crime Concerns," suggests hard evidence of a connection, and the act of publishing the article alone, citing concerns expressed by "senior members of the Ministry of National Security and the police force," as well as Jamaica's national security minister, would lead a casual reader to assume a connection exists even in the absence of evidence. Blaming social ills in Jamaica on deportees effectively acquits the Jamaican government of responsibility for poverty, which is a much more probable cause of high crime rates. As one deportee, Wendy, told me, "Everything that happens in Jamaica they say deportees are doing it." Instead of implementing measures to alleviate poverty, the government can save face and blame deportees. This scapegoating makes reintegration difficult for deportees.

Most Jamaicans are deported on criminal grounds, mostly for drug-related crimes. Jamaican mass media have used this fact to lead many Jamaicans to believe that all deportees are hardened criminals (Headley et al. 2005). When deportees return to Jamaica, people presume they did something illegal, which makes it difficult to obtain employment. One of my respondents, Samuel, told me he has been able to keep his job only because his employer has not yet found out he is a deportee.

The 37 Jamaican deportees I interviewed confirmed for me that the stigma inhibits their survival in Jamaica. They nearly all struggled to make a living. Criminalized by their governments and rejected by their countrymen, these deportees often ended up homeless or near-homeless as they moved from one relative's home to another's.

One of my research assistants, Caleb, who is a deportee himself, told me he knows some Jamaican deportees who lead a life of crime in Jamaica, yet they are in the minority. Only one deportee I interviewed admitted to getting involved in criminal activity in Jamaica. This deportee, Dwayne, had moved to the United States when he was 16. When he was 23, he was convicted on drug charges and deported. He initially lived in his father's home in Kingston. He had trouble getting along with his father, so he moved in with another deportee who was involved in the transnational drug trade. Dwayne worked as a chauffeur for the other deportee until he got into trouble himself and spent six years in a Jamaican prison for having sex with an underage girl. When I

met Dwayne, he had been out of prison for a few months and was working as a loan collector.

Dwayne is one of four deportees whom I met by chance on the streets
of Kingston, instead of through my research assistants. My research
assistants were probably not inclined to introduce me to people involved
in criminal activities. However, it is likely that few deportees are actually
committing crimes in Jamaica. Research by Bernard Headley and colleagues (2005) argues that the widespread perception among Jamaicans
that deportees are to blame for high crime rates in Jamaica is not based
on any evidence that Jamaican deportees are committing crimes.

Financial Hardship

The biggest problem that Jamaican deportees face is poverty. My respondents were either among the working poor or the unemployed
poor. Most were homeless or under constant threat of homelessness.

Many deportees felt obliged to ask their friends and relatives in the
United States for money to survive. Samuel, whose story I told in chapter 3, has great financial difficulty in Jamaica. When I asked how he gets
by, he told me, "You nuh, I beg. I ask relatives in the States that I need a
$50 here, $50 there and, if they can, they will. They extend." Darius, who
also was deported after a long prison sentence, told me that his three
sisters and one brother in the United States correspond regularly with
him and, were it not for them, he would be homeless.

I asked Hakim where he sleeps. He told me the following:

> I am in Rockfort right now. . . . Somebody gave me a place to stay. It is
> like that. I bounce around. My greatest fear is not being able to stay clean;
> that is my greatest fear because you see people walking around unclean
> and I fear that. So I am glad that somebody can say that you can come
> back and take a shower and lend you an iron to iron out some clothes
> and wash some clothes. Everybody has their own little hangup, but my
> thing is that I want to stay clean.

Hakim was unemployed when we met. He had been laid off from a
job as a security guard once his employer realized he was a deportee.
Very few of the Jamaican deportees with whom I spoke had stable

employment. O'Ryan had recently found a stable job, after seven years of on-and-off employment in Jamaica. He earned JA$3,800 (less than US$50) a week for full-time work. Keith found work at a construction company making JA$1,000 a day, but he usually worked three days a week only. I wondered about how deportees could survive on these wages. Jamaica is expensive: A meal in a restaurant, a ride on a bus, and most items at grocery stores tend to cost more than their equivalents in the United States. According to one website, in 2014 the average cost of a one-bedroom apartment in Kingston was JA$56,000 (about US$500).[2] None of my respondents were able to afford their own apartments or houses. Thus, they lived with friends or relatives or in rented rooms.

Most of my respondents dreamed of being able to fend for themselves and hoped to receive money from abroad that would enable them to set up a business. Harry, for example, used money from relatives abroad to purchase a cargo van. He makes a living by charging for cargo services. Others told me they had already set up a business and it had failed. Winslow, for example, set up a fishing business with money he received from U.S. relatives. However, his business failed when drilling began near where he was fishing, scaring all of the fish away. Many deportees who had not yet started a business told me that they planned to do so. Elias, for example, is using the money his family sends him to set up a business on the beach selling jerk chicken: "I'm trying to rent one of the stalls and stock it up. . . . I'm trying to do some jerk chicken. . . . I'm trying to set up this place on the beach. All the money they would send me, that's what I put in the stall, and only thing needed now is for it to get stocked."

With no source of income in Jamaica, Elias relies on his ties to the United States to get his business off the ground. Kareem also awaits money from the United States so that he can buy a vehicle and start a taxi business. In addition to a vehicle, he needs to get his Jamaican driver's license and relevant permits.

I need to get my license. I need a thousand dollars to get my permit. You just need a TRN [Taxpayer Registration Number], you know what I'm sayin'. Because that's my really dream; I always like driving. . . . Driving is my dream, so that is what I am going to do and just start building from there. . . . My mother is suppose to come but I'm really not going to wait on that. I am going to try and get my license and get a car from some-body. When she come, I will ask her to lend me the money to buy one and then I will work and pay her back on it. Whatever if she want to give it to me or whatever. . . . I need the money to buy one and I'll work and give it back to her.

Kareem's dependence on his mother to start a business clearly pains him.

Respondents had generally known poverty in the United States as well. Carl, for example, told me that "landing in Brooklyn, coming from Jamaica, is not an easy place." However, in the United States, these Jamaicans had managed to acquire furnished apartments, cars, and access to modern technology. In Jamaica, in contrast, they lived in rented rooms or from couch to couch. Between the financial setback of deportation itself, the disconnection from family support, and the stigma attached to deportation, they experienced a decline.

Although many of these deportees turned to selling drugs in the United States because of their financial hardship, this was not the case after deportation. Back in Jamaica, financial hardships did not lead my respondents to selling drugs. They explained to me that the reason for this is that they did not have the connections in Jamaica; the payoff was significantly less; and the price—imprisonment in Jamaica—was substantially higher. Many of my respondents expressed that prison in the United States was bearable yet they did not think they could deal with living in prison in Jamaica.

Emotional Hardship

Many deportees spoke with passion about the significance of staying in contact with relatives and friends in the United States in order to hold on to a part of themselves. O'Ryan, whose story I told in chapter 3, has been in Jamaica for seven years, yet still considers Brooklyn home. He maintains constant contact with people in New York to "live his life," as he put it. He still finds it hard to accept that he is permanently exiled to Jamaica and cannot return to New York, where he had lived since he was six years old:

One thing is guaranteed that no matter where I go or what I do I'm born in Jamaica; I am a Jamaican, you know, and I just gotta accept [it]. . . . I keep hearing from my family that you're in Jamaica, you need to start thinking about Jamaica . . . and it's not easy . . . to me. I'm still in America. I mean, that's home . . . regardless of that, I grew [up], I did everything there. I went to school there. I mean, that's everything. Everything that happened to me for the first time happened to me in New York. I have no experiences of Jamaica. . . .

Whenever I think about anything, I really still do think about New York. So it's like I still wanna know how everything is going, if everybody is okay. It's, like, basically, I'm still trying to live my life, but not. . . . I don't get to live it physically, you know what I'm saying. I like to talk to people and find out what's going on.

We can hear O'Ryan trying to convince himself that he wants to come to terms with his Jamaicanness as well as with the fact that he now lives in Jamaica. He bears out Karen Fog Olwig's (2002) point: A migrant's place of birth is not always a "natural place of belonging." O'Ryan struggles with feeling as if New York is where he belongs, even though his official place of belonging is Jamaica. Maintaining ties to Brooklyn has been crucial for his psychological well-being. Like most of my respondents, he had never called anyone in Jamaica when he lived in the United States, but now he calls "home"—New York—on a regular basis.

O'Ryan lives with his great-aunt outside of Kingston, and he told me she had found him crying in the backyard one day. He was ashamed that she had seen him, a grown man, crying. And, worse still, she called his mother in the United States to tell her about it. O'Ryan's affective transnational ties bear some resemblance to the emotional ties parents maintain with their children when they travel abroad to work (Parreñas 2005). But, as a grown man, O'Ryan is ashamed of his dependence. He hung his head and lowered his eyes as he told me about shedding tears, indicating he was ashamed of having been reduced to crying.

Victor, who migrated to the United States when he was four, described similar feelings about his deportation, which happened when he was 27. With no job skills and no connections, Victor could not find work in Jamaica. I asked him what he did to survive, and he replied that he sold whatever he could find. He burned CDs and sold them; he sold used clothes. His mother was barely scraping by in the United States and could not afford to support him. I asked Victor where he slept. He replied, "Here and there."

Like O'Ryan, Victor, considered Brooklyn his home: "I come from Brooklyn. . . . I grew up in Brooklyn all my life." He still talked regularly to his mother in the United States, describing her as "the cornerstone" of his life. Victor used his emotional ties to his mother as a coping strategy to deal with extreme emotional and material duress.

When I asked about his plans for the future, Victor told me he intended to leave Jamaica. In the 10 years since he had been deported, he had tried several times to return illegally to the United States without success, usually with material assistance from someone in the United States. Despite the difficulties involved in traveling illegally, he planned to try again to get "home."

For deportees like Victor and O'Ryan, a gendered shame surrounding their inability to provide for themselves and to cope emotionally with their new situations complicated financial and emotional stresses. Their transnational ties to the United States are coping strategies for alleviating these stresses, but they still experience shame.

Caleb also finds himself reliant on others for the first time. In the United States, Caleb was a legal permanent resident (LPR), a U.S. army veteran, and a software engineer. In addition, he sent money on a regular basis to his grandmother and aunts. Caleb spoke with pride about the fact that he had sent money to support his grandmother. Now that he has been deported, however, he finds himself the receiver of remittances. He depends on his girlfriend for his economic survival.

Alberto had a similar experience. Born in Kingston in 1954, he traveled to the United States at 15 to join his parents. Alberto maintained few ties with Jamaica once he left and never once returned for a visit to Jamaica during the 40 years he lived in the United States. Although Alberto rarely thought of Jamaica during his U.S. residence, he is lucky his parents did. Because they purchased a home in Jamaica, Alberto had a place to live when he was deported. Alberto had a few thousand dollars in savings when he arrived in 2007. When I spoke to him in June 2009, he was still living off his dwindling savings as well as occasional income from music gigs. I asked him if he received remittances from the United States. He seemed insulted, saying, "I am not the type of guy who likes to ask for help."

Living in his parents' home, built with migrant remittances, Alberto actually depended on U.S. help. His savings were also a form of migrant remittances, in that he earned them in the United States. When that money runs out, Alberto likely will find himself asking his U.S. relatives for money, although he will be ashamed to do so.

Carl expressed similar sentiments. He had been financially successful in the United States, able to provide his children with everything they needed and most things they wanted with money he had earned in the drug economy. Now, as a deportee, he was reluctant to depend on them for his survival, as he told me:

> I don't want to depend on my kids and I don't want to put them in no pressure. . . . [My son] said: "Dad, you all right? I'm going to send some phones to you so you could sell the phone." I'm, like, "No, I'm all right, kid; I'm all right. I just want you to work, go to school, and take care of yourself." I got to lie to him. . . . I don't want to put no pressure on any of them. If they got it and they are willing to do it, I'll gladly accept it because I'm broke as hell. But I just want them to be safe and all right.

Carl had only been in Jamaica a few months. He was proud of having filled his gendered role as a provider and breadwinner when he had lived in the United States (Lewis 2007). When we met, Carl wore a gold bracelet and expensive clothes he had bought in the United States, even though he admitted he was broke. He promised that next time we met he would buy me a meal, implying that he still saw himself as a provider. He told me that people called him "boss man," because his clothing and jewelry made it appear that he had money. Carl may be driven to sell his possessions once the reality of his newfound poverty sets in, but with his extensive connections in the transnational drug economy, I wouldn't be surprised to learn that Carl has used his connections to obtain a fake passport to get back to the United States.

Philip, whose story I told in chapters 1 and 4, had been in Jamaica for 11 months when I met him. He found it hard to think about anything other than the United States: his five children, his business, his life. In the United States, he had run a restaurant and worked as a musician in the evenings. In Jamaica, he felt lost and was unable to find gainful employment. He felt useless. He lived with his mother in Kingston, but, having spent the prime of his life in the United States, he was devastated by his banishment. He told me, "It's like I am dead." I asked Philip what he does in his free time. He replied:

> Nothing. Just watch TV and try to reminisce back on America. My mom always tell me, "Why you don't watch the local news?" And I say it can't help me, you know, what I mean. I just watch overseas. . . . My life wasting, wasting, wasting, wasting. . . . Most of the time I spend alone. . . . Me and my mango tree, you know. It's just very weird, very weird to me right now. This is more like stress every day, you know what I mean, hurt every day. I try to pick up my mistake every day, you know. I just leave whatever I leave behind and move forward.

Philip, who once provided for his mother in Jamaica and his family in the United States, now depends on them for his survival. Philip continued to keep in contact both with his wife (they never legally divorced) and his girlfriend—with whom he had another child. Although he found it shameful, he depended on them for financial support. He also was ashamed that he depended on his mother for survival, when he used to send her money. Philip told me:

> Well, my wife sends me money sometimes. My last baby['s] mother sends me money. . . . I feel a way to take money from my wife. I never did that before. Worse, my baby['s] mom, I just met her like a couple of years ago, you know what I mean, and she's my baby['s] mom, and, you know, just like I used to be the person who help them, you know, now I am the dependent one.

Philip's remittances serve as a reminder of what he has lost: his family and his economic well-being. In his newfound position as "dependent" instead of provider, Philip told me he "feel[s] a way to take money" from his wife. Philip had difficulty describing this feeling of shame—calling it "a way"—because to discuss his shame openly would be even more shameful. As Michael Kimmel (1994) has argued, men are often silent regarding threats to their masculinity.

The Jamaican men I interviewed expressed regrets about losing their financial stability and family members. Many of them left very small children behind, and the fact that their children may never know them deeply affects them. Some keep connected to their children through phone calls, but they depend on their children's mothers' good will for that connection.

Deportation may be the end of their story from the U.S. side, but, for many Jamaicans, it is the beginning of a nightmare. Additionally, the children they leave behind have to learn to live with the fact that the U.S. government deported their fathers. The extreme stigmatization that deportees face in Jamaica contributes to their economic and social isolation.

The Dominican Republic: Criminalization and Chronic Unemployment

In the Dominican Republic, officials distinguish between people who are deported on criminal grounds and those who are deported on immigration grounds. Dominicans who are caught crossing the border illegally in the United States or who have overstayed their visas and are deported on those grounds are considered noncriminal deportees in the Dominican Republic. In contrast, Dominicans who are deported after being convicted of a crime in the United States are considered criminal deportees and are subject to further surveillance in the Dominican Republic. The reason for their deportation is recorded, and their deportation shows up on their criminal and credit reports in the Dominican Republic.

In January 2010, I was able to observe the intake process for deportees. The flight landed three hours later than expected and had only 30 deportees when they were expecting 130. I rode in a car driven by a Dominican soldier, and officers from the Deportee Department of the Migration Department (DGM) accompanied me. The plane with deportees in it was a large, white, unmarked plane. It landed in the cargo area of the airport, parked in between a UPS plane and a DHL plane. There were two U.S. Immigrations and Custom Enforcement (ICE) officials on the plane who handed over the list of deportees to the Dominican officials. The Dominican officer called the deportees' names one by one and they came off of the plane and onto a DGM bus, which had bars both on the windows and in the front to protect the drivers from the passengers. The bus took the deportees to the DGM office.

On that day, there were two women and 28 men. Eleven of the passengers had been deported for immigration reasons; the rest, on criminal grounds. When they arrived at the DGM office, the deportees were escorted upstairs and given their possessions—a change of clothes for some, books, photos, makeup, deodorant, and shoelaces.

Next, the officer separated the deportees into two groups. The noncriminal deportees were processed first. They went, one by one, to be fingerprinted and have their names and information recorded both by the DGM and the Departamento Nacional de Investigaciones (DNI). As there were only 11, that process took about 40 minutes. Then it was time to process those who were deported on criminal grounds. They went through the same process but had to be taken from there to the police station in Villa Juana, to be booked again by the police and the drug control division.

At the police station, each deportee is fingerprinted; a photo is taken; and all personal data is recorded. Once this process is finished, deportees are released to a family member, who must bring a photocopy of his or her national ID card, the cedula. Deportees are only released to family members and are not permitted to leave the police station until a family member comes. If a family member does not come for a deportee, he or she will be held for several days in the local jail to ensure his or her own safety, as a local police officer told me.

In the Dominican Republic, citizens and media don't merely stigmatize deportees; the government criminalizes them on arrival, booking them as criminals. Even though they have already served their time in the United States for their convictions, criminal deportees must report monthly, as if they were on parole, to the police officer in charge of deportees. In addition, police officers make field visits to deportees' houses. On those visits, they talk with the deportees, their family members, and their neighbors to find out how each deportee is doing.

After six months of parole visits and without committing a crime, the police issue criminal deportees a carta de buena conducta, which they must present to potential employers. The letter says, "This person has no criminal record in the Dominican Republic, either before or after having been deported." Because of the stigma against deportees, this practice effectively prevents most deportees from getting formal employment. Whereas the Jamaican deportees were often able to hide their deportee status, the requirement of the carta de buena conducta makes this more difficult for Dominicans. Locked out of most jobs, they rely on the informal labor market and remittances from family members in the United States. Some find work in call centers or hotel resorts, where their English fluency and familiarity with U.S. culture are assets.

From the perspective of the Dominican police force, it is necessary to keep track of deportees because of their criminal past.[3] Many deportees, however, feel as though the crimes they committed were a consequence of their circumstances in the United States and do not mean that they would reoffend in the Dominican Republic.

Despite many obstacles to employment, Dominican deportees have a very low rate of recidivism. Of the 14,858 persons deported to the Dominican Republic since 2001, only 122 were convicted of crimes in the Dominican Republic afterward. One government official pointed out to me that there are more former police officers in Dominican jails than deportees—due to widespread corruption among police officers. Despite this, Dominicans profess a widespread belief that deportees have caused a rise in crime. Most of the deportees I spoke with had trouble finding work because of the stigma of criminality attached to being a deportee. The neoliberal concern with crime that divides law-abiding citizens who are responsible for themselves from criminals whom the state must control translates into a punitive response to deportees in the Dominican Republic.

Wealthy people in the Dominican Republic live in tremendous houses behind large gates with personal watchmen and bodyguards. They bar the poor, homeless, and drug addicts from entering these enclaves. Deportees told me that, because they were poor, they could not enter the upscale neighborhood where I was renting an apartment, because the police would beat them if they encountered them there without a valid reason. Respondents will probably be poor as long as they remain in the Dominican Republic. Few make a decent living. Some find work at call centers or as drivers. Many find occasional jobs in construction.

Many deportees, like Harold, dream of returning to the United States. Harold was born in 1965 in Santo Domingo. He does not remember much about the neighborhood he grew up in, because he left the island when he was eight years old. I conducted his interview in English, as his English is better than his Spanish. In 1973, Harold moved with his family to Washington Heights in New York City, as an LPR. Harold finished high school at George Washington High School in that same neighborhood.

Harold qualified for citizenship when he was 13, but his parents never applied for him. He could have applied on his own when he was 18, but he never did. "It never crossed my mind, you know," he told me. Harold tried college out for a while, but after dropping out of City College and then the American Business Institute, he decided to try his lot in the labor force. He worked in grocery stores and at other odd jobs until he landed a stable job in a mailing company. Harold worked there for six years until the company closed down in 1990 and the entire staff was laid off.

Harold found himself unemployed, and he had just had a baby girl with a coworker. Since neither he nor his child's mother had any source of income, Harold began to sell drugs in Washington Heights to support his family. Not too long after he started, Harold was caught and charged with the criminal sale of $5 worth of crack cocaine. He was sentenced to five years' probation. Harold decided that the criminal lifestyle was not for him. He told me he learned his lesson. He reported each week to his probation officer and his sentence was reduced to three years' probation.

Harold never got into trouble with the police again; he went back to working in the formal labor market. He worked at Starbucks, at a construction company, and became a handyman. Things were going well for Harold; he learned how to repair all sorts of home appliances. He split up with the mother of his two children, but they kept in contact. He met another woman, and they bought a house together.

In 2007, Harold was caught with marijuana and charged with simple possession. He purchased a bag of marijuana on the street and was arrested right afterward. He did not do any time for this. He paid a $100 fine and that was it. In 2008, Harold began to have disagreements with his first wife over child support. After a series of court appointments, he missed one of his court dates. In his absence, the judge sentenced Harold to six months in jail for failure to pay child support. Harold served his time. However, instead of being released, he was told he had an immigration hold. Harold had to go to immigration court with regard to his 1990 conviction. Although his case had been closed 18 years before, and, at the time, there were no immigration consequences to his guilty plea, Harold faced deportation because of it.

Harold got a lawyer from inside the detention facility in Louisiana. She advised him to plead guilty to the charge, that the 1990 sale was an aggravated felony, but Harold disagreed. He thought he could win his case. Harold spent 11 months inside an immigration detention facility in Louisiana, fighting his case, sending appeal after appeal. He told me he spent over $300 on stamps. Convinced he eventually would win, he never signed his deportation orders. That did not stop ICE from deporting him. In October 2009, Harold was deported to the Dominican Republic, the country he left when he was eight years old. He had not been back since he left.

The only people he knew in the Dominican Republic were his brother, who also had been deported, and his sister, who lives there for part of the year. Once deported, Harold went to get a national ID card in Santo Domingo, so that he could begin to look for a job. However, when he got to the office, they told him his birth certificate was fake. He had to go to the local office where he was born to get a new one. I asked Harold how he felt when they told him his birth certificate was fake. He said he was scared that he would get in trouble for possession of false documents. But he didn't. They just told him to get an authentic one.

Harold finds it hard to adjust to life in the DR. He is used to the laws, customs, and people of New York City. He expressed awe at the fact that, in the DR, you can drink beer in the park. "It is not like over there, you have get a permit for this, a permit for that, you get a violation. Over here, you're free. You park however you want. You drink beer. This is wild. I don't even like it here 'cause it is too wild, too open." Harold is also used to working all the time, and he is anxious to find employment.

But I have to do something. I have to work or do something 'cause I am not the type of person to lay back. I mean, my sister, every time she comes, she gives us money, but I am not the type of person that I want to rely on somebody else. I want to do on my own. I work seven days a week over there in New York. I want to put an ad in the newspaper, a classified, and then I am going to make some business cards and flyers.

Like many of the Jamaicans and Dominicans I interviewed, Harold was not comfortable relying on his family for his survival, but he had no choice. He desperately wanted to work in the Dominican Republic, but he worried that no Dominicans would trust him to enter their homes and repair appliances. To Harold, it made little sense that Dominicans were scared of him. He had sold drugs decades earlier and then bought marijuana for personal consumption. In the United States, that made him an aggravated felon. But it didn't make him a thief or an untrustworthy person. Nevertheless, the stereotypes were hard to overcome, and they threatened his survival.

Maxwell, like Harold, finds the reality of his deportation hard to confront. Both saw themselves as worthy neoliberal subjects in the United States: people who worked honest jobs and contributed to their own and their family's well-being. In the DR, this has become hard to accomplish.

I asked Maxwell how he felt when he returned to Santo Domingo. He told me:

> I did not feel good, because my life is America. The United States. I went to the United States when I was young. I had my life there. My youth is there, not here. I lived half of my life there. People from my generation are no longer here. They are there. . . . My friends are over there. . . . The job I had over there, I was able to do good. Here, I feel depressed because I don't enjoy my life here. It is not the same. I feel frustrated. All my life is over there, in the United States.

His wife has come to visit him twice in the DR, but she is not willing to move there. Maxwell wants to return to the United States as well. When we spoke, Maxwell had yet to find work in Santo Domingo, although he had been there for one year. He relies on remittances from his wife, and, similar to the Jamaican deportees, because of gendered expectations, he is not happy about that. "Yes, my wife helps me. I am not used to that. She is a woman. I know how it is to live in the United States, to work in the United States. People earn by the hour. Not everyone earns the same. I don't like to ask for money because working over there is hard."

Maxwell hoped the president might pardon him so he could return, owing to his wife's military service. The likelihood that he could get a pardon is very low, because the president almost never issues them. Nevertheless, whenever I asked about his future plans, he said that eventually he would return to the United States. Having lived there from ages 16 to 36, Maxwell feels very tied to the United States. He longs to be with his wife and to start a family with her.

I asked Maxwell what he learned in the United States. He responded, "The United States is great. [It] is like a university where Latino immigrants learn about life, how to live, how to organize your life, how to set goals, how to wake up. The United States teaches you how to live, how to respect people. . . . Over there, I learned English. I broadened my horizons." Maxwell holds the United States in high regard, in spite of feeling he was mistreated by its government. He believes he can get back on the right side of the worthy/unworthy divide among neoliberal subjects. Whereas fellow Dominicans may see him as less trustworthy because he is a deportee, he sees himself as a better person because of what he learned in the United States.

After interviewing scores of deportees who were unemployed in the DR, I began to search for deportees who were able to find a way to make ends meet without relying on remittances. I found a few. I met German, who had found work in a gay bar. German lived with his girlfriend and her children above the bar, and he was able to survive with a combination of his earnings from the gay bar and gifts that regular clients brought him. Many of the customers in the gay bar were either foreigners or people who lived abroad, and German developed friendships with many of them. Given the stigma against homosexuality in the DR, German likely secured this job because many Dominicans would not take the risk of working in a gay bar, lest others suspect them of homosexuality.

Another deportee I met who had steady employment had secured work as a driver. He had used his family connections to avoid getting registered into the database as a deportee, even though he was deported on criminal grounds.

The only Dominican deportee I met who had achieved financial success was Jay, who operates a small call center that he co-owns. I met Jay in his office on the third floor of a building in the business district of Santo Domingo. The call center consists of a row of 10 computers, each equipped with headphones with built-in microphones. When I went, there were four workers seated at the computers, taking calls for a payday loan program in the United States.

Jay shares an air-conditioned office with his co-owner and partner, a Dominican woman he met in Santo Domingo. Jay's sister, who is financially comfortable in the United States, is the third partner in the business. Jay's parents also have retired to the DR, and he lives with them in a middle-class neighborhood in central Santo Domingo called Tropical.

When Jay was deported to the Dominican Republic in 1997, he left his wife and two kids behind. Jay had moved from the Dominican Republic when he was six, and he had few connections. His deportation put stress on his marriage, and he eventually separated from his life partner of 30 years and was unable to watch his children grow up. Without his income, his wife struggled financially. She had to solicit help from the government to maintain the household. Without Jay's encouragement and support, his son never went to college. Jay talked to them on the phone, but the long distance strained their relationship.

Jay spent his first few weeks in Santo Domingo sleeping on a very old bed in his grandmother's house. However, he was able to use his skills, his English, and his business sense to get back on his feet. He found a job at a call center through a newspaper ad, and he moved up in the company. Eventually, he set up his own business, which was slowly growing when I met him in 2010. Even though Jay has achieved financial stability, he still deeply misses his children and his lifestyle in the United States.

Federica, who was deported to the DR in 2001, after living for nearly 20 years in the United States, also deeply misses her children. She was deported as a consequence of a prior felony conviction, which she picked up due to an association with her husband, who was, at the time, addicted to drugs. Federica's conviction was in 1996, and she was released from jail pending a deportation hearing. In 2001, ICE agents came to her workplace and arrested her in front of the senior citizens she was caring for.

When Federica was deported, her youngest children were two and three years old. It breaks her heart that they now barely know her. Her daughters, who are 9 and 12, know her and talk to her, but the younger two don't even want to speak to her on the phone. Tears poured down her cheeks as Federica told me, "I am a mother, and I feel as if I have no children. I am a grandmother, and I have no children. This hurts deeply." Federica has been able to make ends meet by working in call centers, and now she shares expenses with her Dominican husband, thereby making it easier to survive. However, the pain she feels from losing her children is profound. She would love to have her children come visit her. However, neither she nor her two older daughters can afford airfare, and her ex-husband is not willing to send her younger daughters. Her deportation has resulted in what will likely be a permanent separation from her children.

Federica and Jay were able to find work in call centers because of their bilingual and bicultural abilities. This industry—which benefits from having workers who are intimately familiar with the United States—is willing to look past the cartas de buena conducta and employ deportees.

None of the Dominican deportees I met were homeless, because they stayed with family members. However, there certainly are deportees among the most downtrodden in the DR. Yolanda Martín (2013) interviewed scores of Dominican deportees who became addicted to heroin or had experienced a relapse in their drug addiction as a result of the trauma of deportation. Dominican deportees often found themselves yearning for both the financial security they had experienced in the United States and the love and protection of their families. The official stigma of being a deportee prevented them from obtaining a job and the Caribbean Sea made it exceedingly difficult for them to return to the United States illegally. Like the Jamaicans, they experienced deportation as an outsized punishment for bad choices.

Guatemala: Tattooed Deportees and Call-Center Employees

I spent most of a Friday in the fall of 2009 watching three planeloads of deportees—a total of 280 people—being processed back into Guatemala. When the deportees first arrived, they filed into a room packed with people and waited for immigration officials to call their names. I noticed one of the deportees right away because of his sharp clothes and sparkling-clean tennis shoes. At one point, he flashed a wad of bills. He had a shaved head, and his arms were covered with tattoos. He asked another deportee to trade shirts with him, and when he took off his short-sleeved shirt, he revealed a fully tattooed, muscular upper body.

After donning the long-sleeved shirt that covered his tattoos, he went around chatting with various other deportees. When the receiving process was over, he and three others hopped into a cab. Just before getting in the cab, he said, with a Southern California twang, "I am getting up outta here." The cab driver headed straight for the border.

Berlin and colleagues (2008) estimate that the vast majority of Guatemalan tattooed deportees return immediately to the United States. Whereas Guatemalans have the option of taking the risk of going by land to return to the United States, Dominicans and Jamaicans must cross by sea, which presents a different set of obstacles.

Every week, four to six planes full of deported Guatemalans depart the United States. Most of these deportees are men. In 2005, 14,522 Guatemalans were deported, fewer than 15 percent of whom had a criminal conviction in the United States. In 2011, 30,313 Guatemalans were deported, 39 percent of whom had a criminal conviction. In six years, the number of deportees doubled and the percentage of those deported on criminal grounds increased 260 percent. The United States now deports 40,000 Guatemalans—mostly men—every year. Many of these deportees arrive after having lived most of their lives in the United States.

Despite the increase in Guatemalans deported on criminal grounds, Guatemala has no generalized stigma against deportees. Unlike in El Salvador, Jamaica, and the Dominican Republic, Guatemalans do not tend to presume that deportees are criminals. The stigma of criminality is exclusive to deportees who have visible tattoos.

Guatemalan deportees arrive by air at the Guatemalan Air Force base, which is adjacent to the passenger airport. One plane I was able to observe arriving was all white except for a blue tail, an ID number, and the words "Operated by Xtra Airways" written on the side. On the airplane, the deportees are handcuffed and shackled. If officials give them food or water during the flight, the deportees have to figure out how to eat with their handcuffs on. When the plane lands, the U.S. marshals and Department of Homeland Security (DHS) employees accompanying the flight hand a list of passengers to the Guatemalan migration authorities. The deportees are then permitted to deplane and walk single-file into a room where marimba music welcomes them. They are invited to sit in rows of white plastic chairs. On each chair is a paper bag with a sandwich and a drink for them to eat in case they arrive hungry. Once everyone is seated, an immigration agent explains to the deportees the process they must undertake in order to leave the Air Force base. He or she also welcomes them to Guatemala and reminds them to use their real names, as they have nothing to fear, now that they are in their own country.

Each deportee is called by name to be processed by immigration agents. The agents verify that they are indeed Guatemalan. They also ask when they left Guatemala and through which port of exit. Ministry of Health officials verify whether the deportees have any communicable diseases. The Guatemalan police check each deportee's record to see if he has an outstanding warrant for arrest in Guatemala.

Deportees receive a limited number of services. Banrural, a Guatemalan bank, exchanges U.S. dollars for Guatemalan quetzals at the market rate. The Ministry of Foreign Relations provides each deportee with a two-minute phone call to whomever is coming to pick him or her up. The Ministry of Employment also has its liaisons available, who can point deportees to jobs for which they may qualify, although few deportees gain employment in this way.

Finally, deportees are given their bags and are allowed to leave. The Ministry of Foreign Relations supplies a bus that takes the deportees to terminals where they can take buses to their hometowns. People who are unable to contact their relatives are taken on this same bus to the Casa del Migrante shelter, where they can stay for two days as they try to locate their relatives.

The reception of Guatemalan deportees stands in stark contrast to the reception of Dominicans insofar as they are not criminalized upon arrival. However, tattooed Guatemalan deportees face extreme stigma. I interviewed 34 Guatemalan deportees, many of whom had tattoos. In their interviews, they recounted the problems their tattoos caused them yet insisted they liked their inked bodies. For Guatemalans, tattoos mark young men as suspicious and dangerous. Generally, the only job a tattooed deportee can get is in a call center answering phone calls from U.S. customers.

Police officers harass tattooed deportees at every turn: Some reported having to remove their shirts so police officers can photograph their tattoos on a daily basis. Strangers avoid sitting next to them on buses because tattoos provoke fear and loathing. Gang members shoot at them, interpreting their tattoos as rival gang affiliations.

Some deportees experienced police and gang violence as a direct result of their tattoos. Melvin is one example. Melvin, whose story I told in chapter 4, moved to the United States when he was 18 as an LPR. He later married and had two kids with a woman from the United States. He was doing well for himself, with a successful flooring industry, when he was arrested for leaving the scene of a car accident and was deported to Guatemala.

In Guatemala, Melvin stayed with an uncle in Zona 4 de Mixco, a dangerous neighborhood. The tattoos all over his arms and on his neck soon caused problems. Melvin had gotten the tattoos because he liked them, and a friend he knew offered to do them for him. Melvin did not know that Guatemalan gang members considered the spider tattooed on his neck and the spider webs tattooed on his elbows to be symbols of one of the gangs popular in Central America. One day, on his way home to his uncle's house, members of a rival gang spotted Melvin and shot at him. He ducked, but a bullet hit his uncle, injuring him. The injury was not fatal, but the family decided to move out of that area.

Melvin moved to his father's halfway-constructed house in Santa Catalina, a much safer part of the city. Once the house was finished and Melvin was settled in, his wife and children moved to Guatemala City. She sold their house in suburban Virginia, and they had US$200,000 in savings—enough to set up house in Guatemala. Despite their substantial savings, after two years, they had spent all of their money and their relationship was unable to withstand the stress of moving to a new country. Melvin's wife and their two kids returned to the United States. Melvin had to figure out his life in Guatemala on his own.

Having lived in the United States for two decades, Melvin speaks fluent English and thus is able to take calls from U.S. customers at the call center where he works. He earns enough to get by but barely makes in a month what he used to earn in a day. He drives to and from his house and his job and avoids going outside at any other time, fearing gang violence. He is a target for police and gang members alike. He told me that if he is killed in Guatemala City, no one will ever find out. The police will see his tattoos and presume he is a gang member, and no one will ever care to investigate. Melvin explained his fears:

> I don't go out because of my tattoos. . . . I can walk without my jacket here [in the call center]. But if I walk down the street, they shoot me. They see my tattoos, they go, "Oh, he's a gang member." If the gang members don't kill me, the cops will. So, it's bad. But sometimes I'm afraid more of the cops than the gang members 'cause they pull you over, they hit you, they want money. They want to put you in jail. Like, "For what? I didn't do nothing. Here are my papers. I haven't done nothing."

Melvin easily transitioned between talking about fearing violence from gang members to feeling threatened by the police. In my discussions with tattooed deportees, police harassment figured prominently.

Jose, another Guatemalan deportee, learned about the stigma associated with his tattoos almost immediately after getting off the plane. He soon found out that he would face constant police harassment because of the tattoos. He described an incident that had occurred just a few days before our interview, when he was walking to his job at a call center.

> I have a tattoo here on my neck. One day, a cop saw one of my tattoos. I was dressed with my button-up shirt and everything, just coming to work. It was 6:30 in the morning. And they had me all stripped down, taking pictures of my tattoos and my ID and "where do I live?, where do I work?," and I'm like, "I work right there." I had my ID and everything and I'm, like, "I work right there" [pointing to the building where he worked]. And one of them walked me all the way down here just to make sure I came in. It's hard. It's a lot harder. It's the life and you just have to kind of accept it because that is the way life is here and especially with the gang members here and all the trouble they are causing down here. I mean, you just have to accept that and you can't really do anything. The cops are just doing their job, I mean, but they do go way out of line. The cops go way out of line and you're stuck in, like, a box that categorizes you plain and simple. A lot of stores don't want you in their shops. When you take the bus, a lot of bus drivers ask you to get down because there have been a lot of killings and muggings and everything. There were a couple of times when they wouldn't let me get on the bus at night. Especially at night. They were, like, "No." And I would have to walk all the way over here [several miles]. So, it's hard.

Most of my tattooed Guatemalan respondents, like Jose and Melvin, mentioned being stopped by police. They consistently reported having to remove their shirts so that the police could take pictures of them.

Even deportees without tattoos faced violence in Guatemala City. Chris traveled to the United States when he was 11, and he was deported after being convicted of domestic violence. In Guatemala, he went back to his parents' house where, to his surprise, they received him with open arms and a lot of love.

His parents were still living in the neighborhood where he grew up: Villalobos, in Zone 12. The neighborhood has a lot of crime and violence. About a month after Chris arrived, they got a note asking the family for Q10,000 (US$1,200). The neighborhood extortionists had seen that Chris dressed in fancy American clothes. They presumed the family had money. When they didn't pay, armed gunmen shot at Chris. Luckily, he thought quickly and lay flat on the ground. Presuming him dead, they drove off. Chris fled to the countryside town of Xela, where he hid out for four months. In the meantime, his family moved to another house outside of Villalobos. Once they had settled in, Chris moved back to Guatemala City. Now he works at a call center, where his English skills are an asset.

Deportees who arrive in Guatemala City have to learn how to deal with the urban violence, especially gangs, guns, kidnapping, and extortionists. Depending on whose statistics you believe, Guatemala is either the second or fourth most dangerous country in Latin America, and among the top 10 homicide capitals of the world. Although the Peace Accords were signed in 1996, ending the decades-long civil war, homicides have been on the rise since the end of the 20th century in Guatemala City.

The homicide rate in Guatemala was about 53 per 100,000 persons in 2008, 10 times the rate of the United States. Evidence of this high rate of homicides is clear in the newspapers, which provide a more gruesome story each day. One story that appeared in the newspaper while I was in Guatemala involved gang members who allegedly shot the delivery driver bringing Chinese food to their car, because the owner of the restaurant failed to pay the extortionists. Stories of killings on public buses abound, and newspapers often link the killings to gang members and to extortion. Many deportees recounted to me that they are scared to ride on buses, especially at night. Others ride the buses to get to work every day, but still fear violence.

Nearly all of the deportees I spoke to went to a family member's house upon arriving in Guatemala. Some of them are lucky, and their families live in fairly safe parts of the city. Others are less fortunate and have to live in places filled with gangs and urban violence. In these areas, deportees have to learn to navigate the streets of their new barrios to avoid unpleasant confrontations. Some are able to use the street smarts they obtained in the United States to get by. Others rely on the respect neighbors have for their families in Guatemala City to protect them.

Some of the reports on violence in Guatemala City may be overblown by sensationalist media outlets. However, the feeling that Guatemala City is a violent space is pervasive. In the three months I lived there in 2009, three people recounted to me that a close friend or family member was killed by violent means. My landlady told me that a friend of hers was killed during an armed robbery. One of my interviewees told me that her nephew was killed at his house by murderers who came to look for him. Another interviewee told me that her son-in-law had been kidnapped, and her daughter had died in a car accident related to the kidnapping. Two of my 34 interviewees told me that they had been shot at. Others reported witnessing violent crimes. My friend who works for the United Nations told me that she never walks the streets of Guatemala City, by order of her employers. I have traveled all over the world. Guatemala City is the only place I have been where I took off my simple gold wedding band, upon my research assistant's recommendation. Deportees' reports that the city feels unsafe resonated with my own experience in the city. When I returned in 2013, however, a semblance of security had returned—especially in the upper middle-class areas.

Guatemala City is divided into several zones. They start in the middle and then spread out in a spiral, like the shell of a snail, going around from 1 up to 18. The spiral snail pattern is a bit off in some places, but the peripheral neighborhoods tend to have higher numbers. The western outskirts have a few wealthy or upper middle-class neighborhoods, going from the fairly well off Zone 9 to the quite well-off Zone 10 to the elite Zone 15. The city center is in Zone 1. It is a commercial district but has somewhat of a concentration of poverty. Zone 6, a working-class/poor neighborhood, meets Zone 1. This leads out to Zone 18, a poor neighborhood on the southeastern edge of the city. Most of my inter-viewees lived in "red zones," so-called because they are dangerous.

One of my interviewees, Lorenzo, had a huge scar on his face. I asked him about it. He told me he got his scar in Guatemala. He was standing on 18 Calle in a red zone in the evening with his wife when two robbers approached him. When they demanded that he give them his phone, he punched one in the face. The other scratched him with a sharp object, leaving a huge scar across his left cheek. I asked him why he didn't just give him the stuff. He told me, "When you're from L.A., you don't do that." Like many deportees, Lorenzo lives in a rough part of Guatemala City—La Limonada in Zone 5. I asked him if anyone gives him trouble there. He told me they don't. I pointed out that they must know he has family in the United States, and I asked if he has any issues with extor-tionists. He said, thankfully, he does not. It seems that the street smarts he developed in Los Angeles are helping him to survive in Guatemala.

Guatemala City is dangerous enough that some deportees risk the perilous crossing back to the United States. I met a young man, Giancarlo, who had been deported just two weeks before and was plan-ning his imminent return. I asked him why he was leaving, when he knows how dangerous the trip can be. He told me he wanted to leave because he wasn't finding a stable job, and because Guatemala City is dangerous. The job he had required him to ride public transportation at night, and the newspapers are full of accounts of assaults, robberies, and murders on the buses, especially after dark.

While I was in the city, three armed robbers got on the bus in Zone 7 at 8:30 pm and took everyone's belongings. This was front-page news, not because of the robbery but because the passengers on the bus shot and killed two of the assailants. In this case, two of the passengers were armed and fired at the robbers. The third got away with the passen-gers' belongings. Because of the violence in Guatemala City, the lack of opportunities for stable work, and the opportunities available in the United States, Giancarlo planned to risk the trip across Mexico.

On the trip, Giancarlo risks being robbed on the freight trains going north. One of my interviewees explained to me that on the train in tun-nels it is completely dark. You have to hold on tightly lest you fly off and die. Thieves board the train and frisk migrants holding on in the dark. How the pickpockets achieve this without dying themselves is a mystery.

Another danger of returning to the United States illegally is kidnapping. Zetas, narcotrafficking rings in Mexico, often kidnap migrants and hold them for ransom. A family must come up with $6,000 in order to save the migrant's life.

Apart from the violence, one of the most marked aspects of the reintegration of Guatemalan deportees is that they often work in call centers. The irony of this fascinates me. Guatemalans are deported from the United States back to their country of origin. One of the strategies used to deport people is to raid places of employment, and one of the rallying cries for increasing deportations is that "they take our jobs!" However, deportees in Guatemala often find work at U.S.-based companies such as Citibank or Sears, answering phone calls from U.S. customers. Of course, they are paid a fraction of what they would be paid to do the same work in the United States.

Melvin and Chris both worked in call centers, as did Hector. Hector is one of the deportees I met who had attained middle-class status in the United States. He had been in the United States since he was a toddler and was deported after serving 18 months for credit-card fraud.

> I was looking forward to coming back to Guatemala and it wasn't until I started flying over the country and really started seeing the way that the houses looked. . . . And I'm sorry. This is going to make me sound completely superficial and completely self-centered but it looked poor and I'm not used to that. My least expensive pair of jeans is $600, you know what I mean? That is the kind of guy I was in the United States for so long. . . .
>
> And now I am moving to another country where really I'm gonna be . . . I have a lot of advantages over everybody else who lives there, education wise, language wise, and experience wise. You know, I've worked for a billion-dollar company for so long. I know what I'm doing. I'm a responsible business owner. I know what I can do and can't do and, just for the record, because I don't want there to be any misconception about this, my crime in no way involved my work. I really kept the two of them separate. Ethically, I didn't feel like I could [do] that because I still hold that brand very close to my heart. It fed me and clothed me. It taught me everything I know about being a responsible business owner and being a really excellent human being. So, I never touched that. I came

into Guatemala feeling like I was really gonna be that big fish in a small pond all over again, but it wasn't until I flew over close to the airport where it hit me. And I wanted to cry when I realized I'm really stepping into a third world country. Yeah, I am going to be the big fish in a small pond, but this pond barely has water right now. And it was a scary feeling because, all of a sudden, I'm not gonna have the lifestyle that I was used to, at least not right away. And that was more than anything else. That's the point where it hit me, after almost close to 24 months that I'm not in the United States anymore. And that's a frickin' scary feeling. . . .

My aunt picked me [up] and I had kept it together for close to 24 months at that point, up until the point where I realized I walked out of that gate. You know, that black gate that you walk out of at the airport where it really hit me that I am a free person again. I no longer have to report to anybody. I am on my own again. It was a good feeling because I'm an independent individual. I have always been really independent. But at the same time, I had gotten accustomed. I don't like saying institutionalized 'cause I don't think I was institutionalized. I am still the same person in a lot of ways that I wasn't before with a little bit extra with some interesting experiences along the way. But in a lot of ways, those two years were just a learning experience right back to where I was before personality wise. But I had gotten to be really reliant on that system, on that penal system to provide. I had no worries as far as meals, clothing, whatever. You didn't have to, you know what I mean? And all of a sudden it hit me that I'm a free person and all the responsibilities that come with it. . . .

Once I got out of that gate, it hit me that I was free. I started to cry. And I hadn't cried in 24 months.

Although emotionally overwhelmed, like many deportees, Hector's first response was to try and get a job. He found a plethora of ads for call centers who wanted English-speaking employees. Two weeks after arriving, he sent out an email in response to a job ad and got a response that same day, to his surprise. He set an appointment for an interview. When he arrived at the high-rise building, Hector was surprised to see that it looked "pretty American." He was greeted by the receptionist in English, and the whole interview took place in English. At the end of the interview, the manager offered him the job and told him he'd be making Q3,700 a month, with a possible bonus of Q500 a month—for a total of about US$400–500 a month. It was nowhere near the US$80,000 salary he made in the United States, but enough to get by in Guatemala.

Many other deportees, like Hector, told me that it was remarkably easy for them to find jobs in call centers. Deportees, it seems, are a welcome addition to the transnational labor force in Guatemala—with or without tattoos. Just as the Dominican call-center managers are willing to overlook the fact that many of their employees are deportees, Guatemalan call-center managers are willing to hire people with tattoos.

Brazil: The American Dream Deferred

Unlike the process I observed in other countries, Brazil has no formal process for receiving deportees, and Brazilians attach little or no stigma to deportation. For me, this meant it was difficult to find deportees. No one keeps track of them and, without stigma, they integrated into society. One of the few people in government I was able to find that knew anything about deportees was Elie Chidiac, the head of the State Department of the State of Goiás. Mr. Chidiac was very welcoming as I explained to him the purpose of my project—to understand how people deported from the United States to Goiás reintegrate into Brazilian society. He explained to me that Brazil has various social programs that help with education, health, and housing and that deportees can gain priority access to those programs. He pointed out that deportees often arrive disillusioned with their failure to achieve their financial goals. These programs, however, may help them get back on their feet.

I asked Mr. Chidiac whether he knew of data on the demographics of deportees. He explained to me that the Brazilian government does not keep records of arriving deportees because they do not consider them to be criminals. Brazil considers the civil infractions in the United States that prompt deportation, such as entering without inspection or overstaying a visa, not to be the concern of the Brazilian state. Deportees arrive on regular commercial flights and enter Brazil through the same process as any other Brazilian citizen returning home.

Mr. Chidiac serves as an advisor to Goianos abroad. Not all Brazilian states have such an office, but he told me that 200,000 Goianos live

abroad—about 100,000 in the United States and 100,000 in Europe—
more from any other state in Brazil. He also estimated that 80 percent
reside illegally abroad, and that about 2,000 are deported each year to
Goiás. Of the deportees, he estimated that half come from the United
States and half from Europe.

I asked Mr. Chidiac why he thought Goiás has so many emigrants.
He told me that, because there are so many Goianos abroad, migrant
networks lead to more migration. Mr. Chidiac pointed out that Goianos
rarely travel to the United States unless they have specific job offers.
He believes that employers abroad recruit via workers from Goiás, who
typically bring in other Goianos such as relatives or friends. He also
pointed to close connections between Goiás and neighboring Minas
Gerais. Minas Gerais was the quintessential emigration state from Brazil in the 1980s and 1990s, and Goianos have outstripped Mineiros in
recent years.

Mr. Chidiac explained to me that few Brazilians travel to the United
States illegally today for two reasons. The first is the falling value of the
U.S. dollar. The second is the difficulty in attaining a visa to travel to
Mexico. Prior to 2005, Brazilians were able to travel to Mexico without
a visa. Thus, many Brazilians who desired to travel to the United States
took a plane to Mexico and then made their way across the border. Now
that it is not easy to get to Mexico, few Brazilians venture to the United
States illegally. Instead, migrants travel to Europe, where they do not
need a visa to enter.

Although Mr. Chidiac was not able to give me statistics on deportees
in Goiás, he ventured a guess that about 80 percent of deportees are men
and that most lived in the United States or Europe for more than seven
years. Overall in Brazil, three of every ten deportees are from Goiás.

For many Brazilians, deportation is a financial setback. They traveled to the United States with the intention of saving up money and
deportation cut their trip short. Joaquim, for example, traveled to the
United States in 2005 because he was in debt in Brazil and didn't see a
way out of debt other than to go to the United States. Joaquim borrowed
R$25,000—at an interest rate of 7 percent a month—and contracted a
coyote. When Joaquim made it to the United States, he began to work as
many as three shifts a day. He managed to pay off his debt in two years
and purchased 10 cows back in Goiás within two years. Once he had

paid off his debts, he planned to save money to build a home. However, he was caught after just two years in the United States and deported back to Brazil. Despite two years of backbreaking work, his migration journey was pretty much a wash—he bought 10 cows but had to sell his van and thus was without transportation.

Most of the Brazilians I interviewed had similar stories to tell. For some, especially those deportees profiled in chapter 2 who spent thousands of dollars but never made it to the United States, deportation was financially devastating. Unlike the other national origin groups, Brazilians rarely told me that they left children or spouses in the United States. If one spouse was deported, the other typically would return as well. If they had young children born in the United States, they would take them back to Brazil. Once back in Brazil, these deportees struggled to regain a financial footing, yet most eventually did.

João, for example, operated an ice cream shop in Itapuranga. Ice cream shops are popular in this small town where summers get very hot. Since he was a young man, João dreamed of traveling to the United States. He saw people come and go between his town, Itapuranga, and the rich northern neighbor and that they always returned with money to build their houses and buy new cars.

João had enough money to survive, but he wanted more—enough to establish a good life for himself and his wife and children. He tried to get a visa four times in Brasilia and once in São Paulo before deciding in 2004 to go with a coyote. A friend recommended a coyote in Goiânia who advised him to get a visa to go to Mexico. The coyote would help him get to the United States from there for R10,000 (US$6,000). The coyote assured João that he would not have to walk in the desert and that they would not face any danger.

João spent five days in Mexico, traveling from one small town to the next, and was accompanied by different groups of people hoping to get into the United States. He did have to walk in the desert. João walked two nights in the desert and ended up outside of Laredo, Texas. Just as he and his group neared the highway, Border Patrol agents accosted them and João was arrested. They detained João in Laredo for a couple of weeks before transferring him to Austin and then San Antonio. After two months in detention, João was accompanied from San Antonio to Atlanta and deported to São Paulo.

João had sold his ice cream shop in order to travel. When he returned, he bought the shop back and continued with his life in Brazil. I asked João if this trip had changed him. He said, yes, he no longer has any desire to travel to the United States. He didn't mention that he was now R10,000 poorer than he might have otherwise been. For him, deportation was a financial setback, but it was one he was able to overcome.

Laurentino was also able to get back on his feet after his deportation. His house sits right on a plaza in Itapuranga; it is contemporary and nicely furnished. He has a modern kitchen, nice living-room furniture, a computer, and a large flat-screen television. We had the interview at his dining-room table.

Laurentino traveled to the United States when he was 19, around 2000. Laurentino's family owns a plantation, and his parents lived off of this as he grew up. Laurentino did not have to work to support his family while he went to school. He was not wealthy, but not poor either.

When Laurentino was nearly finished with high school, he and a group of four friends decided to travel to the United States. They obtained tourist visas and went to Miami. There, a friend helped them get an apartment and find jobs. They stayed there for two months before deciding to travel to Massachusetts. They heard there were more Brazilians in Massachusetts and that they could earn more money. They purchased a car and drove to Framingham, a suburb of Boston.

In Framingham, Laurentino worked in house painting and did other odd jobs such as pizza delivery. Things went fairly well for him. He only stayed one year, though, as long as his visa allowed. He decided to travel back to Brazil to try and renew his visa. He thought that he could return to Brazil and get a visa that allowed him to work in the United States again. However, the second time his visa was denied.

In 2003, Laurentino decided he wanted to go back to the United States. He paid a coyote US$6,000 and went through Mexico to McAllen, Texas. There, immigration agents caught him. He signed a voluntary departure and was deported. Laurentino tried three more times with a different coyote. On the fourth try he got in.

He went right back to Framingham and worked at the same house-painting job. Laurentino was able to save up enough money to purchase his parents' home from them. He also purchased cows in Brazil to set up a small dairy farm. He stayed in the United States for three years, working and saving up money, sending money to his parents and planning a future in Brazil.

Most of Laurentino's friends were Brazilians. He attended a Brazilian evangelical church and went out on the weekends with other young Brazilians. He still keeps in contact with some of these friends who stayed in Massachusetts. He misses hanging out with them and would like to be able to go back and visit.

Three years after his return to Framingham, Laurentino decided to return to Brazil. He knew he had no opportunity to establish legal residency in the United States. His friends in Brazil were getting married, getting jobs, and setting up their lives. He hadn't even finished high school and didn't see much of a future for himself in the United States. So, he packed up and came home voluntarily.

Laurentino is doing well for himself. He completed high school and is pursuing a degree in literature at a public university. He wakes up each morning to milk his cows, and he lives off of the money from selling the cow milk. Laurentino was very critical of other Brazilians who come back and spend money ostentatiously. Instead of buying a fancy car or fancy clothes, he purchased cows, which provide him with enough money to get by.

Marly, whose story I told in chapter 2, loved her life in Danbury, Connecticut. Her Brazilian boyfriend came illegally through Mexico to be with her and they got married in the United States. Her oldest son came on a visa. Marly and her husband lived in a nice house; they had a car, and both were working. Marly's son was also establishing himself in the United States and had two children there. However, Marly's other two children were unable to acquire visas and Marly came back to attempt to help them. They were unsuccessful, and Marly resolved to return to the United States.

This time—in 2007—the Border Patrol denied Marly entry because she had overstayed her previous tourist visas. Marly was devastated. She loved living in Danbury and could not believe that it had all come to an end, though Border Patrol agents told her she could apply for another visa in five years.

Back in Jaraguá, however, Marly had been able to set up a better life for herself. She built a large, fancy house with a swimming pool. She has a very modern kitchen, new furniture, and a lovely bedroom set.

She also has set up a small clothing company where she makes clothes with her signature design. Her husband has joined her and he set up a small grocery store, a bright, modern-looking enterprise. Together, they have set themselves up financially and are much better off than before they left. Most Brazilians I talked to want to go to the United States to visit or to earn money. In contrast, Marly really enjoyed living there and wants to return with her family, permanently. For now, however, that is not possible.

Marly's son is in the United States. If he is able to get his green card through his marriage to a U.S. citizen, and then attain citizenship, he may be able to bring Marly and her husband over. However, the fact that she has been there already and has overstayed her tourist visa on more than one occasion still could complicate things for them.

Marly expressed regret about her inability to visit the United States, but her regrets pale in comparison to the deep pain felt by deportees in other countries who found themselves separated from all of their loved ones and were then unable to make ends meet.

Tom would also like to return to the United States indefinitely. A Brazilian coyote came to his town when he was 25, in 2005, looking for people interested in traveling to the States. The trip cost US$10,000. Tom borrowed the money at a high interest rate. At the time, Brazilians could obtain a visa at the port of entry in Mexico, and Tom was able to do so, with the help of a bribe.

From Mexico, Tom and his group traveled to the U.S. border. They found a Mexican coyote to take them across the Rio Grande. At that time, the Border Patrol engaged in "catch and release" of anyone trying to cross the border who wasn't Mexican. This meant that, if the Border Patrol caught them, they would be released. When the policy was rescinded not too long afterward, Brazilians and others were detained while waiting for their court cases, making crossing the border illegally much less attractive.

Tom received a court date and made his way to Marietta, Georgia. In Marietta, Tom met up with friends from his hometown. The next day he was working. Tom's friends showed him how to install hardwood flooring, and, soon, he was earning $20 an hour. He did not return to Texas for his hearing. Tom's debt grew from $10,000 to $30,000 because of the high interest. However, he was able to pay it off in two years.

With his debt paid, Tom saved money to purchase a van. With a vehicle, he could take on his own contracts and earned four times as much money. However, he didn't have a valid driver's license. On his way home from the evangelical church he attended, a county sheriff pulled Tom over. The sheriff had run his plates and knew his license was not valid. While Tom was booked, the county sheriff's office ran his information on the immigration database and found out about his immigration warrant.

Tom served 50 days in an immigration prison before being deported back to Brazil. Back in Brazil, Tom found out his knee was bad because of all of the kneeling he had done in the flooring business. He had knee surgery—paid for by the Brazilian public health system—and was on bed rest for a few months. Once Tom recuperated, he found a job as a motorcycle salesman. He supplements his income by buying and selling cattle. Back in Brazil, Tom earns enough money to get by, and he said he hoped to marry and have children.

Tom misses the United States and his friends, his church, and the good money he made there. He is happy to be reunited with his mother and siblings in Brazil but says he would return in a heartbeat if he could do so legally. In the United States, Tom told me, you can work for two days and have an iPhone. In Brazil, you can work all year and still won't have enough extra cash. For Tom, like many Brazilians, the lure of the United States is primarily economic. Since they can get by in Brazil, however, they are not very likely to try and return.

Conclusion

Deportees are, in some ways, the ultimate example of surplus labor. Whereas the United States will eventually free most prisoners, it banishes deportees, typically for life. This keeps them from competing for scarce jobs or diminishing public aid. However, deportees continue to exist in their countries of origin, 97 percent of them in Latin America or the Caribbean. Unable to stop this flow of deportees, countries have responded by finding ways in which deportees can serve another purpose.

In Guatemala, the government blames some deportees for social ills. The Jamaican and the Dominican governments blame deportees for crime generally. In Guatemala and the Dominican Republic, deportees who speak English take jobs in call centers. Jamaica, the Dominican Republic, and Guatemala share contexts of insecurity, inequality, and indigence. In contrast, Brazil is poised to surpass the United Kingdom to become the world's sixth largest economy. Brazil's better treatment of deportees reflects its economic boom, rather than the characteristics of deportees themselves. While the United States may view the relatively small number of Brazilians it deports every year as surplus labor, Brazil does not. The state and the citizens treat deportees accordingly.

In Jamaica, deportees are stigmatized as criminals and as failed migrants. This contributes to their economic and social isolation. Jamaican deportees pay a very high cost for being scapegoats for growing levels of crime and violence. Jamaican deportees are often homeless and many are depressed both because of their inability to make ends meet and because of their separation from the people they love the most.

In the Dominican Republic, deportees face official stigmatization due to the requirement of cartas de buena conducta in order to gain employment. This requirement locks them out of the formal labor market. Many Dominican deportees have skills that potentially could be useful in the Dominican Republic, yet few are given the opportunity to put their skills to use. The only exception to this is that some are employed in call centers.

In Guatemala, there is not a generalized stigma against deportees but the stigma of gang members spills over to deportees who have visible tattoos. Similar to the Dominican Republic, hiring managers at call centers are willing to overlook the tattoos. Deportees who work in call centers are able to earn enough to get by. Working in the call center also gives them access to other deportees with whom they can reminisce about life in the United States. Those deportees who left families behind, however, have a difficult time dealing with this loss.

In Brazil, the government basically ignores the deportee status of deported Brazilians and welcomes them home as it does any other citizen. On a societal level, this has translated into the lack of a stigma for deportees. In addition to this, most Brazilians were planning to return home anyway and kept strong ties to their hometowns and families. For this reason, reintegration was relatively seamless for many Brazilian deportees, even though it often resulted in financial hardship.

A consideration of these four cases together makes it clear that the context of reception matters greatly for the reintegration of deportees. Also of importance are whether or not the deportee left close family members behind, the length of time lived in the United States, the age of departure, and the particular skill set he or she attained while living in the United States.

Conclusion

Global Apartheid

In this book, I have argued that mass deportation is best understood in the context of global capitalism. Every area of the world has been incorporated into the global system of capitalist production, and mass deportation reflects global capitalism's demand for the free flow of goods across borders and the controlled flow of labor. In the late 1970s, capitalism began to enter a crisis. The global elite distanced production from the limitations posed by national boundaries by moving manufacturing to poorer countries. Billions of workers in India, China, Latin America, and elsewhere became producers and consumers within the global commodity chain. These workers and consumers became part of a new capitalist order governed by a neoliberal ideology of self-rule and limited state support.

Late 20th-century global capitalism created a deregulated and flexible workforce. New opportunities to enter the labor market drew peasants from the countryside to cities, where they toiled in sweatshops and gained access to cash, which enabled them to purchase the latest consumer goods. The items they produce and consume flow relatively freely throughout the global commodity chain. Nonwhite workers in Asia, Latin America, and other new sites of global production make up the bulk of this deregulated and flexible workforce. Globalizing forces have thrown them into the global production line, and many seek to move up the global labor hierarchy.

It may appear ironic that global capitalism has facilitated the transnational flows of goods while countries like the United States restrict the transnational flow of labor. However, upon closer consideration, it becomes clear that the sustainability of a system wherein workers in one country earn $10 an hour and those in a neighboring country earn $5 a day depends on the enforcement of national borders. Most people who toil for low wages in the Global South have no legal avenue to sell their labor abroad; undocumented emigration represents an attempt to do just this, often at great human and financial cost. By raising the cost of illegal border crossing, the United States minimizes the number of people who are able to seek out higher wages in wealthier countries. It also contributes to the creation of a vulnerable labor force in the United States.

The global economy depends on a compliant labor force, in both the Global North and the Global South. With a deregulated labor force, companies can easily fire workers or cut wages and benefits without having to worry about strikes, sit-ins, or labor regulations. Many Latin American workers seek out work in the United States after suffering such a loss. When they arrive in the United States, these workers, who are often undocumented, find themselves at the bottom of the social and economic hierarchy. They also work at the whims of their employer; undocumented workers are even less likely to organize and fight for their rights than other low-wage workers.

Undocumented workers, however, are not always complacent. The lack of a legalization program for undocumented workers means there are millions of people who have lived in the United States for decades who have been unable to attain legalization. The last major legalization program was implemented in 1986, and it covered immigrants who had been in the country since 1982 (as well as farmworkers who had been in the country at least six months). This means that undocumented immigrants who arrived later were not eligible. Thus, there are people who have lived in the United States for more than three decades who have never been eligible for legalization. In the spring of 2006, millions of undocumented immigrants and their allies took a major stand against the U.S. government's failure to legalize them by organizing protest marches in many U.S. cities.

Those who arrived as young people and still have no papers were at the forefront of the protests (Nicholls 2013). Rallied by the Sensenbrenner bill (HR 4437), which would have made it a felony to be an undocumented immigrant, these marches were some of the largest political demonstrations in the history of the United States. Protestors demanded comprehensive immigration reform and put the struggles of undocumented immigrants in the national conscience. Several immigrant rights groups were born of this struggle and activists have fought tirelessly since for legalization (Gonzales 2013).

However, official policy has not ceded to demands. Instead, the George W. Bush administration implemented Secure Communities and increased the 287(g) Program in the immediate aftermath of these marches. Such expansion and heightened policing of immigrant communities spanned the Bush and the Obama administrations. As this book has described, every interaction with the police became an opportunity for deportation of undocumented immigrants. The racialization of the undocumented as "Latino" has facilitated this biased policing (Romero 2011). Selective enforcement of immigration laws through racial profiling renders nonwhite immigrants more vulnerable to exploitation (Romero 2011).

People in the United States have long stood up for liberty—even for the right to carry arms in public. At the same time, U.S. citizens have embraced social control and punishment (especially when it comes to black and Latino men). When immigrants are characterized as "terrorists" and "criminals," people in the United States accept the policing and punishment of these groups. Politicians use racialized and gendered discourses of fear to win support for policies that lead to mass deportation. These fear-mongering discourses work best in the context of economically hard times, making the Great Recession an opportunity to launch a war on immigrants.

In 2007, the U.S. economy entered into a recession, which lasted at least until 2009. In the context of the Great Recession, and in the aftermath of the massive immigrant rights marches, interior removals escalated to unprecedented levels. In 2003, when Bush created the Department of Homeland Security (DHS), there were 30,000 interior removals. By 2008, Bush's last year in office, this number had shot up to 140,000. The number of interior removals reached a peak of 188,000 in 2011. They have since fallen and there were 131,000 interior removals in 2013.[1] This rise in interior removals in the context of the Great Recession and the massive immigrant rights marches raises the following question: Is deportation the exportation of the reserve army of labor?

It is hard to make the case that the U.S. government actively colluded with employers to export workers in order to prevent uprisings and maintain social control and a compliant labor force. However, the following conditions made mass deportation possible: (1) a strong coercive state apparatus; (2) a flexible, deregulated, vulnerable, global labor force; and (3) a global market for the production of goods and services.

As I have argued throughout this book, a critical analysis of mass deportation allows us to develop a more nuanced understanding of global capitalism. A strong coercive state and a weak labor force help to sustain global capitalism despite rising inequality and cuts to social benefits. Mass deportation is but one element in the maintenance of global capitalism. However, it is intimately connected to each stage of what I have called the neoliberal cycle.

The neoliberal cycle began when the United States facilitated the entry of countries in the Global South into the global economy. During the 1950s and 1960s, the United States helped to install governments in the Dominican Republic and Guatemala that were more favorable to global capitalist production. In the 1980s, the United States supported Jamaica's and Brazil's integrations into the global economy. As these and other countries became part of the global chain of production and consumption, their economies experienced disruptions. Economic and social turmoil often led to increased emigration. Emigration, in turn, helped to thin the ranks of the unemployed in the sending country and cushion this transition through remittances.

Some emigrants get to the United States through legal channels. For others, however, their only choice is illegal migration. Dominicans risk their lives on fishing boats while Guatemalans cross through Mexico. Brazilians rely on migrant smugglers who transport them through several countries. For each group, as the U.S. border enforcement apparatus has made the passage more difficult, they have sought new, invariably more dangerous, ways to get into the country. When migrants pay thousands of dollars to get into the United States, they become more vulnerable workers who must first work hard to pay off their enormous debts and then begin to save money to send home to their families. With such a tremendous need to earn money, migrant workers become even less likely to rise up against exploitative employers and others.

When immigrants arrive in decrepit urban areas, their chances for success in their new homes are curtailed. The children of immigrants watch their parents toil in low-wage jobs with few benefits and often hope to be able to do better than their parents by getting an education.

While many immigrants and their children achieve this dream, others do not. The stories in chapter 3 shed light on how easy it can be to fall through the cracks when you live in a high-crime area with constant policing. For many of the men interviewed for this book, any misstep can land you in jail, which in turn can lead to deportation.

Chapters 4 and 5 described how the buildup of the criminal and immigration law enforcement apparatus has affected immigrant men of color. Black and Latino immigrant men are often swept up after being accused of minor crimes. Duaine and Kareem were both arrested in their neighborhoods for smoking marijuana and were deported on those same grounds. Just as mass incarceration is not designed to jail every single drug user or seller, mass deportation is not designed to deport every single undocumented immigrant or every legal permanent resident who indulges in marijuana. Instead, both are systems of social control designed to remove surplus labor and keep labor compliant.

After spending time in jails, prisons, and immigration detention, immigrants are sent to their countries of origin, where many face stigmatization and unemployment. In the Dominican Republic and Jamaica, deportees are blamed for the most recent crime wave. In Guatemala, tattooed deportees are shamed and treated as undesirable. In a unique twist, deportees in Spanish-speaking countries like Guatemala and the Dominican Republic are able to get jobs in call centers and then take calls from English-speaking customers from the United States. Those deportees who work in call centers find a new role in the neoliberal cycle as skilled workers in the global economy.

In March 2014, the Obama administration passed the milestone of two million deportations. In response, activists around the country demanded a moratorium on deportations. Attempts to pass comprehensive immigration reform have failed repeatedly in Congress. The stories in this book have made it clear that deportation is often devastating for the deportee and the family left behind. And deportation is only the tip of the iceberg. Deportees are the immigrants who are actually apprehended and forced to leave. Each deportation has reverberating effects for the communities they leave behind as well as the communities in which deportees arrive.

Nearly one quarter of the more than 400,000 people deported in 2012 were parents of U.S. citizens. Tens of thousands of these children will grow up in the United States knowing that the U.S. government has taken away their right to grow up with one or both of their parents. Nearly all of these children are black or Latino.

Deportation involves arrest, detention, and forced removal. Throughout the history of the United States, communities, especially those deemed to be nonwhite, have been subjected to these forms of repression. It is hard to imagine that the United States would allow detention centers to flourish if the detainees were primarily white. The dehumanization of people of color seems to be a necessary prerequisite for these repressive practices. Instead of detaining and deporting fathers, brothers, and community members, the United States is detaining and deporting criminals, terrorists, and illegal aliens.

Global and Local Apartheid

The racialized consequences of mass deportation are undeniable. Mass deportation has disparate consequences for different racial groups in the United States. Moreover, it maintains a system of "global apartheid" (Nevins and Aizeki 2008: 184) where the "relatively rich and largely white of the world are generally free to travel and live wherever they would like and to access the resources they 'need.' Meanwhile, the relatively poor and largely nonwhite are typically forced to subsist in places where there are not enough resources." Mass deportation helps to maintain this system of global apartheid by removing mostly nonwhite people from the United States—a land of plenty—to much poorer nations where most people are not white. Global apartheid is part of the larger system of global capitalism. The role of the United States in the maintenance of global apartheid is a continuation of its highly racialized history of immigration policy.

People from other lands have always sought their fortunes in the United States. Immigrant (and, of course, slave) labor made the country the economic powerhouse it is today. Immigrants have not always been welcomed with open arms, despite their contributions. Just as immigration has been a constant, so has nativism. Moreover, nativism has always been tainted with racism.

Understanding the current moment of mass deportation thus requires a critical race lens—an analysis that recognizes the "historical centrality and complicity of law in upholding white supremacy (and concomitant hierarchies of gender, class, and sexual orientation)" (West 1995: xi). In the post–civil rights era, laws continue to maintain racial inequality, even though racial discrimination is illegal. As Mary Romero (2011: 102) explains, "Laws appearing race neutral become race-based through law enforcement practices."

Although U.S. immigration policy has shifted dramatically over the years, two trends have remained constant: (1) Nativism has been an integral part of debates over immigration policy, and (2) the consequences of immigration policy have been more disadvantageous to people defined as nonwhite than to those considered to be white. What has changed over time is the removal of explicitly discriminatory language from U.S. immigration laws.

The name of the very first piece of U.S. immigration legislation passed, the 1882 Chinese Exclusion Act, reveals the deep roots of anti-immigrant sentiment in the United States. This act was developed at the behest of white farmers in California who did not want competition from Chinese farmers. The 1924 National Origins Act, designed to keep out undesirable immigrants from Asia, Africa, and southern and eastern Europe, followed. In the early 20th century, U.S. legislators had no qualms about openly voicing their concerns with regard to keeping out "undesirable races" (Ngai 2004).

The backdrop to the 1924 National Origins Act was the eugenics movement, which promoted the idea that intelligence, alcoholism, laziness, crime, poverty, and other moral and cultural traits were inherited. Based on this notion, eugenicists advocated for immigration restrictions, selective breeding, and the sterilization of the biologically unfit as a way of creating a superior breed of people. During this period, many Americans believed that the U.S. population was in decline due to immigration and the high fertility of poor and unfit people (Lindsay 1998).

One of the main proponents of eugenics was Madison Grant (1865–1937), the author of *The Passing of the Great Race*, in which he posited that Europe could be divided into three races: "Nordics," "Alpines," and "Mediterraneans." He argued, forcefully, that Nordics were the most fit and that measures should be taken to ensure their racial purity and survival. As the chairman of the United States Committee on Selective Immigration, he advocated for a reduction in the numbers of Alpines and Mediterraneans admitted into the United States. The views of Madison Grant and other eugenicists played an important role in the development of immigration policy in the 1920s, as these new laws placed limits on the immigration of "undesirable" groups (Jacobson 1998).

The preference for immigrants from western European countries encoded in the 1924 act reflected Grant's views; the intent was to improve the racial composition of the United States. The National Origins Act was the practical implementation of eugenicist theories with regard to undesirable races. The Nazi death camps ultimately engendered a cultural rejection of the utility and morality of eugenics, but racism remained.

In 1943, Congress repealed the Chinese Exclusion Act, and in 1946 it extended the right of citizenship to other Asians (Reimers 1981; Ngai 2004). The Immigration and Nationality Act of 1952 revised the quotas, and then the Immigration and Nationality Act of 1965 completely revamped the quota system, making it more equitable and nondiscriminatory. By 1965, openly voiced concerns about the racial composition of migrant flows would imperil legislators' reputation and claim to office.

The 1965 act was meant to end an era of exclusionary immigration policies. And it did. The family reunification and employment provisions of the act translated into new waves of Latin American and Asian immigrants. Since 1965, the proportion of people of European descent in the United States has gradually decreased while the arrival of people of Latin American and Asian ancestry has increased (Massey et al. 2002). Some social scientists predict that, by 2050, whites will no longer be a majority in this country (Golash-Boza and Darity 2008). The new racial composition of immigrants in the 21st century has stoked nativist fears, as it did in the 20th century.

In this context, the United States has gradually built up an immense immigration law enforcement apparatus. More people have been removed from the United States in the 21st century than in the entire history of U.S. immigration law enforcement. The massive 21st-century removal stands out because it involves the deportation of millions of people from the country in addition to border fortification, which has kept millions more out. The relative exceptionality of this interior enforcement raises the question as to why it has happened.

On the face of it, no clearly expressed racial agenda underlies mass deportation, but today 97 percent of all deportees are sent to Latin America and the Caribbean. Mainstream politicians no longer openly deplore the racial composition of immigrant flows, yet people of color disproportionately bear the consequences of today's immigration policy enforcement. As is typical in a society that claims to be colorblind, policies disproportionately affect one segment of the population, even though the policies do not mention race.

Despite the relative absence of racial rhetoric, race continues to be the backdrop—as it was during the eugenics movement. The United States has a long history of marginalizing people deemed to be "other." This othering justified the mass internment of the Japanese, the enslavement of Africans and African Americans, and the mass repatriation of Mexicans in the 1930s. Similarly, insofar as the public perceives deportees as members of an undesirable group, it applauds their removal.

As much as many Americans would like to think they have buried racially discriminatory episodes deep in their history, contemporary mass deportation proves otherwise. It primarily affects nonwhite people; is carried out without due process; and separates millions of children from their parents. It is on par with other racially tainted tragedies in history: Indian boarding schools that kept Native American children from their parents; internment camps where Japanese citizens and Japanese Americans were forced to live during World War II; and the Jim Crow laws that denied equal opportunities to African Americans. Like these travesties, deportation laws primarily affect one group of people: More than 97 percent of people deported in 2012 were Caribbean or Latin American immigrants, even though they only account for 60 percent of noncitizens.

Many of these deportees are like O'Ryan, Hakim, Maximo, and Vern. They barely know the countries to which they are deported, and they face police brutality, gang violence, homelessness, and a life of poverty and isolation in their native countries. Like Jim Crow laws, deportation laws reflect the U.S. racial hierarchy; the deportation of legal permanent residents has hit black immigrants particularly hard: One of every 12 Jamaican and Dominican male legal permanent residents has been deported since 1996. Like the more than 120,000 people interned by the United States during World War II, 30,000 immigrants detained in the

United States have no legal right to a speedy hearing before a judge or the right to counsel. Like Native American children taken from their parents in the early 20th century, immigrant children lose contact with one or both of their parents due to deportation. The law actually prevents judges from accounting for family ties before ordering a deportation. Men like Diallo, a legal permanent resident found with a marijuana cigarette on two occasions, receive the same treatment as a convicted of murderer with no papers, even though Diallo has a U.S. citizen daughter. The law considers them both guilty of aggravated felonies, entitled to no due process prior to deportation.

Mass deportation is only possible because of the current moment in global capitalism where goods flow relatively freely across borders while people face tremendous restrictions. The prosperity of the richer countries depends on these border restrictions. The acceptance of these restrictions by people in the United States relies on racist and nativist logics. However, if it is true, as Dr. Martin Luther King famously stated, "that the arc of the moral universe is long, but bends towards justice," then this global apartheid is unsustainable.

NOTES

INTRODUCTION: MASS DEPORTATION AND THE NEOLIBERAL CYCLE

1   "Más de 44 mil deportados de Estados Unidas durante 2013," *Prensa Libre*, 2013, accessed October 14, 2014, http://www.prensalibre.com/noticias/justicia/Deportados-Estados_Unidos-2013_0_1031896954.html.

2   Department of Homeland Security, *"Fiscal Year 2011 Budget in Brief,"* accessed February 16, 2012, http://www.dhs.gov/xlibrary/assets/budget_bib_fy2011.pdf.

3   Department of Education, *"Fiscal Year 2011 Budget Summary and Background Information,"* accessed October 17, 2014, http://www2.ed.gov/about/overview/budget/budget11/summary/11summary.pdf; Department of Justice, *"Fiscal Year 2011 Budget,"* accessed February 20, 2012, http://www.justice.gov/opa/pr/2010/February/10-ag-109.html.

4   Ginger Thompson and Sarah Cohen, "More Deportations Follow Minor Crimes, Records Show," *New York Times*, April 6, 2014, accessed September 9, 2014, http://www.nytimes.com/2014/04/07/us/more-deportations-follow-minor-crimes-data-shows.html?_r=0.

5   TRAC Immigration, *"Secure Communities and ICE Deportation: A Failed Program?,"* April 8, 2014, accessed September 9, 2014, http://trac.syr.edu/immigration/reports/349/.

6   Department of Homeland Security, *"2010 Yearbook of Immigration Statistics,"* accessed March 7, 2014, http://www.dhs.gov/yearbook-immigration-statistics-2010#.

7   International Bank for Reconstruction and Development/World Bank, *Migration and Remittances Factbook, Second Edition* (Washington, D.C.: World Bank, 2011), 290, accessed October 14, 2014, http://issuu.com/world.bank.publications/docs/9780821382189/41?e=1107022/2728353.

8   Michael Spence, *"Globalization and Unemployment: The Downside of Integrating Markets,"* *Foreign Affairs*, July/August, accessed August 14, 2014, http://www.foreignaffairs.com/articles/67874/michael-spence/globalization-and-unemployment.

9   AFL-CIO: America's Unions, "Trends in CEO Pay and S&P 500 Index Companies," 2013, accessed October 14, 2014, http://www.aflcio.org/Corporate-Watch/Paywatch-Archive/CEO-Pay-and-You/Trends-in-CEO-Pay.

10 AGC of America, "Construction Employment Experiences Largest Decline in Two Years and May Even as Spending on Construction Activity Inched Up by 0.3 Percent in April," June 1, 2012, accessed September 9, 2014, http://www.agc.org/cs/news_media/press_room/press_release?pressrelease.id=1089.

11 Scott Bittle, Jon Rochkind, and Amber Ott, "Slip-Sliding Away: An Anxious Public Talks about Today's Economy and the American Dream," 2011, accessed October 12, 2014, http://www.publicagenda.org/pages/slipsliding-away.

12 Branko Milanovic, World Bank, "Global Income Inequality by the Numbers: In History and Now," 2012, accessed October 22, 2014, https://openknowledge .worldbank.org/bitstream/handle/10986/12117/wps6259.pdf?sequence=2.

13 Mary Dougherty, Dennis Wilson, and Amy Wu, Department of Homeland Security, "Immigration Enforcement Actions: 2005," November 2005, accessed July 26, 2010, http://www.dhs.gov/xlibrary/assets/statistics/yearbook/2005/Enforcement_ AR_05.pdf.

CHAPTER 1. GROWING UP

1 Lina Bassarsky *et al.*, United Nations Department of Economic and Social Affairs, "*International Migration Policies: Government Views and Priorities*," 2013, http:// www.un.org/en/development/desa/population/publications/policy/international -migration-policies-report-2013.shtml.

2 United Nations Human Development Programme, "Human Development Report," 2009, accessed October 18, 2014, http://hdr.undp.org/en/media/HDR_ 20072008_EN_Complete.pdf; Department of Homeland Security, DHS Table 03 for 2009, "Persons Obtaining Legal Permanent Resident Status by Region and Country of Birth: Fiscal Years 2000 to 2009," Yearbook of Immigration Statistics, accessed October 20, 2014, http://www.dhs.gov/yearbook-immigration-statistics -2009-3.

3 Department of Homeland Security, "Persons Obtaining Legal Permanent Resident Status by Region and Country of Birth: Fiscal Years 1997 to 2006," http://www.dhs .gov/xlibrary/assets/statistics/yearbook/2006/table03d.xls; Department of Homeland Security, "Estimates of the Unauthorized Immigrant Population Residing in the United States: January 2006 August 2007," 2007, accessed September 9, 2014, http://www.dhs.gov/xlibrary/assets/statistics/publications/ill_pe_2006.pdf.

4 Quentin Delpech, "Guate-Mara: The Extortion Economy in Guatemala," *Americas Quarterly*, Spring 2013, accessed October 1, 2014, http://www.americasquarterly .org/content/guate-mara-extortion-economy-guatemala.

CHAPTER 2. CROSSING OVER

1 Jo Tuckman, "Survivor Tells of Escape from Mexican Massacre in Which 72 Were Left Dead," *Guardian*, August 25, 2010, accessed October 16, 2014, http:// www.theguardian.com/world/2010/aug/25/mexico-massacre-central-american -migrants.

2 Jo Tuckman, "Mexican Mass Grave Toll Rises to 116," *Guardian*, April 13, 2011, accessed October 16, 2014, http://www.theguardian.com/world/2011/apr/13/ mexico-mass-grave-matamoros-tamaulipas.

3 Maria Jimenez, American Civil Liberties Union of San Diego, "Humanitarian Crisis: Migrant Deaths at the U.S.-Mexico Border," October 1, 2009, accessed

September 9, 2014, http://www.aclu.org/files/pdfs/immigrants/humanitarian crisisreport.pdf.

4 "Stowaway Problem in the U.S.," *Social Contract Press*, Fall 1994, accessed October 16, 2014, http://www.thesocialcontract.com/artman2/publish/tsc0501/article_399 .shtml; Immigration and Customs Enforcement, "Jamaican Citizen Sentenced to Prison for Illegally Re-entering U.S.," November 5, 2012, accessed October 18, 2014, http://www.ice.gov/news/releases/1211/121105roanoke.htm.

5 Kevin Thomas, "A Demographic Profile of Black Caribbean Immigrants in the United States," *Migration Policy Institute*, April 2012, accessed October 16, 2014, http://www.migrationpolicy.org/research/CBI-demographic-profile-black -caribbean-immigrants.

6 U.S. State Department, "Adjusted Refusal Rate—B-Visas Only by Nationality Fiscal Year 2013," 2013, accessed October 15, 2014, http://travel.state.gov/content/ dam/visas/Statistics/Non-Immigrant-Statistics/RefusalRates/FY13.pdf.

7 Julia Preston, "**Young** and Alone, Facing Court and Deportation," New York Times, August 25, 2012, accessed October 17, 2014, http://www.nytimes .com/2012/08/26/us/more-young-illegal-immigrants-face deportation.html? pagewanted=all&_r=0.

8 Customs and Border Patrol, "United States Border Patrol Nationwide Illegal Alien Apprehensions Fiscal Years 1925–2013," 2014, accessed October 15, 2014, http:// www.cbp.gov/sites/default/files/documents/U.S.%20Border%20Patrol%20Fiscal %20Year%20Apprehension%20Statistics%201925–2013.pdf.

9 Customs and Border Patrol, "United States Border Patrol: Border Patrol Agent Staffing by Fiscal Year (Oct. 1st through Sept. 30th)," 2014, accessed October 15, 2014, http://www.cbp.gov/sites/default/files/documents/U.S.%20Border%20 Patrol%20Fiscal%20Year%20Staffing%20Statistics%201992–2013.pdf.

10 Wayne Cornelius *et al.*, Immigration Policy Center, "Controlling Unauthorized Immigration from Mexico: The Failure of 'Prevention through Deterrence' and the Need for Comprehensive Reform," June 10, 2008, accessed October 17, 2014, http://www.immigrationforum.org/images/uploads/CCISbriefing061008.pdf.

11 "El Rio Bravo senda fatal para migrantes," *El Universal Nacion*, December 23, 2007, accessed October 17, 2014, http://www.eluniversal.com.mx/nacion/156688.html.

12 Raquel Rubio-Goldsmith *et al.*, Immigration Policy Center, "A Humanitarian Crisis at the Border: New Estimates of Deaths among Unauthorized Immigrants," February 2007, accessed October 17, 2014, http://www.800milewall.org/Resources/ Crisis%20at%20the%20Border%20Deaths.pdf.

13 Chris Kraul and Nicole Gaoutte, "No-Visa Agreement Backfired on Mexico," *Los Angeles Times*, September 14, 2005, accessed October 17, 2014, http://articles .latimes.com/2005/sep/14/world/fg-mexbrazil14.

14 Blas Nuñez-Neto, Alison Siskin, and Stephen Viña, Congressional Research Service, "Border Security: Apprehensions of 'Other Than Mexican' Aliens," September 22, 2005, accessed October 17, 2014, http://trac.syr.edu/immigration/library/ P1.pdf.

15 Department of Homeland Security, "FY 2012 Budget in Brief," 2012, accessed October 16, 2014, http://www.dhs.gov/xlibrary/assets/budget-bib-fy2012.pdf.

16 Doris Meissner, Migration Policy Institute, "Immigration Enforcement in the United States—The Rise of a Formidable Machinery," 2013, http://www.migration policy.org/pubs/enforcementpillars.pdf.

CHAPTER 3. BECOMING (BLACK AND LATINO) AMERICAN

1 I did meet some Brazilian deportees whose Brazilian-born children continue to live in the United States. Most of these children were adults and had obtained legalization, usually through marriage to a U.S. citizen. Most important, the Brazilians often did not arrive in heavily policed neighborhoods, making it less likely for them to get into trouble with law enforcement. In chapter 5, I discuss in more detail the different pathways immigrants have into the deportation dragnet.

2 Renee Feltz and Amy Goodman, "'If the Risk Is Low, Let Them Go': Elderly Prison Population Skyrockets Despite Low Risk to Society," *Truthout News*, December 24, 2013, accessed October 17, 2014, http://www.truth-out.org/news/ item/20825-if-the-risk-is-low-let-them-go-elderly-prison-population-skyrockets -despite-low-risk-to-society.

CHAPTER 4. THE WAR ON DRUGS

1 My calculations are based on Bernard Headley's estimates in his book (Headley et al. 2005), Department of Homeland Security data releases, Migration Policy Institute numbers (Glennie and Chappell 2010), and a report by Human Rights Watch, Forced Apart: By the Numbers. The report by Human Rights Watch indicates that 14,501 Jamaicans were deported on criminal grounds between 1997 and 2007. My calculation is that about 10,000 of the criminal deportees were legal permanent residents. Human Rights Watch obtained their data from the Department of Homeland Security through a Freedom of Information request. Headley obtained his data from the U.S. embassy in Jamaica. Glennie and Chappell obtained theirs from the Department of Homeland Security and Jamaican data sources.

2 Nancy Rytina, "Estimates of the Legal Permanent Resident Population in 2007," 2009, accessed October 16, 2014, http://www.dhs.gov/xlibrary/assets/statistics/ publications/lpr_pe_2007.pdf.

3 University of California, Berkeley, School of Law, Chief Justice Earl Warren Institute on Race, Ethnicity and Diversity; University of California, Berkeley, School of Law, Immigration Law Clinic; and University of California, Davis, School of Law, "In the Child's Best Interest? The Consequences of Losing a Lawful Immigrant Parent to Deportation," March 2010, accessed October 16, 2014, http://www.law .berkeley.edu/files/Human_Rights_report.pdf.

4 U.S. Census Bureau, "State and County Quick Facts," July 8, 2014, accessed October 17, 2014, http://quickfacts.census.gov/qfd/states/00000.html.

5 Department of Homeland Security, "Estimates of the Legal Permanent Resident

Population in 2012," 2013, accessed October 17, 2014, http://www.dhs.gov/sites/default/files/publications/ois_lpr_pe_2012.pdf.

6 Department of Homeland Security, "Fiscal Year 2013 ICE Immigration Removals," 2014, accessed October 18, 2014, http://www.ice.gov/removal-statistics/.

7 Immigration and Customs Enforcement, "ICE Removal Statistics, Fiscal Year 2013," 2014, accessed October 16, 2014, http://www.ice.gov/removal-statistics/.

8 "NYC Marijuana Possession Arrests Skyrocket, Illustrate NYPD Racial Bias, New Report Shows," *New York Civil Liberties Union*, 2008, accessed October 16, 2014, http://www.nyclu.org/node/1736.

9 *Carachuri-Rosendo v. Holder*, Attorney General, Certiorari to the United States Court of Appeals for the Fifth Circuit No. 09–60, argued March 31, 2010 — decided June 14, 2010, accessed October 16, 2014, http://www.supremecourt.gov/opinions/09pdf/09-60.pdf.

CHAPTER 5. GETTING CAUGHT

1 Department of Homeland Security, "Fiscal Year 2013 ICE Immigration Removals," 2014, accessed October 16, 2014, https://www.ice.gov/doclib/about/offices/ero/pdf/2013-ice-immigration-removals.pdf.

2 U.S. Department of Justice, "Justice Department Releases Investigative Findings on the Alamance County, N.C., Sheriff's Office," 2012, accessed October 16, 2014, http://www.justice.gov/opa/pr/2012/September/12-crt-1125.html.

3 "DOJ: Alamance Sheriff Shows Pattern of Discrimination against Latinos," *WFMY News*, September 18, 2012, accessed October 17, 2014, http://archive.digtriad.com/news/local/article/246062/57/DOJ-Alamance-Sheriff-Shows-Pattern-Of-Bias-Against-Latinos.

4 "Georgia Teen, a Plaintiff in SPLC Suit, Tells House Subcommittee about Terrifying Immigration Raid," *Southern Poverty Law Center*, February 2008, accessed October 16, 2014, http://www.splcenter.org/get-informed/news/georgia-teen-a-plaintiff-in-splc-suit-tells-house-subcommittee-about-terrifying-im.

5 Tamara's comment indicates that she, like many Brazilians, sees the United States as a place where one can earn money and live comfortably. It also indicates that my social location as a white, North American, middle-class woman influenced our interactions. Insofar as this research is primarily interview-based and not ethnographic, it is difficult for me to give many details on how my social location influenced my respondents, but I am sure that my social location did have an influence. I am less sure how — primarily because many of the people profiled in this book are people whom I only met once. I learned in my first book that an understanding of the researcher's positionality comes primarily from informal comments that respondents make outside of the context of the interview. For this project, I had minimal access to that kind of information.

6 Walter Ewing, Immigration Policy Center, "Growth of the U.S. Deportation Machine," 2014, accessed October 18, 2014, http://www.immigrationpolicy.org/just-facts/growth-us-deportation-machine.

7 Kimber Solana, "Illegal Immigrants Give Billions to Medicare, Social Security with No Hope of Benefit," *USC Annenberg*, January 13, 2007, accessed October 18, 2014, http://www.reportingonhealth.org/2013/01/07/illegal-immigrants -give-billions-medicare-social-security-no-hope-benefit.

8 Foundation for Advancing Alcohol Responsibility, "Drunk Driving Fatalities— National Statistics," 2012, accessed October 18, 2014, http://responsibility.org/ drunk-driving/drunk-driving-fatalities-national-statistics.

9 Immigration Justice Clinic, Cardozo Law School, "Constitution on ICE: A Report on Immigration Home Raid Operations," 2009, accessed October 16, 2014, http:// cdm16064.contentdm.oclc.org/cdm/ref/collection/p266901coll4/id/2049.

CHAPTER 6. BEHIND BARS

1 Detention Watch Network, "The Influence of the Private Prison Industry in Immigration Detention," 2012, accessed October 27, 2014, http://www.detention watchnetwork.org/privateprisons.

2 Department of Corrections and Community Supervision, New York State, "New York State Department of Corrections and Community Supervision Announces Prison Reforms That Will Save Taxpayers Over $30 Million Annually Following Decline in Crime Rate and Inmate Population," 2013, accessed October 18, 2014, http://www.doccs.ny.gov/PressRel/2013/Prison_Closure_Announcement .html.

3 Detention Watch Network, "About the U.S. Detention and Deportation System," http://www.detentionwatchnetwork.org/aboutdetention; National Immigrant Justice Center. "Isolated in Detention," September 2010, accessed April 11, 2011, http://www.immigrantjustice.org/download-document/793-isolated-in-detention -full-report.html.

4 Detention Watch Network, "The Influence of the Private Prison Industry in Immigration Detention," 2012, accessed October 27, 2014, http://www.detention watchnetwork.org/privateprisons.

5 *Zadvydas v. Davis et al.* U.S. 99-7791 (2001), accessed October 18, 2014, http:// www.law.cornell.edu/supct/html/99-7791.ZS.html.

6 *Demore v. Kim* U.S. 01-1491 (2003), accessed April 15, 2011, http://www.law.cornell .edu/supct/pdf/01-1491P.ZO.

7 *Demore v. Kim* U.S. 01-1491 (2003), Opinion of Souter, accessed April 15, 2011, http://www.law.cornell.edu/supct/pdf/01-1491P.ZX.

8 "Immigrant Groups Complain of 'Icebox' Detention Cells," *Los Angeles Times*, December 5, 2013, accessed October 20, 2014, http://articles.latimes.com/2013/ dec/05/nation/la-na-ff-detention-centers-20131206.

CHAPTER 7. BACK HOME

1 "Statistics Fuel Deportee-Crime Concerns," *Gleaner*, April 15, 2010, accessed October 18, 2014, http://jamaica-gleaner.com/gleaner/20100415/lead/lead3.html.

2 NUMBEO, "Cost of Living in Kingston, Jamaica," August 2014, accessed October 18, 2014, http://www.numbeo.com/cost-of-living/city_result.jsp?country=Jamaica &city=Kingston.

3 Marianella Belliard and Bridget Wooding, "Deportados: El rostro humano de una realidad social," *Observatorio Migrantes del Caribe*, August 2011, accessed October 13, 2014, http://www.obmica.org/images/Publicaciones/MigrationPolicyBrief/ Deportados_espaol_final_mpb.pdf.

CONCLUSION. GLOBAL APARTHEID

1 Marc R. Rosenblum and Kristen McCabe, "Deportation and Discretion: Reviewing the Record and Options for Change," Migration Policy Institute, October 2014, accessed October 30, 2014, http://www.migrationpolicy.org/research/ deportation-and-discretion-reviewing-record-and-options-change.

BIBLIOGRAPHY

Alexander, Michelle. 2010. *The New Jim Crow: Mass Incarceration in the Age of Color-blindness*. New York: New Press.

Amann, Edmund, and Werner Baer. 2002. "Neoliberalism and Its Consequences in Brazil." *Journal of Latin American Studies* 34(4): 945–959.

Anderson, Tammy L. 2005. "Dimensions of Women's Power in the Illicit Drug Economy." *Theoretical Criminology* 9(4): 371–400.

Azmy, Baher, Bassina Farbenblum, Scott Michelman, et al. 2008. U.S. District Court. District of New Jersey. *Argueta el al v. ICE*. Retrieved from http://www.clearing house.net/chDocs/public/IM-NJ-0007-0008.pdf.

Balderrama, Francisco E., and Raymond Rodríguez. 2006. *Decade of Betrayal: Mexican Repatriation in the 1930s*. Albuquerque: University of New Mexico Press.

Berlin, Daniel, Erin Brizius, Micah Bump, Daren Garshelis, Niloufar Khonsari, Erika Pinheiro, Kate Rhudy, Rebecca Shaeffer, Sarah Sherman-Stokes, and Thomas Smith. 2008. "Between the Border and the Street: A Comparative Look at Gang Reduction Policies and Migration in the United States and Guatemala." Accessed October 20, 2014. Retrieved from https://www.law.georgetown.edu/academics/centers -institutes/human-rights-institute/fact-finding/upload/Guatemala-report.pdf.

Bloch, Alice, and Liza Schuster. 2005. "At the Extremes of Exclusion: Deportation, Detention and Dispersal." *Ethnic and Racial Studies* 28(3): 491–512.

Bobo, Lawrence D., and Victor Thompson. 2010. "Racialized Mass Incarceration: Poverty, Prejudice, and Punishment." In *Doing Race: 21 Essays for the 21st Century*, edited by Hazel R. Markus and Paula Moya. New York: W. W. Norton. 322–355.

Boehme, Eric. 2011. "Recession and the Risks of Illegality: Governing the Undocumented in the United States." *New Political Science* 33(4): 541–554.

Bonilla-Silva, Eduardo. 2013. *Racism without Racists: Color-blind Racism and the Persistence of Racial Inequality in America*. Lanham, Md.: Rowman and Littlefield.

Bosworth, Mary. 2011. "Deportation, Detention and Foreign-national Prisoners in England and Wales." *Citizenship Studies* 15(5): 583–595.

———. 2014. *Inside Immigration Detention*. Oxford: Oxford University Press.

Bourgois, Philippe. 2003. *In Search of Respect: Selling Crack in El Barrio*. Cambridge: Cambridge University Press.

Brands, Henry. 1987. "Decisions on American Armed Intervention: Lebanon, Dominican Republic, and Grenada." Political Science Quarterly 102(4): 607–624.

Brotherton, David, and Luis Barrios. 2011. *Banished to the Homeland: Dominican Deportees and Their Stories of Exile*. New York: Columbia University Press.

Brotherton, David, and Yolanda Martin. 2009. "The War on Drugs and the Case of Dominican Deportees." *Journal of Crime and Justice* 32(2): 21–48.

Castles, Stephen. 2011. "Migration, Crisis, and the Global Labour Market." *Globalizations* 8(3): 311–324.

Clarke, Colin, and David Howard. 2006. "Contradictory Socio-economic Consequences of Structural Adjustment in Kingston, Jamaica." *Geographical Journal* 172(2): 106–129.

Collins, Patricia Hill. 1998. "It's All in the Family: Intersections of Gender, Race, and Nation." *Hypatia* 13(3): 62–82. Retrieved from http://www.jstor.org/stable/3810699.

———. 2004. *Black Sexual Politics*. New York: Routledge.

Collyer, Michael. 2012. "Deportation and the Micropolitics of Exclusion: The Rise of Removals from the UK to Sri Lanka." *Geopolitics* 17(2): 276–292.

Comfort, Megan. 2007. "Punishment beyond the Legal Offender." Annual Review of Law and Social Science 3: 271–296.

Contreras, Randol. 2012. *The Stickup Kids: Race, Drugs, Violence, and the American Dream*. Berkeley: University of California Press.

Cooper, Dereck W. 1985. "Migration from Jamaica in the 1970s: Political Protest or Economic Pull?" International Migration Review 18(4): 728–745.

Cornelius, Wayne A. 2006. "*Impacts of Border Enforcement on Unauthorized Mexican Migration to the United States*." Accessed January 15, 2013. Retrieved from http://borderbattles.ssrc.org/Cornelius/.

Davis, Angela. 1998. "*Masked Racism: Reflections on the Prison Industrial Complex*." Colorlines 2. Accessed October 10, 2008. Retrieved from http://www.colorlines.com/article.php?ID=309&p=1.

De Genova, Nicholas. 2002. "Migrant 'Illegality' and Deportability in Everyday Life." *Annual Review of Anthropology* 31: 419–447.

———. 2005. *Working the Boundaries: Race, Space, and "Illegality" in Mexican Chicago*. Durham, N.C.: Duke University Press.

DeVeaux, Mika'il. 2013. "The Trauma of the Incarceration Experience." Harvard Civil Rights-Civil Liberties Law Review 48(1): 257–277.

Dolovich, Sharon. 2012. "Two Models of the Prison: Accidental Humanity and Hypermasculinity in the L.A. County Jail." *Journal of Criminal Law and Criminology* 102: 965.

Dow, Mark. 2004. *American Gulag: Inside America's Immigration Detention*. Berkeley: University of California Press.

Dreby, Joanna. 2010. *Divided by Borders*. Berkeley: University of California Press.

———. 2012. "The Burden of Deportation on Children in Mexican Immigrant Families." *Journal of Marriage and Family* 74: 829–845.

Duany, Jorge. 2004. "Los Países: Transnational Migration from the Dominican Republic to the United States." In *Dominican Migration: Transnational Perspectives*, edited by Ernesto Sagás and Sintia E. Molina. Gainesville: University Press of Florida.

Dunn, Timothy J. 1996. *The Militarization of the U.S.-Mexico Border, 1978–1992: Low-intensity Conflict Doctrine Comes Home*. CMAS Border Migration Studies

Series. University of Texas at Austin. Retrieved from http://www.loc.gov/catdir/description/texas041/94042964.html.

———. 2009. *Blockading the Border and Human Rights: The El Paso Operation That Remade Immigration Enforcement.* Austin: University of Texas Press.

Espinal, Rosario. 1995. "Economic Restructuring, Social Protest, and Democratization in the Dominican Republic." *Latin American Perspectives* 22(3): 63–79.

Feagin, Joe. 2000. *Racist America.* Routledge: New York.

Foner, Nancy. 2009. "Gender and Migration: West Indians in Comparative Perspective." *International Migration* 47(1): 3–30.

Foucault, Michel. 1977. *Discipline and Punish: The Birth of the Prison.* New York: Random House.

Fragomen, Austin T., and Steven Bell. 2007. *Immigration Fundamentals: A Guide to Law and Practice.* New York: Practicing Law Institute.

García, Angela S., and David Keyes. 2012. "Life as an Undocumented Immigrant: How Restrictive Local Immigration Policies Affect Daily Life." Washington, D.C.: Center for American Progress.

García, Maria Cristina. 2006. *Seeking Refuge: Central American Migration to Mexico, the United States and Canada.* Berkeley: University of California Press.

Garland, David. 2012. *The Culture of Control: Crime and Social Order in Contemporary Society.* Chicago: University of Chicago Press.

Gibney, Matthew J. 2008. "Asylum and the Expansion of Deportation in the United Kingdom." *Government and Opposition* 43(2): 146–167.

Gilmore, Ruth. 2007. *Golden Gulag: Prisons, Surplus, Crisis and Opposition in Globalizing California.* Berkeley: University of California Press.

Glennie, Alex, and Laura Chappell. 2010. *Jamaica: From Diverse Beginning to Diaspora in the Developed World.* Migration Information Source. Retrieved from http://www.migrationinformation.org/Profiles/display.cfm.

Goffman, Erving. 1961. "On the Characteristics of Total Institutions." Presented at the Symposium on Preventive and Social Psychiatry.

Golash, Deirdre. 2005. *The Case against Punishment.* New York: NYU Press.

Golash-Boza, Tanya. 2012. *Immigration Nation: Raids, Detentions and Deportations in Post-911 America.* Boulder, Colo.: Paradigm.

Golash-Boza, Tanya, and William Darity. 2008. "Latino Racial Choices: The Effects of Skin Colour and Discrimination on Latinos' and Latinas' Racial Self-identifications." *Ethnic and Racial Studies* 31(5): 899–934.

Golash-Boza, Tanya, and Pierrette Hondagneu-Sotelo. 2013. "Latino Immigrant Men and the Deportation Crisis: A Gendered Racial Removal Program." *Latino Studies* 11(3): 271–292.

Golub, Andrew, Bruce D. Johnson, and Eloise Dunlap. 2007. "The Race/Ethnicity Disparity in Misdemeanor Marijuana Arrests in New York City." *Criminology and Public Policy* 6(1): 131–164.

Gonzales, Alberto. 2013. *Reform without Justice: Latino Migrant Politics and the Homeland Security State.* New York: Oxford University Press.

Goza, Franklin. 1994. "Brazilian Immigration to North America." *International Migration Review* 28(1): 136–152.

Gray, Obika. 2004. *Demeaned but Empowered: The Social Power of the Urban Poor in Jamaica*. Kingston: University of West Indies Press.

Gunst, Laurie. 1995. *Born fi' Dead: A Journey into the Jamaican Posse Underworld*. Edinburgh: Cannongate.

Hacker, Jacob, S. Philip Rehm, and Mark Schlesinger. 2013. "The Insecure American: Economic Experience, Financial Worries, and Policy Attitudes." Perspectives on Politics 11: 23–49.

Hagan, John, and Alberto Palloni. 1999. "Sociological Criminology and the Mythology of Hispanic Immigration and Crime." *Social Problems* 46(4): 617–632. doi:10.1525/sp.1999.46.4.03x0265e.

Hahamovitch, Cindy. 2011. *No Man's Land: Jamaican Guestworkers in America and the Global History of Deportable Labor*. Princeton: Princeton University Press.

Haller, William, Alejandro Portes, and Scott M. Lynch. 2011. "Dreams Fulfilled, Dreams Shattered: Determinants of Segmented Assimilation in the Second Generation." *Social Forces* 89(3): 733–762.

Harris, Anita. 2004. "Jamming Girl Culture: Young Women and Consumer Citizenship." In *All about the Girl: Culture, Power, and Identity*, edited by Anita Harris. New York: Routledge. 163–172.

Harrison, Jill Lindsey, and Sarah E. Lloyd. 2012. "Illegality at Work: Deportability and the Productive New Era of Immigration Enforcement." *Antipode* 44(2): 365–385. doi:10.1111/j.1467-8330.2010.00841.x.

Harvey, David. 2005. *A Brief History of Neoliberalism*. Oxford: Oxford University Press.

Headley, Bernard, Michael Gordon, and Andrew MacIntosh. 2005. *Deported: Entry and Exit Findings*. Jamaica: Stephenson Litho Press.

Hernandez, Kelly Lytle. 2010. *Migra: A History of the U.S. Border Patrol*. Berkeley: University of California Press.

Hoefer, Michael, Nancy Rytina, and Bryan C. Baker. 2009. "Estimates of the Unauthorized Immigrant Population Residing in the United States: January 2008." U.S. Department of Homeland Security. Office of Immigration Statistics. Policy Directorate. Retrieved from http://www.dhs.gov/xlibrary/assets/statistics/publications/ois_ill_pe_2008.pdf.

Hoffman, Abraham. 1974. *Unwanted Mexican Americans in the Great Depression: Repatriation Pressures, 1929–1939*. Tucson: University of Arizona Press.

Hondagneu-Sotelo, Pierrette, and Ernestine Avila (1997). "'I'm Here, but I'm There': The Meanings of Latina Transnational Motherhood." *Gender and Society* 11(5): 548–571.

Inda, Jonathan. 2013. "Subject to Deportation: IRCA, 'Criminal Aliens,' and the Policing of Immigration." *Migration Studies* 1(3): 292–310.

Jackall, Robert. 1997. *Wild Cowboys: Urban Marauders and the Forces of Order*. Cambridge: Harvard University Press.

Jacobson, Matthew. 1998. Whiteness of a Different Color. Cambridge: Harvard University Press.

Johnson, Kevin. 2004. The "Huddled Masses" Myth: Immigration and Civil Rights. Philadelphia: Temple University Press.

Kanstroom, Dan. 2007. Deportation Nation: Outsiders in American History. Cambridge: Harvard University Press.

Kao, Grace, and Marta Tienda. 1995. "Optimism and Achievement: The Educational Performance of Immigrant Youth." Social Science Quarterly 76(1): 1–19. Accessed October 20, 2014. Retrieved from http://search.ebscohost.com/login.aspx?direct=true&db=buh&AN=9504181 06&site=ehost-live.

Kasinitz, Philip. 1992. Caribbean New York: Black Immigrants and the Politics of Race. Ithaca, N.Y.: Cornell University Press.

Kasinitz, Philip, John H. Mollenkopf, Mary C. Waters, and Jennifer Holdaway. 2008. Inheriting the City: The Children of Immigrants Come of Age. Cambridge: Harvard University Press.

Kimmel, M. 1994. "Masculinity as Homophobia: Fear, Shame and Silence in the Construction of Gender Identity." In Theorizing Masculinities. Thousand Oaks, Calif.: Sage. 119–141.

King, Ryan D., Michael Massoglia, and Christopher Uggen. 2012. "Employment and Exile: U.S. Criminal Deportations, 1908–2005." American Journal of Sociology 117: 1786–1825.

Kretsedemas, Philip. 2012. The Immigration Crucible: Transforming Race, Nation and the Limits of the Law. New York: Columbia University Press.

Lacayo, A. Elena. 2010. "The Impact of Section 287(g) of the Immigration and Nationality Act on the Latino Community." National Council of La Raza. Accessed October 20, 2014. Retrieved from http://www.nclr.org/images/uploads/publications/287gReportFinal.pdf.

Lawston, Jodie, and Martha Escobar. 2009–10. "Policing, Detention, Deportation, and Resistance: Situating Immigrant Justice and Carcerality in the 21st Century." Social Justice 36(2): 1–6.

Lay, Sody. 2004. "Lost in the Fray: Cambodian American Youth in Providence, Rhode Island." In Asian American Youth, Culture, and Identity, edited by Jennifer Lee and Min Zhou. New York: Routledge. 221–234.

Levitt, Peggy. 2001. Transnational Villagers. Berkeley: University of California Press.

Lewis, Linden. 2007. "Man Talk, Masculinity, and a Changing Social Environment." Caribbean Review of Gender Studies 1(1): 1–20.

Lindsay, Matthew. 1998. "Reproducing a Fit Citizenry: Dependency, Eugenics, and the Law of Marriage in the United States, 1860–1920." Law and Social Inquiry 23(3): 541–585.

Lopez, Nancy. 2003. Hopeful Girls, Troubled Boys: Race and Gender Disparity in Urban Education. New York: Routledge.

Louie, Miriam. 2001. Sweatshop Warriors. Boston: South End Press.

Margolis, Maxine. 1993. *Little Brazil: An Ethnography of Brazilian Immigrants in New York City*. Princeton: Princeton University Press.

Marshall, T. H. 1950. *Citizenship and Social Class*. Cambridge: Cambridge University Press.

Martín, Yolanda C. 2013. "The Syndemics of Removal: Trauma and Substance Abuse." In *Outside Justice*. New York: Springer. 91–107.

Massey, Douglas, Jorge Durand, and Nolan J. Malone. 2002. *Beyond Smoke and Mirrors: Mexican Immigration in an Era of Economic Integration*. New York: Russell Sage Foundation.

Master, Maureen. 2003. "Due Process for All: Redressing Inequities in the Criminal Provisions of the 1996 Immigration Laws." Presented at the United States Conference for Catholic Bishops. Accessed October 23, 2008. Retrieved from http://www.usccb.org/mrs/dueprocessforall.shtml.

Mastman, Michael. 2008. "Undocumented Entrepreneurs: Are Business Owners Employees under the Immigration Laws?" *NYU Journal of Legislation and Public Policy* 70(1999): 225–258. Accessed October 20, 2014. Retrieved from http://heinonlinebackup.com/hol-cgi-bin/get_pdf.cgi?handle=hein.journals/nyulpp12&section=9.

Mau, Steffen. 2010. "Mobility Citizenship, Inequality, and the Liberal State." *International Political Sociology* 4(4): 339–361.

Mauer, Mark. 2007. "Racial Impact Statements as a Means of Reducing Unwarranted Sentencing Disparities." Ohio State Journal of Criminal Law 5(19): 19–46. Retrieved from http://www.sentencingproject.org/doc/publications/rd_racialimpact statements.pdf.

McCall, Leslie, and Christine Percheski. 2010. "Income Inequality: New Trends and Research Directions." *Annual Review of Sociology* 36(1): 329–347.

McDowell, Meghan, and Nancy Wonders. 2009–10. "Keeping Migrants in Their Place: Technologies of Control and Racialized Public Space in Arizona." Social Justice 36(2): 54–72.

Mendelson, Margot, Shayna Strom, and Michael Wishnie. 2009. "*Collateral Damage: An Examination of ICE's Fugitive Operations Program.*" Washington, D.C.: Migration Policy Institute.

Menjívar, Cecilia. 2006. "Liminal Legality: Salvadoran and Guatemalan Immigrants' Lives in the United States." *American Journal of Sociology* 111(4): 999–1037.

———. 2007. "Men's Migration and Women's Lives: Views from Rural Armenia and Guatemala." *Social Science Quarterly* 88(5): 1243–1262.

Menjívar, Cecilia, and Leisy Abrego. 2012. "Legal Violence: Immigration Law and the Lives of Central American Immigrants." *American Journal of Sociology* 117(5): 1380–1421. Accessed October 20, 2014. Retrieved from http://www.jstor.org/stable/10.1086/663575.

Miles, Thomas J., and Adam B. Cox. 2014. "Does Immigration Enforcement Reduce Crime? Evidence from 'Secure Communities.'" Journal of Law and Economics 57(4): 937–973.

Miller, Teresa. 2008. "A New Look at Neo-liberal Economic Policies and the Criminalization of Undocumented Migration." *Southern Methodist University School of Law Review* 61: 171–188.

Model, Suzanne. 2008. *West Indian Immigrants: A Black Success Story?* New York: Russell Sage Foundation.

Morawetz, Nancy. 2000. "Understanding the Impact of the 1996 Deportation Laws and the Limited Scope of Proposed Reforms." *Harvard Law Review* 113(8): 1936–1962.

Morris, Martina, and Bruce Western. 1999. "Inequality in Earnings at the Close of the Twentieth Century." *Annual Review of Sociology* 25(1): 623–657.

National Research Council. 2014. "The Growth of Incarceration in the United States: Exploring Causes and Consequences." Washington, D.C.: National Academies Press. Accessed September 15, 2014. Retrieved from http://www.vtlex.com/wp-content/uploads/2014/06/18613.pdf.

Nazario, Sonia. 2007. *Enrique's Journey: The Story of a Boy's Dangerous Odyssey to Reunite with His Mother*. New York: Random House.

Nevins, Joseph. 2002. *Operation Gatekeeper: The Rise of the "Illegal Alien" and the Remaking of the US-Mexico Boundary*. New York: Routledge.

Nevins, Joseph, and Mizue Aizeki. 2008. *Dying to Live: A Story of US Immigration in an Age of Global Apartheid*. San Francisco: City Lights.

Ngai, Mai. 2004. *Impossible Subjects*. Princeton: Princeton University Press.

Nicholls, Walter. 2013. *The DREAMers: How the Undocumented Youth Movement Transformed the Immigrant Rights Debate*. Stanford, Calif.: Stanford University Press.

Norton, Michael I., and Dan Ariely. 2011. "Building a Better America—One Wealth Quintile at a Time." *Perspectives on Psychological Science* 6(1): 9–12.

Ogbu, John U. 1990. "Minority Education in Comparative Perspective." *Journal of Negro Education* 59(1): 45–57.

Olivo, Antonio. 2011. "Pilsen Store Has Design on History." *Chicago Tribune*, November 26. Accessed October 20, 2014. Retrieved from http://articles.chicagotribune.com/2011-11-26/news/ct-met-latino-museum-20111126_1_pilsen-color-barrier-mexican-american.

Olwig, K. F. 2002. "A Wedding in the Family: Home Making in a Global Kin Network." *Global Networks* 2(3): 205–218.

Pager, Devah. 2007. *Marked: Race, Crime, and Finding Work in an Era of Mass Incarceration*. Chicago: University of Chicago Press.

Pakulski, Jan. 1997. "Cultural Citizenship." *Citizenship Studies* 1(1): 73–86.

Parenti, Christian. 2000. *Lockdown America: Police and Prisons in the Age of Crisis*. London: Verso.

Parreñas, Rhacel Salazar. 2005. *Children of Global Migration: Transnational Families and Gendered Woes*. Stanford, Calif.: Stanford University Press.

Passas, Nikos. 2000. "Global Anomie, Dysnomie, and Economic Crime: Hidden Consequences of Neoliberalism and Globalization in Russia and around the World." *Social Justice* 27(2): 16–44. Accessed October 20, 2014. Retrieved from http://elibrary.ru/item.asp?id=8333177.

Petersilia, J. 2003. *When Prisoners Come Home: Parole and Prisoner Reentry*. New York: Oxford University Press.

Pettit, Betty, and Bruce Western. 2004. "Mass Imprisonment and the Life Course: Race and Class Inequality in U.S. Incarceration." *American Sociological Review* 69: 151–169.

Pierre, Jemima. 2004. "Black Immigrants in the United States and the 'Cultural Narratives' of Ethnicity." *Identities: Global Studies in Culture and Power* 11(2): 141–170.

Portes, Alejandro, Patricia Fernandez-Kelly, and William Haller. 2005. "Segmented Assimilation on the Ground: The New Second Generation in Early Adulthood." *Ethnic and Racial Studies* 28(6): 1000–1040.

Portes, Alejandro, and Rubén G. Rumbaut. 2001. *Legacies: The Story of the Immigrant Second Generation*. Berkeley: University of California Press.

Portes, Alejandro, and Richard Schauffler. 1994. "Language and the Second Generation: Bilingualism Yesterday and Today." *International Migration Review* 28(4): 640–661.

Portes, Alejandro, and Min Zhou. 1993. "The New Second Generation: Segmented Assimilation and Its Variants." *Annals of the American Academy of Political and Social Science* 530(1): 74–96.

Pottinger, Audrey M. 2005. "Children's Experience of Loss by Parental Migration in Inner-city Jamaica." *American Journal of Orthopsychiatry* 75(4): 485–496. doi:10.1037/0002-9432.75.4.485.

Reimers, D. M. 1981. "Post–World War II Immigration to the United States: America's Latest Newcomers." Annals of the American Academy of Political and Social Science 454(1): 1–12.

Rios, Victor M. 2011. *Punished: Policing the Lives of Black and Latino Boys*. New York: NYU Press.

Robinson, William I. 2000. "Neoliberalism, the Global Elite, and the Guatemalan Transition: A Critical Macrosocial Analysis." *Journal of Interamerican Studies and World Affairs* 42(4): 89–107.

———. 2004. "Global Crisis and Latin America." *Bulletin of Latin American Research* 23(2): 135–153.

———. 2008. *Latin America and Global Capitalism: A Critical Globalization Perspective*. Baltimore, Md.: John Hopkins University Press.

———. 2014. *Global Capitalism and the Crisis of Humanity*. Cambridge: Cambridge University Press.

Romero, Mary 2011. "Keeping Citizenship Rights White: Arizona's Racial Profiling Practices in Immigration Law Enforcement." Law Journal for Social Justice 1(1): 97–113.

Rosas, Gilberto. 2012. *Barrio Libre: Criminalizing States and Delinquent Refusals of the New Frontier*. Durham, N.C.: Duke University Press.

Rumbaut, Rubén. 1994. "Origins and Destinies: Immigration to the United States since World War II." *Sociological Forum* 9(4): 583–621.

——. 2005. "Turning Points in the Transition to Adulthood: Determinants of Educational Attainment, Incarceration, and Early Childbearing among Children of Immigrants." *Ethnic and Racial Studies* 28(6): 1041–1086.

Rytina, Nancy. 2009. "Estimates of the Legal Permanent Resident Population in 2008." U.S. Department of Homeland Security. Office of Immigration Statistics. Policy Directorate. Retrieved from http://www.dhs.gov/xlibrary/assets/statistics/publications/ois_lpr_pe_2008.pdf.

Sabin, Miriam, Barbara Lopes Cardozo, Larry Nackerud, Reinhard Kaiser, and Luis Varese. 2003. "Factors Associated with Poor Mental Health among Guatemalan Refugees Living in Mexico 20 Years after Civil Conflict." *Journal of the American Medical Association* 290(5): 635–642.

Sabo, Donald, Terry Allen Kupers, and Willie James London. 2001. *Prison Masculinities*. Philadelphia: Temple University Press.

Sagás, Ernesto, and Sintia E. Molina, eds. 2004. *Dominican Migration: Transnational Perspectives*. Gainesville: University Press of Florida.

Sanderson, Matthew R. 2014. "Networks of Capital, Networks for Migration: Political–Economic Integration and the Changing Geography of Mexico–US Migration." *Global Networks* 14(1): 23–43.

Sassen, Saskia. 1989. "America's 'Immigration Problem.'" *World Policy* 6(Fall): 811–832.

Schmalzbauer, L. 2008. "Family Divided: The Class Formation of Honduran Transnational Families." *Global Networks* 8(3): 329–346. doi:10.1111/j.1471-0374.2008.00198.x.

Simanski, John, and Lesley Sapp. 2012. "Immigration Enforcement Actions: 2011." Office of Immigration Statistics. Accessed October 20, 2014. Retrieved from http://www.dhs.gov/sites/default/files/publications/immigration-statistics/enforcement_ar_2011.pdf.

Simon, Johnathan. 2007. *Governing through Crime: How the War on Crime Transformed American Democracy and Created a Culture of Fear*. New York: Oxford University Press.

Singer, Audrey. 2012. *Investing in the Human Capital of Immigrants: Strengthening Regional Economies*. Washington, D.C.: Brookings Institution. Accessed October 20, 2014. Retrieved from http://www.brookings.edu/research/papers/2012/09/20-immigrants-human-capital-singer.

Siqueira, Sueli. 2007a. "Emigracao internacional e o retorno a terra natal: Realizacoes e frustracoes." XV Encontro Nacional Sobre Emigracao. Minas Gerais, Brazil: Universidad Vale do Rio Doce. Accessed February 7, 2008. Retrieved from http://www.abep.nepo.unicamp.br/docs/anais/outros/5EncNacSobreMigracao/comunic_sec_2_emi_int_ret.pdf.

——. 2007b. "O sonho frustrado e o sonho realizado: As duas faces da migração para os EUA." *Nuevo Mundo* 7. Posted June 7. Accessed February 7, 2008. Retrieved from http://nuevomundo.revues.org/document5973.html.

Siulc, Nina. 2009. "Unwelcome Citizens." PhD diss., New York University.

Sládková, J., S. M. G. Mangado, and J. R. Quinteros. 2012. "Lowell Immigrant Communities in the Climate of Deportations." *Analyses of Social Issues and Public Policy* 12(1): 78–95. doi:10.1111/j.1530-2415.2011.01253.x.

Spener, David. 2009. *Clandestine Crossings: Migrants and Coyotes on the Texas–Mexico Border*. Ithaca, N.Y.: Cornell University Press.

Stanton-Salazar, R., and Sanford M. Dornbusch. 1995. "Social Capital and the Reproduction of Inequality: Information Networks among Mexican-Origin High School Students." *Sociology of Education* 68(April): 116–135. Accessed October 21, 2014. Retrieved from http://ed-share.educ.msu.edu/scan/TE/danagnos/te9204B.PDF.

Steger, Manfred. 2010. *Globalization*. Oxford: Oxford University Press.

Steger, Manfred, and Ravi K. Roy. 2010. *Neoliberalism: A Very Short Introduction*. Oxford: Oxford University Press.

Sudbury, Julia. 2002. "Celling Black Bodies: Black Women in the Global Prison Industrial Complex." *Feminist Review* 70(1): 57–74.

Sun, Yongmin. 1999. "The Contextual Effects of Community Social Capital on Academic Performance." *Social Science Research* 28: 403–426.

Thomas, Deborah A. 2009. "The Violence of Diaspora: Governmentality, Class Cultures, and Circulations." *Radical History Review* 103: 83–104.

Torres-Saillant, Silvio, and Ramona Hernández. 1998. *The Dominican Americans*. Santa Barbara, Calif.: Greenwood.

Valdez, Zulema. 2011. *The New Entrepreneurs: How Race, Class, and Gender Shape American Enterprise*. Stanford, Calif.: Stanford University Press.

Varsanyi, Monica W. 2008. "Rescaling the 'Alien,' Rescaling Personhood: Neoliberalism, Immigration and the State." *Annals of the Association of American Geographers* 98(4): 877–896.

Vickerman, Milton. 1999. *Crosscurrents: West Indian Immigrants and Race*. New York: Oxford University Press.

Vigil, James Diego, Steve Yun, and Jesse Cheng. 2004. "A Shortcut to the American Dream? Vietnamese Youth Gangs in Little Saigon." In *Asian American Youth, Culture, and Identity,* edited by Jennifer Lee and Min Zhou. New York: Routledge. 207–220.

Wacquant, Loïc. 2009. *Punishing the Poor: The Neoliberal Government of Social Insecurity*. Durham, N.C.: Duke University Press.

Waters, Mary C. 1999. *Black Identities: West Indian Immigrant Dreams and American Realities*. Cambridge: Harvard University Press.

Weis, T. 2004. "Restructuring and Redundancy: The Impacts and Illogic of Neoliberal Agricultural Reforms in Jamaica." *Journal of Agrarian Change* 4(4): 461–491. doi:10.1111/j.1471-0366.2004.00088.x.

Welch, Michael. 2002. *Detained: Immigration Laws and the Expanding INS Jail Complex*. Philadelphia: Temple University Press.

Wessler, Seth. 2011. "U.S. Deports 46K Parents with Citizen Kids in Just Six Months." Colorlines, November 3. Retrieved from http://colorlines.com/archives/2011/11/shocking_data_on_parents_deported_with_citizen_children.html.

West, Cornel. 1995. "Foreword." In *Critical Race Theory: The Key Writings That Formed the Movement*, edited by Kimberlé Williams Crenshaw. New York: New Press. xi–xiii.

Western, Bruce. 2006. *Punishment and Inequality in America*. New York: Russell Sage Foundation.

———. 2007. "Testimony before the Joint Economic Committee." October 4. Retrieved from http://www.wjh.harvard.edu/soc/faculty/western/pdfs/western_jec_testimony .pdf.

Wiarda, Howard. 1980. "Review: The United States and the Dominican Republic: Intervention, Dependency and Tyrannicide." *Journal of Interamerican Studies and World Affairs* 22(2): 247–260.

Wilkinson, Deanna. L., Amanda Magora, Marie Garcia, and Atika Khurana. 2009. "Fathering at the Margins of Society: Reflections from Young, Minority, Crime-Involved Fathers." *Journal of Family Issues* 30(7): 945–967. doi:10.1177/0192513X 09332354.

Wolford, Wendy. 2005. "Agrarian Moral Economies and Neoliberalism in Brazil: Competing Worldviews and the State in the Struggle for Land." *Environment and Planning A* 37(2): 241–261. doi:10.1068/a3745.

Zhou, Min. 1997. "Segmented Assimilation: Issues, Controversies, and Recent Research on the New Second Generation." International Migration Review 31(4): 975–1008.

Zhou, Min, and Carl L. Bankston. 1994. "Social Capital and the Adaptation of the Second Generation: The Case of Vietnamese Youth in New Orleans." *International Migration Review* 28(4): 821–845. Retrieved from http://www.jstor.org/stable/ 10.2307/2547159.

Zhou, Min, Jennifer Lee, Jody Agius Vallejo, Rosaura Tafoya-Estrada, and Yang Sao Xiong. 2008. "Success Attained, Deterred, and Denied: Divergent Pathways to Social Mobility in Los Angeles's New Second Generation." *Annals of the American Academy of Political and Social Science* 620(1): 37–61.

INDEX

Abrego, Leisy, 167–68

AEDPA. *See* Anti-Terrorism and Effective Death Penalty Act

Aggravated felonies, 105–6, 162–63, 265

Aizeki, Mizue, 16

Alberto, 64, 100–102; immigration detention of, 212–13; as Jamaican deportee, 226–27

Alcoholism, 99

Alex, 138–40, 160

Alexander, Michelle, 144–45, 190–91

Alfonso, 170–71

American Creed, 160–62

American Dream, 57, 125, 161–62

Anti-Terrorism and Effective Death Penalty Act (AEDPA), 105

Antonio, 54, 60, 85–86, 214

Appeals process: of Diallo, 215–16; of Elias, 216; of Harold, 233; immigration detention and, 214–17

Apprehension, 71, 168; Alfonso, 170–71; collateral arrests in, 195–96; of fugitive aliens, 176–78; Katy, 165–66, 179–81; Maximo, 195–96; Philip, 172–73; by police, 172–74, *174*, 176–77; Vern, 196–97

Arbenz Guzman, Jacobo, 44, 59

Assault, 191–93

Athletics visa, 36

Bad luck, 77–80

Balaguer, Joaquín, 38–39, 60

Balderrama, Francisco E., vii

Banished to the Homeland (Brotherton and Barrios), 115–16

Bankston, Carl L., 107

Barrel children, 33–34

Barrios, Luis, 67, 115–16, 128

Bauxite industry, 30–31, 59

Ben, 190–91

Berlin, Daniel, 238

Betty, 121–24

Black male immigrants, 143–44, 163, 174

Blanco, Jorge, 38

Boats, 42, 58–59; border crossing by, 41, 61–63, *63*, 66–67

Boat work, 41–42, 58–59

Boehme, Eric, 169

Border control, ix, 20–23, 182–83

Border crossing: by boat, 41, 61–63, *63*, 66–67; catch-and release program in, 84, 252; cost of, 87–88; deaths from, 61–62; drugs and, 85, 90; enhanced border security in, 71, 76–77, 87–88, 90; poverty and, 62

Border Patrol, 71, 77, 79, 85–86; police with, 171–72; roundups by, vii–viii; size of, 90

Bosch, Juan, 37–38, 59

Bosworth, Mary, 217

Bourgois, Philippe, 95, 124

Bracero program, 27

Brain drain, 35

Brazil, 49; milk for, 54, 60

Brazilian apprehensions, 82–87, 187–88; by CBP, *174*, 174–75

Corrections Corporation of America (CCA), 2, 210
Cost: of border crossing, 87–88; of coyotes, 78–80, 82–83, 87, 170, 248–49; for deportees, 218; of DHS, 7; of DoJ, 7; of education, 7; of illegal entry, 81, 88, 259; of immigration detention, 209; for immigration policing, 7, 90; for interior removals, 177
Côte d'Ivoire, 20
Cox, Adam, 173–75, *174*
Coyotes (smugglers), 46; in Brazilian border-crossing, 82–87, 249; cost of, 78–80, 82–83, 87, 170, 248–49; for Guatemalan border-crossing, 73–74, 76, 79–80, 89; linkages of, 89–90
Crimes, 244; by Dominican deportees, 231; homicides, 61, 77, 242–43; Jamaican deportees and, 220–22; kidnappings, 61, 71, 245
Criminal Alien Program (CAP), 176–77; assault and, 191–93; Ben, 190–91; Caleb, 193, 198; Chris, 192; Diallo, 189–91, 265; DUI and, 188–91; Emanuel, 192–93; guns and, 192–93; identity theft and, 187–88; immigration fraud and, 185–88; Manuel, 187–88; Melvin, 181–82; race and gender in, 193–94; Walter, 185–87
Criminal aliens, 141–42. *See also* Fugitive aliens
Criminalization: of Dominican deportees, 229–31; of immigrants, 168–69; of Latinos, 182–83
Criminal records: drugs in, 9–10, *11*; immigration in, 9–10, *11*; INS related to, 8–10; lack of, 10; Obama and, 8–10; traffic offenses as, 9–10, *11*
Cristobal, 66–67
Crystal meth, 120, 122
Cultural citizenship, 108
Cultural differences, 99–102

Customs and Border Patrol (CBP), 7, 90, *174*, 174–75

Darius, 67, 222
Deaths, 61–62, 77, 242–43
de Genova, Nicholas, 8, 168
Deindustrialization, 203
Delroy, 152–53
Demore v. Kim, 210–11
Department of Defense (DoD), 201–2
Department of Education, 7
Department of Homeland Security (DHS), viii, 8, 90, 175, 209, 258
Department of Justice (DoJ), 7, 146, 210
Deportation, 23; aggravated felonies and, 105–6, 162–63, 265; definition of, 6; due process and, 106, 210–11; feelings from, 57; judicial review and, 106, 127; location related to, 175, 184, 260; of LPRs, 142–43, 264; as outsourcing, 132; as social control, 167, 175; warrants for, 187, 195–96, 239, 253
Deportation and neoliberalism: economic crisis in, 18–19; incarceration in, 17–18; law enforcement in, 17–18; low-wage jobs or, 19; public expenditure reduction in, 18–19; unemployment and, 18–19
Deportee Department of the Migration Department (DGM), 229–30
Deportees, 1–2, 25; at call centers, 219, 235–37, 240, 245–47, 254; context of, 5; cost for, 218; gender of, 8, 21, *106*, 107, 121–24; home countries of, 21–22, *22*; as scapegoats, 218–19; as surplus labor, 253–54; terrorism related to, 10; women, 121–24
Deregulation, 12, 256–57
Desert, 86–87
Detention: of children, 70–71. *See also* Immigration detention
Detention rate, 199
DeVeaux, Mika'il, 209

34–35; tourist, 50–52, 81, 84, 251; wealth and, 62

Vulnerability, ix, 62, 90, 259

Wacquant, Loïc, 17, 19, 147

Walter, 153, 185–87

War on Drugs, 17, 24, 133, 163–64; targeting in, 143; War on Terror with, 145–46

War on Drugs and mass deportation, 147–48; drug fringe in, 155–62; drug sellers in, 151–55; drug users in, 149–51

War on Terror, 24, 145–46

Warrants, 187, 195–96, 239, 253

Waters, Mary, 101, 103–4, 115, 124, 132

Wealth, 51, 251–52; income and, 14–15, 20; visas and, 62

Welcome, 238–39, 247

Wendy, 221

Wessin, Elias, 37

West Indian immigrants, 101

Whites, 3, 263; as drug sellers, 104–5; as drug users, 149; incarceration of, 109–10, 143–44

White supremacy, 261–62

Wild Cowboys (Jackall), 116, 129

William, 53

Women deportees, 123–24; sexual abuse of, 121–22

Wonders, Nancy, 168

Work permits, 196

World Bank, 12–13

Yolas (fishing boats), 41, 61, 66–68

Zelda and Octavio, 51–53, 60

Zetas, 61

Zhou, Min, 103, 109

ABOUT THE AUTHOR

Tanya Maria Golash-Boza is Associate Professor of Sociology at the University of California, Merced. She is the author of several books, including *Immigration Nation* and *Race and Racisms*.

Made in the USA
Monee, IL
22 August 2020